The Enquirer

THE

ENQUIRER.

REFLECTIONS

ON

EDUCATION, MANNERS,

AND

LITERATURE.

THE

ENQUIRER.

REFLECTIONS

ON

EDUCATION, MANNERS,

AND

LITERATURE.

THE

ENQUIRER.

BY WILLIAM GODWIN.

——Ingenuas didicisse fideliter artes,
Emollit mores, nec sinit esse feros. OVID.

A NEW EDITION.

JOHN ANDERSON, JUN. EDINBURGH.
55, NORTH BRIDGE STREET;
AND SIMPKIN AND MARSHALL, LONDON.

MDCCCXXIII.

G. Woodfall, Printer,
Angel-Court, Skinner Street, London.

ADVERTISEMENT.

MORE than twenty-five years have passed since these Essays were written. It is perhaps twenty years since I have perused them. My bookseller has invited me to the task; and I owe it to the public not again to commit them to the press without some revision. But I have little leisure for the business. My mind is at this moment wholly engrossed in a work, which, if my life and my faculties are sufficiently prolonged, and the precariousness of my outward circumstances will admit it, I should gladly finish, and make it perhaps my last legacy to my fellow men.

In reading over these Essays, I find scarcely a thought that is my present thought, of which, at least, if I were now called upon to write upon their subjects for the first time, I should not express somewhat differently from the way in which it is here expressed. Our minds change like our bodies by insensible degrees, till they cannot, but with some looseness of phraseology, be called the same. Twenty-five years ago I was in the full vigour of animal life; I am so no longer, but in a green old age. When I wrote these Essays, I was a bachelor; I have since become a husband and a father. Yet the difference between the thoughts here expressed, and the thoughts I now entertain, is not fundamental; and to a careless observer would in most instances be imperceptible. Nor do I wish to change the texture of the publication. To those who feel any interest in my writings, such a change would scarcely be acceptable. In the volume to which these lines are prefixed, I appear such as I then was, and in a dress correspondent to the period of life I had reached. In what I may yet publish, there may perhaps be found something of the garrulity of age, and I hope also something of grey-headed reflection, and a more mature and well-ripened cast of thought.

But, alas! to what does it all amount? The toys of childhood, the toys of manhood, and the toys of old age, are still toys. And, if it were hereafter possible for me to look down upon them from a future state, I should find them to be all alike laborious trifles. As it is, and seeing with my present imperfect organs, I am more than half inclined to despise them. But I know not that I could have done any better.

The alterations which I have introduced into the present edition are not considerable. They are greatest in the concluding Essay, as my opinions in some respects on the subject of that Essay have sustained a material change; and I was not willing to contribute, however slightly, to give permanence to notions which now appeared to me erroneous.

I have added two pages to the end of the Essay on Beggars. And, if it may be allowed, I would particularly solicit the reader's attention to a note now added, in page 256, on the character of Brutus.

July 16, 1823.

PREFACE.

THE volume here presented to the reader, is upon a construction totally different from that of a work upon the principles of political science, published by the same author four years ago.

The writer deems himself an ardent lover of truth; and, to increase his chance of forcing her from her hiding-place, he has been willing to vary his method of approach.

There are two principal methods according to which truth may be investigated.

The first is by laying down one or two simple principles, which seem scarcely to be exposed to the hazard of refutation; and then developing them, applying them to a number of points, and following them into a variety of inferences. From this method of investigation, the first thing we are led to hope is, that there will result a system consentaneous to itself; and, secondly, that, if all the parts shall thus be brought into agreement with a few principles, and if those principles be themselves true, the whole will be found conformable to truth. This is the method of investigation attempted in the Enquiry concerning Political Justice.

An enquiry thus pursued is undoubtedly in the highest style of man. But it is liable to many disadvantages; and, though there be nothing that it involves too high for our pride, it is perhaps a method of investigation incommensurate to our powers. A mistake in the commencement is fatal. An error in almost any part of the process is attended with extensive injury; where every thing is connected, as it were, in an indissoluble chain, and an oversight in one step vitiates all that are to follow. The intellectual eye of man, perhaps, is formed rather for the inspection of minute and near, than of immense and distant objects. We proceed most safely, when we enter upon each portion of our process, as it were, *de novo;* and there is danger, if we are too exclusively anxious about consistency of system, that we may forget the perpetual attention we owe to experience, the pole-star of truth.

An incessant recurrence to experiment and actual observation, is the second method of investigating truth, and the method adopted in the present volume. The author has attempted only a short excursion at a time; and then, dismissing that, has set out afresh upon a new pursuit. Each of the Essays he has written, is intended in a considerable degree to stand by itself. He has carried this principle so far, that he has not been severely anxious relative to inconsistencies that may be discovered between the speculations of one Essay and the speculations of another.

The Essays are principally the result of conversations, some of them held many years ago, though the Essays have all been composed for the present occasion. The author has always had a passion for colloquial discussion; and, in the various opportunities that have been afforded him in different scenes of life, the result seemed frequently to be fruitful both of amusement and instruction. There is a vivacity, and, if he may be permitted to say it, a richness, in the hints struck out in conversation, that are with difficulty attained in any other method. In the subjects of several of the most considerable Essays, the novelty of idea they may possibly contain, was regarded with a kind of complacence by the author, even when it was treated with supercilious inattention in its first communication. It is very possible, in these instances, that the public may espouse the party of the original auditor, and not of the author. Wherever that shall be strikingly the case, the complacence he mentions will be radically affected. An opinion peculiar to a single individual, must be expected, to that individual to appear pregnant with dissatisfaction and uncertainty.

From what has been said the humble pretensions of the contents of the present volume are sufficiently obvious. They are presented to the contemplative reader, not as *dicta*, but as the materials of thinking. They are committed to his mercy. In themselves they are trivial; the hints of enquiry rather than actual enquiries: but hereafter perhaps they may be taken under other men's protection, and cherished to maturity. The utmost that was here proposed, was to give, if possible, a certain perspicuity and consistency to each detached member of enquiry. Truth was the object principally regarded; and the author endeavoured to banish from his mind every modification of prepossession and prejudice.

There is one thought more he is desirous to communicate; and it may not improperly find a place in this Preface. It relates to the French Revolution; that inexhaustible source of meditation to the reflecting and inquisitive. While the principles of Gallic republicanism were yet in their infancy, the friends of innovation were somewhat too imperious in their tone. Their minds were in a state of exaltation and ferment. They were too impatient and impetuous. There was something in their sternness that savoured of barbarism. The barbarism of our adversaries was no adequate excuse for this. The equable and independent mind should not be diverted from its bias by the errors of the enemy with whom it may have to contend.

The author confesses that he did not escape the contagion. Those who range themselves on the same party, have now moderated their intemperance, and he has accompanied them also in their present stage. With as ardent a passion for innovation as ever, he feels himself more patient and tranquil. He is desirous of assisting others, if possible, in perfecting the melioration of their temper. There are many things discussed in the following Essays, upon which perhaps, in the effervescence of his zeal, he would have disdained to have written. But he is persuaded that the cause of political reform, and the cause of intellectual and literary refinement, are inseparably connected. He has also descended in his investigations into the humbler walks of private life. He ardently desires that those who shall be active in promoting the cause of reform, may be found amiable in their personal manners, and even attached to the cultivation of miscellaneous enquiries. He believes that this will afford the best security, for our preserving kindness and universal philanthropy, in the midst of the operations of our justice.

London,
February 4, 1797.

CONTENTS

PART II.

I. Of Riches and Poverty 145
II. Of Avarice and Profusion 146
III. Of Beggars 165

CONTENTS.

PART I.

Essay		Page
I.	Of Awakening the Mind	1
II.	Of the Utility of Talents	6
III, IV.	Of the Sources of Genius	10, 16
V.	Of an Early Taste for Reading	25
VI.	Of the Study of the Classics	31
VII.	Of Public and Private Education	50
VIII.	Of the Happiness of Youth	58
IX.	Of the Communication of Knowledge	67
X.	Of Domestic or Family Life	76
XI.	Of Reasoning and Contention	83
XII.	Of Deception and Frankness	89
XIII.	Of Manly Treatment and Behaviour	98
XIV.	Of the Obtaining of Confidence	105
XV.	Of Choice in Reading	114
XVI.	Of Early Indications of Character	131

PART II.

I.	Of Riches and Poverty	143
II.	Of Avarice and Profusion	149
III.	Of Beggars	165

Essay		Page
IV.	Of Servants	181
V.	Of Trades and Professions	191
VI.	Of Self-Denial	217
VII.	Of Individual Reputation,	
	§. 1. Sources of Popular Applause	228
	§. 2. Sources of Popular Disapprobation	237
	§. 3. Use of Popularity	247
VIII.	Of Posthumous Fame	255
IX.	Of Difference in Opinion.	
	§. 1. Principles of Equitable Interpretation	269
	§. 2. Illustrations	286
X.	Of Politeness.	
	§. 1. Benefits of Politeness	295
	§. 2. Reciprocal Claims of Politeness and Sincerity	305
XI.	Of Learning	317
XII.	Of English Style.	
	Introduction	332
	§. 1. Age of Queen Elizabeth	335
	§. 2. Milton and Clarendon	351
	§. 3. Age of Charles the Second	360
	§. 4. Age of Queen Anne	373
	§. 5. Age of George the Second	391
	§. 6. Conclusion	404

THE

ENQUIRER.

PART I.

ESSAY I.

OF AWAKENING THE MIND.

The true object of education, like that of every other moral process, is the generation of happiness.

Happiness to the individual in the first place. If individuals were universally happy, the species would be happy.

Man is a social being. In society the interests of individuals are intertwisted with each other, and cannot be separated. Men should be taught to assist each other. The first object should be to train a man to be happy; the second to train him to be useful, that is, to be virtuous.

There is a further reason for this. Virtue is essential to individual happiness. There is no transport equal to that of the performance of virtue. All other happiness, which is not connected with self-approbation and sympathy, is unsatisfactory and frigid.

To make a man virtuous we must make him wise. All virtue is a compromise between opposite motives and inducements. The man of genuine virtue, is a man of vigorous comprehension and long views. He who would be eminently useful, must be eminently instructed. He must be endowed with a sagacious judgement, and an ardent zeal.

The argument in favour of wisdom, or a cultivated intellect, like the argument in favour of virtue, when closely considered, shews itself to be twofold. Wisdom is not only directly a means to virtue; it is also directly a means to happiness. The man of enlightened understanding and persevering ardour, has many sources of enjoyment which the ignorant man cannot reach; and it may at least be suspected that these sources are more exquisite, more solid, more durable, and more constantly accessible, than any which the wise man and the ignorant man possess in common.

Thus it appears that there are three leading objects of a just education, happiness, virtue, wisdom; including, under the term wisdom, both extent of information and energy of pursuit.

When a child is born, one of the earliest purposes of his institutor ought to be, to awaken his mind, to breathe a soul into the, as yet, unformed mass.

What may be the precise degree of difference with respect to capacity that children generally bring into the world with them, is a problem that it is perhaps impossible completely to solve.

But, if education cannot do every thing, it can do much. To the attainment of any accomplishment what is principally necessary is, that the accomplishment should be ardently desired. How many instances is it reasonable to suppose there are, where this ardent desire exists, and the means of attainment are clearly and skilfully pointed out, where yet the accomplishment remains finally unattained? Give but sufficient motive, and you have given every thing. Whether the object be to shoot at a mark, or to master a science, this observation is equally applicable.

The means of exciting desire are obvious. Has the proposed object desirable qualities? Exhibit them. Delineate them with perspicuity, and delineate them with ardour. Shew your object from time to time under every point of view which is calculated to demonstrate its loveliness. Criticise, commend, exemplify. Nothing is more common than for a master to fail in infusing the passions

into his pupil tl
is there that re
to be ascribed t
the master, not

The more ii
mind of the in
It is not to be t
or otherwise, ar
qualities, favour
the world with
other qualities i
probably of mc
diseased state ot
treatment, the r
derable degree,
those around hin
implant seeds of
stances, may acco

Reasoning from
it would be a gros
sole object to be
education is to pro
happiness of the in
is one of the most
tion, and it is a purp
into the views of the
It seems probable
matter, in itself consid

[illegible] is. Learn to think, to discrimi-
[illegible] to remember, and to enquire*.

ESSAY II.

OF THE [illegible] OF TALENTS.

[illegible] have sometimes been suggested as to the
[illegible] of talents. "Give to a child," it has
[illegible] said, "good sense and a virtuous
[illegible] more. Talents are often
[illegible] their possessor.
[illegible] leading us astray;
[illegible] with the sober
[illegible]

tion. Is it to be feared that a man should too much for his happiness? Knowledge most part consists in added means of plea- enjoyment, and added discernment to se- ose means.

must probably be partial, not extensive, in- ion, that is calculated to lead us astray. The t of knowledge bewilders, and infuses a false ence; its clear and perfect day must exhibit in their true colours and dimensions. The cure of mistake, must be to afford me more ation; not to take away that which I have.

ents in general, notwithstanding the excep- ntioned in the outset, hold a higher esti- among mankind than virtues. There are who had not rather you should say of that they are knaves, than that they are But folly and wisdom are to a great de- ative terms. He who passes for the oracle scure club, would perhaps appear igno- onfused, and vapid, and tedious, in a of genius. The only complete pro- appellation of fool, is to be the capacity. A self-satisfied, most ridiculous of all

favour

shou

dicious education is, Learn to think, to discriminate, to remember, and to enquire*.

ESSAY II.

OF THE UTILITY OF TALENTS.

DOUBTS have sometimes been suggested as to the desirableness of talents. "Give to a child," it has frequently been said, "good sense and a virtuous propensity; I desire no more. Talents are often rather an injury than a benefit to their possessor. They are a sort of *ignis fatuus* leading us astray; a fever of the mind incompatible with the sober dictates of prudence. They tempt a man to the perpetration of bold, bad deeds; and qualify him rather to excite the admiration, than promote the interests, of society."

This may be affirmed to be a popular doctrine; yet where almost is the affectionate parent who would seriously say, "Take care that my child do not turn out a lad of too much capacity?"

The capacity which it is in the power of education to bestow, must consist principally in in-

* Conjectures respecting the studies to be cultivated in youth, not so much for their own sake, as for that of the habits they produce, are stated in Essay VI.

formation. Is it to be feared that a man should know too much for his happiness? Knowledge for the most part consists in added means of pleasure or enjoyment, and added discernment to select those means.

It must probably be partial, not extensive, information, that is calculated to lead us astray. The twilight of knowledge bewilders, and infuses a false confidence; its clear and perfect day must exhibit things in their true colours and dimensions. The proper cure of mistake, must be to afford me more information; not to take away that which I have.

Talents in general, notwithstanding the exception mentioned in the outset, hold a higher estimation among mankind than virtues. There are few men who had not rather you should say of them that they are knaves, than that they are fools. But folly and wisdom are to a great degree relative terms. He who passes for the oracle of an obscure club, would perhaps appear ignorant, and confused, and vapid, and tedious, in a circle of men of genius. The only complete protection against the appellation of fool, is to be the possessor of uncommon capacity. A self-satisfied, half-witted fellow, is the most ridiculous of all things.

The decision of common fame, in favour of talents in preference to virtues, is not so absurd as has sometimes been imagined. Talents are the instruments of usefulness. He that has them, is capable of producing uncommon benefit; he that has them not, is destitute even of the power. A tool with a fine edge may do mischief; but a tool that neither has an edge nor can receive it, is merely lumber.

Again; the virtues of a weak and ignorant man scarcely deserve the name. They possess it by way of courtesy only. I call such a man good, somewhat in the same way as I would call my dog good. My dog seems attached to me; but change his condition, and he would be as much attached to the stupidest dunce, or the most cankered villain. His attachment has no discrimination in it; it is merely the creature of habit.

Just so human virtues without discrimination, are no virtues. The weak man neither knows whom he ought to approve, nor whom to disapprove. Dazzled by the lustre of uncommon excellence, he is frequently one of the first to defame it. He wishes me well. But he does not know how to benefit me. He does not know what benefit is. He does not understand the nature of happiness or good. He cannot therefore be very zealous to promote it. He applies as much ardour to the thought of giving me a trinket, as to the thought of giving me liberty, magnanimity, and independence.

The idea of withholding from me capacity, lest

I should abuse it, is just as rational as it would be to shut me up in prison, lest, by going at large, I should be led into mischief.

I like better to be a man than a brute; and my preference is just. A man is capable of giving more and enjoying more. By parity of reason I had rather be a man with talent, than a man without. I shall be so much more a man, and less a brute. If it lie in my own choice, I shall undoubtedly say, Give me at least the chance of doing uncommon good, and enjoying pleasures uncommonly various and exquisite.

The affairs of man in society are not of so simple a texture, that they require only common talents to guide them. Tyranny grows up by a kind of necessity of nature; oppression discovers itself; poverty, fraud, violence, murder, and a thousand evils, follow in the rear. These cannot be extirpated without great discernment and great energies. Men of genius must rise up, to shew their brethren that these evils, though familiar, are not therefore the less dreadful, to analyse the machine of human society, to demonstrate how the parts are connected together, to explain the immense chain of events and consequences, to point out the defects and the remedy. It is thus only that important reforms can be produced. Without talents, despotism would be endless, and public misery incessant. Hence it follows, that he who is a friend to general happiness, will neglect no chance of producing, in his pupil or his child, one of the long-looked-for saviours of the human race.

ESSAY III.

OF THE SOURCES OF GENIUS.

It is a question which has but lately entered into philosophical disquisition, whether genius be born with a man, or may be subsequently infused. Hitherto it was considered as a proposition too obvious for controversy, that it was born and could not be infused. This is however by no means obvious.

That some differences are born with children, cannot reasonably be denied. But to what do these differences amount? Look at a new-born infant. How unformed and plastic is his body; how simple the features of his mind!

The features of the mind depend upon perceptions, sensations, pleasure, and pain. But the perceptions, the pleasures, and pains of a child previous to his birth, must make a very insignificant catalogue. If his habits at a subsequent period can be changed and corrected by opposite impressions, it is not probable that the habits generated previous to birth can be inaccessible to alteration.

If therefore there be any essential and decisive difference in children at the period of birth, it must consist in the structure of their bodies, not in the effects already produced upon their minds. The senses, or sensibility, of one body may be radically more acute than those of another. We do not find however that genius is inseparably connected with any particular structure of the organs of sense. The man of genius is not unfrequently deficient in one or more of these organs; and a very ordinary man may be perfect in them all. Genius however may be connected with a certain state of nervous sensibility originally existing in the frame. Yet the analogy from the external organs is rather unfavourable to this supposition. Dissect a man of genius, and you cannot point out those differences in his structure which constitute him such; still less can you point out original and immutable differences. The whole therefore seems to be a gratuitous assumption.

Genius appears to signify little more, in the first instance, than a spirit of prying observation and incessant curiosity. But it is reasonable to suppose that these qualities are capable of being generated. Incidents of a certain sort in early infancy will produce them; nay, may create them in a great degree, even at a more advanced period.

If nothing occur to excite the mind, it will become torpid; if it be frequently and strongly excited, unless in a manner that, while it excites, engenders aversion to effort, it will become active, mobile, and turbulent. Hence it follows, that an adequate cause for the phenomenon of genius may be found, in the incidents that occur to us subsequent to birth. Genius, it should seem, may be produced after this method; have we any sufficient reason to doubt of its being always thus produced?

All the events of the physical and intellectual world happen in a train, take place in a certain order. The voluntary actions of men are as the motives which instigate them. Give me all the motives that have excited another man, and all the external advantages he has had to boast, and I shall arrive at an excellence not inferior to his.

This view of the nature of the human mind, is of the utmost importance in the science of education. According to the notions formerly received, education was a lottery. The case would be parallel, if, when we went into battle in defence of our liberties and possessions, ninety-nine in a hundred of the enemy were musket-proof.

It would be an instructive speculation to enquire, under what circumstances genius is generated, and whether, and under what circumstances, it may be extinguished.

It should seem that the first indications of genius ordinarily disclose themselves at least as early, as at the age of five years. As far therefore as genius is susceptible of being produced by education, the production of it requires a very early care.

In infancy the mind is peculiarly ductile. We bring into the world with us nothing that deserves the name of habit; are neither virtuous nor vicious, active nor idle, inattentive nor curious. The infant comes into our hands a subject capable of certain impressions, and of being led on to a certain degree of improvement. His mind is like his body. What at first was cartilage, gradually becomes bone. Just so the mind acquires its solidity; and what might originally have been bent in a thousand directions, becomes stiff, unmanageable, and unimpressible.

This change however takes place by degrees, and probably is never complete. The mind is probably never absolutely incapable of any impressions and habits we might desire to produce. The production grows more and more difficult, till the effecting it becomes a task too great for human strength, and exceeds perhaps the powers and contrivance of the wisest man that ever existed. These remarks may contribute to explain the case of genius breaking out, at a late period, in an unpromising subject. If genius be nothing more, in the first instance, than a spirit of prying observation and incessant curiosity, there seems to be no impossibility, though there may be a greatly increased difficulty, in generating it after the period above assigned.

There seems to be a case, more frequent than that of post-dated genius, though not so much remarked; and not dissimilar to it in its circumstances. This is the case of genius, manifesting itself, and afterwards becoming extinct. There is one appearance of this kind that has not escaped notice; the degradation of powers of mind sometimes produced in a man, for the remainder of his life, by severe indisposition.

But the case is probably an affair of very usual occurrence. Examine the children of peasants. Nothing is more common than to find in them a promise of understanding, a quickness of observation, an ingenuousness of character, and a delicacy of tact, at the age of seven years, the very traces of which are obliterated at the age of fourteen. The cares of the world fall upon them. They are enlisted at the crimping-house of oppression. They are brutified by immoderate and unintermitted labour. Their hearts are hardened, and their spirits broken, by all that they see, all that they feel, and all that they look forward to. This is one of the most interesting points of view in which we can consider the present order of society. It is the great slaughter-house, of genius and of mind. It is the unrelenting murderer of hope and gaiety, of the love of reflection and the love of life.

Genius requires great care in the training, and the most favourable circumstances to bring it to perfection. Why should it not be supposed that, where circumstances are eminently hostile, it will languish, sicken, and die?

There is only one remark to be added here, to guard against misapprehension. Genius, it seems to appear from the preceding speculations, is not born with us, but generated subsequent to birth. It by no means follows from hence, that it is the produce of education, or ever was the work of the preceptor. Thousands of impressions are made upon us, for one that is designedly produced. The child receives twenty ideas *per diem* perhaps from the preceptor; it is not impossible that he may have a million of perceptions in that period, with which the preceptor has no concern. We learn, it may be, a routine of barren lessons from our masters; a circumstance occurs perhaps, in the intercourse of our companions, or in our commerce with nature, that makes its way directly to the heart, and becomes the fruitful parent of a thousand projects and contemplations.

ESSAY IV.

OF THE SOURCES OF GENIUS.

TRUE philosophy is probably the highest improvement and most desirable condition of human understanding.

But there is an insanity among philosophers, that has brought philosophy itself into discredit. There is nothing in which this insanity more evidently displays itself, than in the rage of accounting for every thing.

> Nature well known, no prodigies remain,
> Comets are regular, and Wharton plain. POPE.

It may be granted that there is much of system in the universe; or, in other words, it must be admitted, that a careful observer of nature will be enabled by his experience, in many cases, from an acquaintance with the antecedent, to foretel the consequent.

If one billiard-ball strike another in a particular manner, we have great reason to suppose that the result will be similar to what we have already observed in like instances. If fire be applied to gunpowder, we have great reason to expect an explosion. If the gunpowder be compressed in a tube, and a ball of lead be placed over it nearer the mouth of the tube, we have great reason to suppose that the explosion will expel the ball, and cause it to move in the air in a certain curve. If the event does not follow in the manner we expected, we have great reason to suppose that, upon further examination, we shall find a difference in the antecedents correspondent to the difference in the consequents.

This uniformity of events, and power of prediction, constitute the entire basis of human knowledge.

But there is a regularity and system in the speculations of philosophers, exceeding any that is to be found in the operations of nature. We are too confident in our own skill, and imagine our science to be greater than it is.

We perceive the succession of events, but we are never acquainted with any secret virtue by means of which two events are bound to each other.

If any man were to tell me that, if I pull the trigger of my gun, a swift and beautiful horse will immediately appear starting from the mouth of the tube; I can only answer that I do not expect it, and that it is contrary to the tenor of my former experience. But I can assign no reason, why this is an event intrinsically more absurd, or less likely, than the event I have been accustomed to witness.

This is well known to those who are acquainted

with the latest speculations and discoveries of philosophers. It may be familiarly illustrated to the unlearned reader by remarking, that the process of generation, in consequence of which men and horses are born, has obviously no more perceivable correspondence with that event, than it would have for me to pull the trigger of a gun.

It was probably this false confidence and presumption among philosophers, that led them indiscriminately to reject the doctrine of instinct among the animal tribes. There is a uniformity in some of the spontaneous actions of animals, and a promptitude in others, which nothing that has yet been observed in the preceding circumstances would have taught us to expect. It is this proposition, that the term instinct, accurately considered, is calculated to express. Instinct is a general name for that species of actions in the animal world, that does not fall under any series of intellectual processes with which we are acquainted.

Innumerable events are in like manner daily taking place in the universe, that do not fall under any of those rules of succession that human science has yet delineated.

The world, instead of being, as the vanity of some men has taught them to assert, a labyrinth of which they hold the clue, is in reality full of enigmas which no penetration of man has hitherto been able to solve.

The principle above mentioned, which affirms that we are never acquainted with any secret virtue by means of which two events are bound to each other, is calculated to impress upon us a becoming humility in this respect.

It teaches us that we ought not to be surprised, when we see one event regularly succeeding another, where we suspected least of what is apprehended by the vulgar as a link of connection between them. If our eyes were open, and our prejudices dismissed, we should perpetually advert to an experience of this sort.

That the accidents of body and mind should regularly descend from father to son, is a thing that daily occurs, yet is little in correspondence with the systems of our philosophers.

How small a share, accurately speaking, has the father in the production of the son? How many particles is it possible should proceed from him, and constitute a part of the body of the child descended from him? Yet how many circumstances they possess in common?

It has sometimes been supposed that the resemblance is produced by the intercourse which takes place between them after their birth. But this is an opinion which the facts by no means authorize us to entertain.

The first thing which may be mentioned as descending from father to son is his complexion; fair, if a European; swarthy or black, if a negro. Next, the son frequently inherits a strong resemblance to his father's distinguishing features. He inherits diseases. He often resembles him in stature. Persons of the same family are frequently found to live to about the same age. Lastly, there is often a striking similarity in their temper and disposition.

It is easy to perceive how these observations will apply to the question of genius. If so many other things be heritable, why may not talents be so also? They have a connection with many of the particulars above enumerated; and especially there is a very intimate relation between a man's disposition and his portion of understanding. Again; whatever is heritable, a man must bring into the world with him, either actually, or in the seminal germ from which it is afterwards to be unfolded. Putting therefore the notion of inheritance out of the question, it should seem that complexion, features, diseases, stature, age and temper, may be, and frequently are, born with a man. Why may not then his talents, in the same sense, be born with him?

Is this argument decisive against the generability of talents in the human subject, after the period of birth?

It is the madness of philosophy only, that would undertake to account for every thing, and to trace out the process by which every event in the world is generated. But let us beware of falling into the opposite extreme. It will often happen that events, which at first sight appear least to associate with that regularity and that precise system to which we are accustomed, will be found upon a minuter and more patient inspection really to belong to it. It is the madness of philosophy to circumscribe the universe within the bounds of our narrow system; it is the madness of ignorance to suppose that every thing is new, and of a species totally dissimilar from what we have already observed.

That a man brings a certain character into the world with him, is a point that must readily be conceded. The mistake is to suppose that he brings an immutable character.

Genius is wisdom; the possessing a great store of ideas, together with a facility in calling them up, and a peculiar discernment in their selection or rejection. In what sense can a new-born child be esteemed wise?

He may have a certain predisposition for wisdom. But it can scarcely be doubted that every child, not peculiarly defective in his make, is susceptible of the communication of wisdom, and consequently, if the above definition be just, of genius.

The character of man is incessantly changing.

One of the principal reasons why we are so apt to impute the intellectual differences of men to some cause operating prior to their birth, is that we are so little acquainted with the history of the early years of men of talents. Slight circumstances at first determined their propensities to this or that pursuit. These circumstances are irrecoverably forgotten, and we reason upon a supposition as if they never existed.

When the early life of a man of talents can be accurately traced, these circumstances generally present themselves to our observation.

The private memoirs of Gibbon the historian have just been published. In them we are able to trace with considerable accuracy the progress of his mind. While he was at college, he became reconciled to the Roman Catholic faith. By this circumstance he incurred his father's displeasure, who banished him to an obscure situation in Switzerland, where he was obliged to live upon a scanty provision, and was far removed from all the customary amusements of men of birth and fortune. If this train of circumstances had not taken place, would he ever have been the historian of the Decline and Fall of the Roman Empire? Yet how unusual were his attainments in consequence of these events, in learning, in acuteness of research, and intuition of genius!

Circumstances decide the pursuits in which we shall engage. These pursuits again generate the talents that discover themselves in our progress.

We are accustomed to suppose something mysterious and supernatural in the case of men of genius.

But, if we will dismiss the first astonishment of ignorance, and descend to the patience of investigation, we shall probably find that it falls within the ordinary and established course of human events.

If a man produce a work of uncommon talents, it is immediately supposed that he has been through life an extraordinary creature, that the stamp of divinity was upon him, that a circle of glory, invisible to profaner eyes, surrounded his head, and that every accent he breathed contained an indication of his elevated destiny.

It is no such thing.

When a man writes a book of methodical investigation, he does not write because he understands the subject, but he understands the subject because he has written. He was an uninstructed tyro, exposed to a thousand foolish and miserable mistakes when he began his work, compared with the degree of proficiency to which he has attained when he has finished it.

He who is now an eminent philosopher or a sublime poet, was formerly neither the one nor the other. Many a man has been overtaken by a premature death, and left nothing behind him but compositions worthy of ridicule and contempt, who, if he had lived, would perhaps have risen to the highest literary eminence. If we could examine the school-exercises of men who have afterwards done honour to mankind, we should often find them inferior to those of their ordinary competitors. If we could dive into the port-folios of their early youth, we should meet with abundant matter for laughter at their senseless incongruities, and for contemptuous astonishment.

There is no "divinity that hedges"* the man of genius. There is no guardian spirit that accompanies him through life. If you tell me that you are one of those who are qualified to instruct and guide mankind, it may be that I admit it; but I may reasonably ask, When did you become so, and how long has this been your character?

There is no man knows better than the man of talents, that he was a fool: for there is no man that finds in the records of his memory such asto-

* Shakespear.

nishing disparities to contrast with each other. He can recollect up to what period he was jejune, and up to what period he was dull. He can call to mind the innumerable errors of speculation he has committed, that would almost disgrace an idiot. His life divides itself in his conception into distinct periods, and he has said to himself ten times in his course, From such a time I began to live; the mass of what went before, was too poor to be recollected with complacence. In reality each of these stages was an improvement upon that which went before; and it is perhaps only at the last of them that he became, what the ignorant vulgar supposed he was from the moment of his birth.

ESSAY V.

OF AN EARLY TASTE FOR READING.

The first indications of genius disclose themselves at a very early period. A sagacious observer of the varieties of intellect, will frequently be able to pronounce with some confidence upon a child of tender years, that he exhibits marks of future eminence in eloquence, invention or judgment.

The embryon seed that contains in it the premise of talent, if not born with a man, ordinarily takes its station in him at no great distance from the period of birth. The mind is then, but rarely afterwards, in a state to receive and to foster it.

The talents of the mind, like the herbs of the ground, seem to distribute themselves at random. The winds disperse from one spot to another the invisible germs; they take root in many cases without a planter; and grow up without care or observation.

It would be truly worthy of regret, if chance, so to speak, could do that, which all the sagacity of man was unable to effect *; if the distribution of the noblest ornament of our nature, could be subjected to no rules, and reduced to no system.

He that would extend in this respect the province of education, must proceed, like the improvers of other sciences, by experiment and observation. He must watch the progress of the dawning mind, and discover what it is that gives it its first determination.

The sower of seed cannot foretel which seed shall fall useless to the ground, destined to wither and to perish, and which shall take root, and display the most exuberant fertility. As among the

* This suggestion is by no means inconsistent with the remark in Essay III. that the production of genius perhaps never was the work of the preceptor. What never yet has been accomplished, may hereafter be accomplished.

seeds of the earth, so among the perceptions of the human mind, some are reserved, as it were, for instant and entire oblivion, and some, undying and immortal, assume an importance never to be superseded. For the first we ought not to torment ourselves with an irrational anxiety; the last cannot obtain from us an attention superior to their worth.

There is perhaps nothing that has a greater tendency to decide favourably or unfavourably respecting a man's future intellect, than the question whether or not he be impressed with an early taste for reading.

Books are the depositary of every thing that is most honourable to man. Literature, taken in all its bearings, forms the grand line of demarcation between the human and the animal kingdoms. He that loves reading, has every thing within his reach. He has but to desire; and he may possess himself of every species of wisdom to judge, and power to perform.

The chief point of difference between the man of talent and the man without, consists in the different ways in which their minds are employed during the same interval. They are obliged, let us suppose, to walk from Temple-Bar to Hyde-Park-Corner. The dull man goes straight forward; he has so many furlongs to traverse. He observes if he meets any of his acquaintance; he enquires respecting their health and their family. He glances perhaps the shops as he passes; he admires the fashion of a buckle, and the metal of a tea-urn. If he experience any flights of fancy, they are of a short extent; of the same nature as the flights of a forest-bird, clipped of his wings, and condemned to pass the rest of his life in a farm-yard. On the other hand the man of talent gives full scope to his imagination. He laughs and cries. Unindebted to the suggestions of surrounding objects, his whole soul is employed. He enters into nice calculations; he digests sagacious reasonings. In imagination he declaims or describes, impressed with the deepest sympathy, or elevated to the loftiest rapture. He makes a thousand new and admirable combinations. He passes through a thousand imaginary scenes, tries his courage, tasks his ingenuity, and thus becomes gradually prepared to meet almost any of the many-coloured events of human life. He consults by the aid of memory the books he has read, and projects others for the future instruction and delight of mankind. If he observe the passengers, he reads their countenances, conjectures their past history, and forms a superficial notion of their wisdom or folly, their virtue or vice, their satisfaction or misery. If he observe the scenes that occur, it is with the eye of a connoisseur or an artist. Every object is capable of suggesting to him a volume of reflections. The time of these two persons in one respect resembles; it has brought them both to Hyde-Park-Corner. In almost every other respect it is dissimilar.

What is it that tends to generate these very opposite habits of mind?

Probably nothing has contributed more than an early taste for reading. Books gratify and excite our curiosity in innumerable ways. They force us to reflect. They hurry us from point to point. They present direct ideas of various kinds, and they suggest indirect ones. In a well-written book we are presented with the maturest reflections, or the happiest flights, of a mind of uncommon excellence. It is impossible that we can be much accustomed to such companions, without attaining some resemblance of them. When I read Thomson, I become Thomson; when I read Milton, I become Milton. I find myself a sort of intellectual camelion, assuming the colour of the substances on which I rest. He that revels in a well-chosen library, has innumerable dishes, and all of admirable flavour. His taste is rendered so acute, as easily to distinguish the nicest shades of difference. His mind becomes ductile, susceptible to every impression, and gaining new refinement from them all. His varieties of thinking baffle calculation, and his powers, whether of reason or fancy, become eminently vigorous.

Much seems to depend in this case upon the period at which the taste for reading has commenced. If it be late, the mind seems frequently to have acquired a previous obstinacy and untractableness. The late reader makes a superficial acquaintance with his author, but is never admitted into the familiarity of a friend. Stiffness and formality are always visible between them. He does not become the creature of his author; neither bends with all his caprices, nor sympathises with all his sensations. This mode of reading, upon which we depend for the consummation of our improvement, can scarcely be acquired, unless we begin to read with pleasure at a period too early for memory to record, lisp the numbers of the poet, and in our unpractised imagination adhere to the letter of the moralising allegorist. In that case we shall soon be induced ourselves to "build" the unpolished "rhyme*," and shall act over in fond imitation the scenes we have reviewed.

An early taste for reading, though a most promising indication, must not be exclusively depended on. It must be aided by favourable circumstances, or the early reader may degenerate into an unproductive pedant, or a literary idler. It seemed to appear in a preceding essay, that

* Milton.

genius, when ripened to the birth, may yet be extinguished. Much more may the materials of genius suffer an untimely blight and terminate in an abortion. But what is most to be feared, is that some adverse gale should hurry the adventurer a thousand miles athwart into the chaos of laborious slavery, removing him from the genial influence of a tranquil leisure, or transporting him to a dreary climate where the half-formed blossoms of hope shall be irremediably destroyed *. That the mind may expatiate in its true element, it is necessary that it should become neither the victim of labour, nor the slave of terror, discouragement, and disgust. This is the true danger; as to pedantry, it may be questioned whether it is the offspring of early reading, or not rather of a taste for reading taken up at a late and inauspicious period.

ESSAY VI.

OF THE STUDY OF THE CLASSICS.

A QUESTION which has of late given rise to considerable discussion, is, whether the study of the

* The canker galls the infants of the spring,
Too oft before their buttons be disclos'd;
And in the morn and liquid dew of youth
Contagious blastments are most imminent.—SHAKESPEAR.

classics ought to form a part of the education of youth? In the sixteenth and seventeenth centuries the very proposal of such a question would have been regarded as a sort of blasphemy; classical learning was regarded as the first of all literary accomplishments. But in the present day inquisitive and active spirits are little inclined to take any thing upon trust; prescription is not admitted as giving any sanction in matters of opinion; no practice, that is not fastened upon us by decrees and penalties, can hope to maintain its full measure of influence in civil society, except so far as it can be supported by irrefragable arguments.

An obvious ground of presumption in favour of classical learning will suggest itself in tracing its history. The study of the Latin and Greek authors will scarcely be thought to deserve this appellation, so long as their language was the vernacular tongue of those who studied them. Classical learning then may be said to have taken its rise in the fifteenth century, at which time the human mind awoke from a slumber that threatened to be little less than eternal. The principal cause of this auspicious event was the study of the classics. Suddenly men were seized with the desire of rescuing them from the oblivion into which they had fallen. It seemed as if this desire had arisen just in time to render its gratification not impracticable. Some of the most valuable remains of antiquity now in our possession, were upon the point of being utterly lost. Kings and princes considered their recovery as the most important task in which they could be engaged; scholars travelled without intermission, drawn from country to country by the faintest hope of encountering a classical manuscript; and the success of their search afforded a more guiltless, but not a less envied triumph, than the defeat of armies and the plunder of millions. The most honoured task of the literati of that day, was the illustration of an ancient author; commentator rose upon commentator; obscurities were removed; precision acquired; the Greek and Roman writers were understood and relished in a degree scarcely inferior to the improvement and pleasure derived from them by their contemporaries; nor were they only perused with avidity, their purity and their beauties were almost rivalled at the distance of almost fifteen hundred years.

Such is the history of one of the most interesting æras in the annals of mankind. We are indebted to the zeal, perhaps a little extravagant and enthusiastic, of the revivers of letters, for more than we can express. If there be in the present age any wisdom, any powers of reasoning, any acquaintance with the secrets of nature, any refinement of language, any elegance of composition, any love of all that can adorn and benefit the human race, this is the source from which they ultimately flowed*. From the Greek and Roman authors the moderns learned to think. While they investigated with unconquerable perseverance the ideas and sentiments of antiquity, the feculence of their own understanding subsided. The shackles of superstition were loosened. Men were no longer shut up in so narrow boundaries; nor benumbed in their faculties by the sound of one eternal monotony. They saw; they examined; they compared. Intellect assumed new courage, shook its daring wings, and essayed a bolder flight. Patience of investigation was acquired. The love of truth displayed itself, and the love of liberty.

Shall we then discard that, to which our ancestors owed every thing they possessed? Do we not fear lest, by removing the foundations of intellect, we should sacrifice intellect itself? Do we not fear lest, by imperceptible degrees, we should bring back the dark ages, and once again plunge our species in eternal night?

This however, though a plausible, is not a strict and logical argument in favour of classical learning; and, if unsupported by direct reasoning, ought not probably to be considered as deciding

* I do not infer that they could have flowed from no other source; I relate a fact.

the controversy. The strongest direct arguments are as follow. They will be found to apply with the most force to the study of Latin.

The Latin authors are possessed of uncommon excellence. One kind of excellence they possess, which is not to be found in an equal degree in the writers of any other country: an exquisite skill in the use of language; a happy selection of words; a beautiful structure of phrase; a transparency of style; a precision by which they communicate the strongest sentiments in the directest form; in a word, every thing that relates to the most admirable polish of manner. Other writers have taken more licentious flights, and produced greater astonishment in their readers. Other writers have ventured more fearlessly into unexplored regions, and cropped those beauties which hang over the brink of the precipice of deformity. But it is the appropriate praise of the best Roman authors, that they scarcely present us with one idle and excrescent clause, that they continually convey their meaning in the choicest words. Their lines dwell upon our memory; their sentences have the force of maxims, every part vigorous, and seldom any thing that can be changed but for the worse. We wander in a scene where every thing is luxuriant, yet every thing vivid, graceful and correct.

It is commonly said, that you may read the works of foreign authors in translations. But the excellencies above enumerated are incapable of being transfused. A diffuse and voluminous author, whose merit consists chiefly in his thoughts, and little in the manner of attiring them, may be translated. But who can translate Horace? who endure to read the translation? Who is there, acquainted with him only through this medium, but listens with astonishment and incredulity to the encomiums he has received from the hour his poems were produced?

The Roman historians are the best that ever existed. The dramatic merit and the eloquence of Livy; the profound philosophy of Sallust; the rich and solemn pencil of Tacitus, all ages of the world will admire; but no historian of any other country has ever been able to rival.

Add to this, that the best ages of Rome afford the purest models of virtue that are any where to be met with. Mankind are too apt to lose sight of all that is heroic, magnanimous and public-spirited. Modern ages have formed to themselves a virtue, rather polished, than sublime, that consists in petty courtesies, rather than in the tranquil grandeur of an elevated mind. It is by turning to Fabricius, and men like Fabricius, that we are brought to recollect what human nature is, and of what we are capable. Left to ourselves, we are apt to sink into effeminacy and apathy.

But, if such are the men with whose actions it

is most our interest to familiarise ourselves, we cannot do this so successfully as by studying them in the works of their countrymen. To know them truly, we must not content ourselves with viewing them from a distance, and reading them in abridgment. We must watch their minutest actions, we must dwell upon their every word. We must gain admission among their confidents, and penetrate into their secret souls. Nothing is so wretched a waste of time as the study of abridgments.

If it be allowable to elucidate the insufficiency of the modern writers of ancient history by instances, it might be remarked, that Rollin takes care repeatedly to remind his reader that the virtues of the heathens were only so many specious vices, and interlards his history with an exposition of the prophecies of Daniel; that Hooke calumniates all the greatest characters of Rome to exalt the reputation of Cæsar; and that Mitford and Gillies are at all times ready to suspend their narrative for a panegyric upon modern despotism. No persons seem to have been more utter strangers to that republican spirit which is the source of our noblest virtues, than those moderns who have assumed to be the historiographers of the ancient republics.

A second argument in favour of the study of the Latin classics may be thus stated. Language is the great medium of communication among mankind. He that desires to instruct others, or to gain personal reputation, must be able to express himself with perspicuity and propriety. Most of the misunderstandings which have existed, in sentiment or in science, may be traced to some obscurity or looseness of expression as their source. Add to this, that the taste of mankind is so far refined, that they will not accept an uncouth and disgustful lesson, but require elegance and ornament. One of the arts that tend most to the improvement of human intellect, is the art of language; and he is no true friend to his species, who would suffer them from neglect to fall back, from their present state of advancement in this respect, into a barbarous and undisciplined jargon.

But it is perhaps impossible to understand one language, unless we are acquainted with more than one. It is by comparison only that we can enter into the philosophy of language. It is by comparison only that we separate ideas, and the words by which those ideas are ordinarily conveyed. It is by collating one language with another, that we detect all the shades of meaning through the various inflections of words, and all the minuter degradations of sense which the same word suffers, as it shall happen to be connected with different topics. He that is acquainted with only one language, will probably always remain in some degree the slave of language. From the imperfectness of his knowledge, he will feel himself at one time seduced to say the thing he did not mean, and at another time will fall into errors of this sort without being aware of it. It is impossible he should understand the full force of words. He will sometimes produce ridicule, where he intended to produce passion. He will search in vain for the hidden treasures of his native tongue. He will never be able to employ it in the most advantageous manner. He cannot be well acquainted with its strength and its weakness. He is uninformed respecting its true genius and discriminating characteristics. But the man who is competent to and exercised in the comparison of languages, has attained to his proper elevation. Language is not his master, but he is the master of language. Things hold their just order in his mind, ideas first, and then words. Words therefore are used by him as the means of communicating or giving permanence to his sentiments; and the whole magazine of his native tongue is subjected at his feet.

The science of etymology has been earnestly recommended, as the only adequate instrument for effecting the purpose here described; and undoubtedly it is of high importance for the purpose of enabling us more accurately to judge of the value of the words we have occasion to employ.

But the necessity and the use of etymology have perhaps been exaggerated. However extensive are our researches, we must stop somewhere; and he that has traced a word half-way to its source, is subject to a portion of the same imperfection, as he that knows nothing of it beyond the language in which he has occasion to use it. It is here perhaps as in many other intellectual acquisitions; the habit of investigating, distinguishing and subtilising, is of more importance than any individual portions of knowledge we may chance to have accumulated. Add to which, that the immediate concern of the speaker or writer, is not with the meaning his words bore at some distant period or the materials of which they are compounded, but with the meaning that properly belongs to them according to the purest standard of the language he uses. Words are perpetually fluctuating in this respect. The gradations by which they change their sense are ordinarily imperceptible; but from age to age their variations are often the most memorable and surprising. The true mode therefore of becoming acquainted with their exact force, is to listen to them in the best speakers, and consider them as they occur in the best writers that have yet appeared.

Latin is indeed a language that will furnish us with the etymology of many of our own words; but it has perhaps peculiar recommendations as a praxis in the habits of investigation and analysis. Its words undergo an uncommon number of variations and inflections. Those inflections are more philosophically appropriated, and more distinct in their meaning, than the inflections of any language of a more ancient date. As the words in Latin composition are not arranged in a philosophical or natural order, the mind is obliged to exert itself to disentangle the chaos, and is compelled to yield an unintermitted attention to the inflections. It is therefore probable that the philosophy of language is best acquired by studying this language. Practice is superior to theory; and this science will perhaps be more successfully learned, and more deeply imprinted, by the perusal of Virgil and Horace, than by reading a thousand treatises on universal grammar.

Example seems to correspond to what is here stated. Few men have written English with force and propriety, who have been wholly unacquainted with the learned languages. Our finest writers and speakers have been men who amused themselves during the whole of their lives with the perusal of the classics. Nothing is generally more easy than to discover by his style, whether a man has been deprived of the advantages of a literary education.

A further argument in favour of the study of the Latin language, may be deduced from the nature of logic, or the art of thinking. Words are of the utmost importance to human understanding. Almost all the ideas employed by us in matters of reasoning have been acquired by words. In our most retired contemplations we think for the most part in words; and upon recollection can in most cases easily tell in what language we have been thinking. Without words, uttered, or thought upon, we could not probably carry on any long train of deduction. The science of thinking therefore is little else than the science of words. He that has not been accustomed to refine upon words, and discriminate their shades of meaning, will think and reason after a very inaccurate and slovenly manner. He that is not able to call his idea by various names, borrowed from various languages, will scarcely be able to conceive his idea in a way precise, clear and unconfused. If therefore a man were confined in a desert island, and would never again have occasion so much as to hear the sound of his own voice, yet if at the same time he would successfully cultivate his understanding, he must apply himself to a minute and persevering study of words and language.

Lastly, there is reason to believe that the study of Latin would constitute a valuable part of education, though it were applied to no practical use, and were to be regarded as an affair of intellectual discipline only.

There are two qualities especially necessary to any considerable improvement of human understanding; an ardent temper, and a habit of thinking with precision and order. The study of the Latin language is particularly conducive to the production of the last of these qualities.

In this respect the study of Latin and of geometry might perhaps be recommended for a similar reason. Geometry it should seem would always form a part of a liberal course of studies. It has its direct uses and its indirect. It is of great importance for the improvement of mechanics and the arts of life. It is essential to the just mastery of astronomy and various other eminent sciences. But its indirect uses are perhaps of more worth than its direct. It cultivates the powers of the mind, and generates the most excellent habits. It eminently conduces to the making man a rational being, and accustoms him to a closeness of deduction, that is not easily made the dupe of ambiguity, and carries on an eternal war against prejudice and imposition.

A similar benefit seems to result from the study of language and its inflections. All here is in order. Every thing is subjected to the most inflexible laws. The mind therefore which is accustomed to it, acquires habits of order, and of regarding things in a state of clearness, discrimination and arrangement.

The discipline of mind here described is of inestimable value. He that is not initiated in the practice of close investigation, is constantly exposed to the danger of being deceived. His opinions have no standard; but are entirely at the mercy of his age, his country, the books he chances to read, or the company he happens to frequent. His mind is a wilderness. It may contain excellent materials, but they are of no use. They oppress and choak one another. He is subject to a partial madness. He is unable to regulate his mind, and sails at the mercy of every breath of accident or caprice. Such a person is ordinarily found incapable of application or perseverance. He may form brilliant projects; but he has neither the resolution nor the power to carry any of them to its completion.

All talent may perhaps be affirmed to consist in analysis and dissection, the turning a thing on all sides, and examining it in all its variety of views. An ordinary man sees an object just as it happens to be presented to him, and sees no more. But a man of genius takes it to pieces, enquires into its cause and effects, remarks its internal structure, and considers what would have been the result, if its members had been combined in a different way, or subjected to different influences. The man of genius gains a whole magazine of thoughts, where the ordinary man has received only one idea; and his powers are multiplied in proportion to the number of ideas upon which they are to be employed. Now there is perhaps nothing that contributes more eminently to this subtilising and multiplication of mind, than an attention to the structure of language.

In matters of science and the cultivation of the human mind it is not always sufficiently attended to, that men are often essentially benefited by processes, through which they have themselves never actually passed, but which have been performed by their companions and contemporaries. The literary world is an immense community, the intercourse of whose members is incessant; and it is very common for a man to derive eminent advantage from studies in which he was himself never engaged. Those inhabitants of any of the enlightened countries of Europe, who are accustomed to intellectual action, if they are not themselves scholars, frequent the society of scholars, and thus become familiar with ideas, the primary source of which is only to be found in an acquaintance with the learned languages. If therefore we would make a just estimate of the loss that would be incurred by the abolition of classical learning, we must not build our estimate upon persons of talent among ourselves who have been deprived of that benefit. We must suppose the indirect, as well as the direct improvement that arises from this species of study, wholly banished from the face of the earth.

Let it be taken for granted that the above arguments sufficiently establish the utility of classical learning; it remains to be determined whether it is necessary that it should form a part of the education of youth. It may be alleged, that, if it be a desirable acquisition, it may with more propriety be made when a man is arrived at years of discretion, that it will then be made with less expence of labour and time, that the period of youth ought not to be burthened with so vexatious a task, and that our early years may be more advantageously spent in acquiring the knowledge of things, than of words.

In answer to these objections it may however be remarked, that it is not certain that, if the acquisition of the rudiments of classical learning be deferred to our riper years, it will ever be made. It will require strong inclination and considerable leisure. A few active and determined spirits will surmount the difficulty; but many who would derive great benefit from the acquisition, will certainly never arrive at it.

Our early years, it is said, may be more advantageously spent in acquiring the knowledge of things, than of words. But this is by no means so certain as at first sight it may appear. If you attempt to teach children science, commonly so called, it will perhaps be found in the sequel that you have taught them nothing. You may teach them, like parrots, to repeat, but you can scarcely make them able to weigh the respective merits of contending hypotheses. Many things that we go over in our youth, we find ourselves compelled to recommence in our riper years under peculiar disadvantages. The grace of novelty they have for ever lost. We are encumbered with prejudices with respect to them; and, before we begin to learn, we must set ourselves with a determined mind to unlearn the crude mass of opinions concerning them that were once laboriously inculcated on us. But in the rudiments of language, it can scarcely be supposed that we shall have any thing that we shall see reason to wish obliterated from our minds.

The period of youth seems particularly adapted to the learning of words. The judgment is then small; but the memory is retentive. In our riper years we remember passions, facts and arguments; but it is for the most part in youth only that we retain the very words in which they are conveyed. Youth easily contents itself with this species of employment, especially where it is not inforced with particular severity. Acquisitions, that are insupportably disgustful in riper years, are often found to afford to young persons no contemptible amusement.

It is not perhaps true that, in teaching languages to youth, we are imposing on them an unnecessary burthen. If we would produce right habits in the mind, it must be employed. Our early years must not be spent in lethargic indolence. An active maturity must be preceded by a busy childhood. Let us not from a mistaken compassion to infant years, suffer the mind to grow up in habits of inattention and irresolution.

If the study of the classics have the effect above ascribed to it, of refining and multiplying the intellectual powers, it will have this effect in a greater degree, the earlier it is introduced, and the more pliable and ductile is the mind that is employed on it. After a certain time the mind that was neglected in the beginning, grows aukward and unwieldy. Its attempts at alertness and grace are abortive. There is a certain slowness and stupidity that grow upon it. He therefore that would enlarge the mind and add to its quantity of existence, must enter upon his task at an early period.

The benefits of classical learning would perhaps never have been controverted, if they had not been accompanied with unnecessary rigours. Children learn to dance and to fence, they learn French and Italian and music, without its being found necessary to beat them for that purpose. A reasonable man will not easily be persuaded that there is some mysterious quality in classical learning that should make it an exception to all other instances.

There is one observation arising from the view here taken on the subject, that probably deserves to be stated. It has often been said that classical learning is an excellent accomplishment in men devoted to letters, but that it is ridiculous, in parents whose children are destined to more ordinary occupations, to desire to give them a superficial acquaintance with Latin, which in the sequel will infallibly fall into neglect. A conclusion opposite to this, is dictated by the preceding reflections. We can never certainly foresee the future destination and propensities of our children. But let them be taken for granted in the present argument, yet, if there be any truth in the above reasonings, no portion of classical instruction, however small, need be wholly lost. Some refinement of mind and some clearness of thinking will almost infallibly result from grammatical studies. Though the language itself should ever after be neglected, some portion of a general science has thus been acquired, which can scarcely be forgotten. Though our children should be destined to the humblest occupation, that does not seem to be a sufficient reason for our denying them the acquisition of some of the most fundamental documents of human understanding.

ESSAY VII.

OF PUBLIC AND PRIVATE EDUCATION.

INNUMERABLE are the discussions that have originated in the comparative advantages of public and private education. The chief benefit attendant on private instruction seems to be the following.

There is no motive more powerful in its operations upon the human mind, than that which originates in sympathy. A child must labour under peculiar disadvantages, who is turned loose among a multitude of other children, and left to make his way as he can, with no one strongly to interest himself about his joys or his sorrows, and no one eminently concerned as to whether he makes any improvement or not. In this unanimating situation, alone in the midst of a crowd, there is great danger that he should become sullen and selfish. Knowing nothing of his species, but from the austerity of discipline or the shock of contention, he must be expected to acquire a desperate sort of firmness and inflexibility. The social affections are the chief awakeners of man. It is difficult for me to feel much eagerness in the pursuit of that, by which I expect to contribute to no man's gratification or enjoyment. I cannot entertain a generous complacency in myself, unless I find that there are others that set a value on me. I shall feel little temptation to the cultivation of faculties in which no one appears to take an interest. The first thing that gives spring and expansion to the infant learner, is praise; not so much perhaps because it gratifies the appetite of vanity, as from a liberal satisfaction in communicated and reciprocal pleasure. To give pleasure to another produces in me the most animated and unequivocal consciousness of existence. Not only the passions of men, but their very judgments, are to a great degree the creatures of sympathy. Who ever thought highly of his own talents, till he found those talents obtaining the approbation of his neighbour? Who ever was satisfied with his own exertions, till they had been sanctioned by the suffrage of a bystander? And, if this scepticism occur in our maturest years, how much more may it be expected to attend upon inexperienced childhood? The greatest stimulus to ambition is for me to conceive that I am fitted for extraordinary things; and the only mode perhaps to inspire me with self-value, is for me to perceive that I am regarded as extraordinary by another. Those things which are censured in a child, he learns to be ashamed of; those things for which he is commended, he contemplates in himself with pleasure. If therefore you would have him eagerly desirous of any attainment, you must thoroughly convince him that it is regarded by you with delight.

This advantage however of private education it is by no means impossible in a great degree to combine with public. Your child may be treated with esteem and distinction in the intervals of his school education, though perhaps these can scarcely follow him when he returns to the roof of instruction. Praise, to produce its just effect, ought not to be administered in too frequent doses.

On the other hand, there is an advantage in public education similar in its tendency to that just described. Private education is almost necessarily deficient in excitements. Society is the true awakener of man; and there can be little true society, where the disparity of disposition is so great as between a boy and his preceptor. A kind of lethargy and languor creeps upon this species of studies. Why should he study? He has neither rival to surpass, nor companion with whom to associate his progress. Praise loses its greatest charm when given in solitude. It has not the pomp and enchantment, that under other circumstances would accompany it. It has the appearance of a cold and concerted stratagem, to entice him to industry by indirect considerations. A boy, educated apart from boys, is a sort of unripened hermit, with all the gloom and lazy-pacing blood incident to that character.

A second advantage attendant upon public education, will be explained by the observation, that a real scholar is seldom found to be produced in any other way. This is principally owing to the circumstance that, in private education, the rudiments are scarcely ever so much dwelt upon; the inglorious and unglittering foundations are seldom laid with sufficient care. A private pupil is too much of a man. He dwells on those things which can be made subjects of reasoning or sources of amusement; and escapes from the task of endless repetition. But public education is less attentive and complaisant to this species of impatience. Society chears the rugged path, and beguiles the tediousness of the way. It renders the mechanical part of literature supportable.

Thirdly, public education is best adapted for the generation of a robust and healthful mind. All education is despotism. It is perhaps impossible for the young to be conducted without introducing in many cases the tyranny of implicit obedience. Go there; do that; read; write; rise; lie down; will perhaps for ever be the language addressed to youth by age. In private education there is danger that this superintendence should extend to too many particulars. The anxiety of individual affection watches the boy too narrowly, controls him too much, renders him too poor a slave. In public education there is comparative liberty. The boy knows how much of his time is subjected to his task-master, and how much is sacredly his own. "Slavery, disguise it as we will, is a bitter draught*;" and will always excite a mutinous and indignant spirit. But the most wretched of all slaveries is that which I endure alone; the whole weight of which falls upon my own shoulders, and in which I have no fellow-sufferer to share with me a particle of my burthen. Under this slavery the mind pusillanimously shrinks. I am left alone with my tyrant, and am utterly hopeless and forlorn. But, when I have companions in the house of my labour, my mind begins to erect itself. I place some glory in bearing my sufferings with an equal mind. I do not feel annihilated by my condition, but find that I also am something. I adjust the account in my own mind with my task-master, and say, Thus far you may proceed; but there is a conquest that you cannot atchieve. The control exercised in private education is a contention of the passions; and I feel all the bitterness of being obliged unmurmuring to submit the turbulence of my own passions to the turbulence of the passions of my preceptor.

* Sterne.

Anger glows in the breast of both the contending parties; my heart pants with indignation against the injustice, real or imaginary, that I endure; in the final triumph of my Brobdingnagian persecutor I recognise the indulgence of hatred and revenge. But in the discipline of a public school I submit to the inflexible laws of nature and necessity, in the administration of which the passions have little share. The master is an object placed in too distant a sphere for me to enter into contention with him. I live in a little world of my own of which he is no member; and I scarcely think more of quarrelling with him, than a sailor does of bearing malice against a tempest.

The consequences of these two modes of education are usually eminently conspicuous, when the scholar is grown up into a man. The pupil of private education is commonly either aukward and silent, or pert, presumptuous and pedantical. In either case he is out of his element, embarrassed with himself, and chiefly anxious about how he shall appear. On the contrary, the pupil of public education usually knows himself, and rests upon his proper centre. He is easy and frank, neither eager to shew himself, nor afraid of being observed. His spirits are gay and uniform. His imagination is playful, and his limbs are active. Not engrossed by a continual attention to himself, his generosity is ever ready to break out; he is eager to fly to the assistance of others, and intrepid and bold in the face of danger. He has been used to contend only upon a footing of equality; or to endure suffering with equanimity and courage. His spirit therefore is unbroken; while the man, who has been privately educated, too often continues for the remainder of his life timid, incapable of a ready self-possession, and ever prone to prognosticate ill of the contentions in which he may unavoidably be engaged.

We shall perhaps perceive a still further advantage in public education, if we reflect that the scene which is to prepare us for the world, should have some resemblance to the world. It is desirable that we should be brought in early life to experience human events, to suffer human adversities, and to observe human passions. To practise upon a smaller theatre the business of the world, must be one of the most desirable sources of instruction and improvement. Morals cannot be effectually taught, but where the topics and occasions of moral conduct offer themselves. A false tenderness for their children sometimes induces parents to wish to keep them wholly unacquainted with the vices, the irregularities and injustice of their species. But this mode of proceeding seems to have a fatal effect. They are introduced to temptation unprepared, just in that tumultuous season of human life when temptation has the greatest power. They find men treacherous, deceitful and selfish; they find the most destructive and hateful purposes every where pursued; while their minds, unwarned of the truth, expected universal honesty. They come into the world, as ignorant of every thing it contains, as uninstructed in the scenes they have to encounter, as if they had passed their early years in a desert island. Surely the advantages we possess for a gradual initiation of our youth in the economy of human life, ought not to be neglected. Surely we ought to anticipate and break the shock, which might otherwise persuade them that the lessons of education are an antiquated legend, and the practices of the sensual and corrupt the only practices proper to men.

The objections to both the modes of education here discussed are of great magnitude. It is unavoidable to enquire, whether a middle way might not be selected, neither entirely public, nor entirely private, avoiding the mischiefs of each, and embracing the advantages of both. This however is perhaps a subordinate question, and of an importance purely temporary. We have here considered only the modes of education at this time in practice. Perhaps an adventurous and undaunted philosophy would lead to the rejecting them altogether, and pursuing the investigation of a mode totally dissimilar. There is nothing so fascinating in either, as should in reason check the further excursions of our understanding*.

ESSAY VIII.

OF THE HAPPINESS OF YOUTH.

A SUBJECT upon which the poets of all ages have delighted to expatiate, is the happiness of youth.

This is a topic which has usually been handled by persons advanced in life. I do not recollect that it has been selected as a theme for description by the young themselves.

It is easy to perceive why the opinion upon which it proceeds, has been so generally entertained.

The appearance of young persons is essentially gratifying to the eye. Their countenances are usually smooth; unmarked with wrinkles, unfurrowed by time. Their eye is sprightly and roving. Their limbs elastic and active. Their temper kind, and easy of attachment. They are frank and inartificial; and their frankness shews itself in their very voice. Their gaiety is noisy and obtrusive. Their spirits are inexhaustible; and their sorrows and their cares are speedily dismissed.

* The subject here treated of, may be considered as taken up, at the point where the present disquisition leaves it, in Essay IX.

Such is frequently the appearance of youth. Are they happy? Probably not.

A reasonable man will entertain a suspicion of that eulogium of a condition, which is always made by persons at a distance from it, never by the person himself.

I never was told, when a boy, of the superior felicity of youth, but my heart revolted from the assertion. Give me at least to be a man!

Children, it is said, are free from the cares of the world. Are they without their cares? Of all cares those that bring with them the greatest consolation, are the cares of independence.

There is no more certain source of exultation, than the consciousness that I am of some importance in the world. A child usually feels that he is nobody. Parents, in the abundance of their providence, take good care to administer to them the bitter recollection. How suddenly does a child rise to an enviable degree of happiness, who feels that he has the honour to be trusted and consulted by his superiors?

But of all the sources of unhappiness to a young person the greatest is a sense of slavery. How grievous the insult, or how contemptible the ignorance, that tells a child that youth is the true season of felicity, when he feels himself checked, controled, and tyrannised over in a thousand ways? I am rebuked; and my heart is ready to burst with indignation. A consciousness of the power assumed over me, and of the unsparing manner in which it is used, is intolerable. There is no moment free from the danger of harsh and dictatorial interruption; the periods, when my thoughtless heart began to lose the sense of its dependence, seem of all others most exposed to it. There is no equality, no reasoning, between me and my task-master. If I attempt it, it is considered as mutiny. If it be seemingly conceded, it is only the more cutting mockery. He is always in the right; right and power in these trials are found to be inseparable companions. I despise myself for having forgotten my misery, and suffered my heart to be deluded into a transitory joy. Dearly indeed, by twenty years of bondage, do I purchase the scanty portion of liberty, which the government of my country happens to concede to its adult subjects!

The condition of a negro-slave in the West Indies, is in many respects preferable to that of the youthful son of a free-born European. The slave is purchased upon a view of mercantile speculation; and, when he has finished his daily portion of labour, his master concerns himself no further about him. But the watchful care of the parent is endless. The youth is never free from the danger of its grating interference.

If he be treated with particular indulgence, and made what is called a spoiled child, this serves in some respects to aggravate the misery of occasional control. Deluded with the phantom of independence, he feels with double bitterness that he is only bound in fetters of gold.

Pain is always more vividly remembered than pleasure, and constitutes something more substantial in my recollections, when I come to cast up the sum of my life.

But not only are the pains of youth more frequent and galling, their pleasures also are comparatively slight and worthless. The greatest pleasures of which the human mind is susceptible, are the pleasures of consciousness and sympathy. Youth knows nothing of the delights of a refined taste; the softest scenes of nature and art, are but lines and angles to him. He rarely experiences either self-complacence or self-approbation. His friendships have for the most part no ardour, and are the mere shadows and mimicry of friendship. His pleasures are like the frisking and frolic of a calf.

These pleasures however, which have so often been the subject of lying exaggeration, deserve to be stated with simplicity and truth. The organs of sense are probably in a state of the greatest sensibility in an early period of life. Many of their perceptions are heightened at years of maturity, by means of the association of ideas, and of the manner in which ideas of sense and ideas of intellect are melted into a common mass. But the simple pleasures of sense, that is, as many of them as are within the reach of youth, are at that age most exquisitely felt. This is particularly obvious in the pleasures of the palate. The case is the same with simple sounds, light, colours, and every thing that agreeably impresses the organs of sight.

Another circumstance conducive to the pleasures of youth, is the pliability and variableness of their minds. In the case of the adult, circumstances make a durable impression. The incidents that happen in the morning, modify my temper through the whole course of the evening. Grief does not easily yield its place to joy. If I have suffered to-day from the influence of unjust control, my temper becomes embittered. I sit down in thoughtful silence, and abhor to be amused. What has once strongly seized the affections, either of exultation or sorrow, does not easily loosen its grasp, but pertinaciously retains its seat upon my heart.

In young persons it is otherwise. Theirs is the tear, in many instances at least, "forgot as soon as shed*." Their minds are like a sheet of white paper, which takes any impression that it is proposed to make upon it. Their pleasures therefore

* Gray.

are, to a great degree, pure and unadulterated. This is a circumstance considerably enviable.

The drawbacks to which it is subject, are, first, that their pleasures are superficial and worthless. They scarcely ever swell and elevate the mind. Secondly, they are pleasures which cannot, to a child of any sagacity, when reflected upon and summed together, constitute happiness. He sees that he was pleased, only because he was seduced to forget himself. When his thoughts return home, he is pleased no longer. He is perhaps indignant against himself for having suffered so gross a delusion. He abhors the slavery that constitutes his lot; and loaths the nothingness of his condition.

Those persons have made a satire of life, but a satire impotent and nugatory, who have represented youth as the proper season of joy. Though the world is a scene full of mixture and alloy, it is yet not so completely an abortion as this sentiment would represent it. If you ask men in general, whether they regard life as a blessing, they will perhaps hesitate: but they will recollect some feelings of exultation, some moments in which they felt with internal pride what it was to exist, and many of them will hereby be induced to pronounce in favour of life. But who can suppose himself a child, and look with exultation upon that species of existence? The principal sources of manly pleasure probably are, the feeling that we also are of some importance and account, the conscious power of conforming our actions to the dictates of our own understanding, an approving sense of the rectitude of our determinations, and an affectionate and heroical sympathy in the welfare of others. To every one of these young persons are almost uniformly strangers.

This is probably a fair and impartial view of the pleasures and pains of the young. It would be highly unjust to suppose that the adult who inflict these pains, are generally actuated by malignity. In some instances, where the miscarriage has been most complete, the kindness and disinterested zeal of its author has been eminent. But kindness and disinterested zeal must be in a great measure nugatory, where the methods pursued are founded in error. If the condition of the young is to be pitied, the condition of those who superintend them, is sometimes equally worthy of compassion. The object of true philosophy will never be to generate the hateful passions; it enters impartially into the miseries of the tyrant and the slave. The intention therefore of these speculations, ought to be considered as that of relieving, at once, the well-meaning, but misguided oppressor, and the unfortunate and helpless oppressed.

Considerations, such as we are here discussing, may indeed terrify the timid and cowardly parent or instructor; they will not have that effect upon the generous and the wise. Such is the condition of terrestrial existence. We cannot move a limb without the risk of destroying animal life, and, which is worse, producing animal torture. We cannot exist without generating evil. The more active and earnest we are, the more mischief shall we effect. The wisest legislator, the most admirable and exemplary author, has probably, by his errors, occasioned a greater sum of private misery, than ever flowed from the agency of any supine and torpid, however worthless, individual. We must therefore steel ourselves against this inevitable circumstance of our lot; and exert our understandings in sober deliberation, to discover how we may be made authors of the greatest overbalance of good.

But, some will say, this depressing condition of human life, ought carefully to be concealed from us, not obtruded upon our view.

The brave man will never shrink from a calm and rational responsibility. Let us put him in the place of the instructor in question; he will say to his pupil, I know I shall occasion you many calamities; this with all my diligence and good will I cannot avoid. But I will endeavour to procure for you a greater sum of happiness than it is probable any other person, who should be substituted in my place, would do; I will endeavour ultimately to render you wise, and virtuous, and active, and independent, and self-approving, and contented.

There is a very obvious reason why such discussions as that in which we are engaged, if pursued with an adventurous and scrutinising spirit, should have an appearance of partiality, and seem to espouse the cause of the young against the adult. There are certain modes of education established in society; these are open to our inspection; we may investigate them with accuracy and minuteness. The hypothetical modes which appear in speculation to have some advantages over them, are for the most part yet untried; we cannot follow them in their detail; we have often but an imperfect view of their great outline. Defects therefore we can point out with confidence, while it is only in an obscure and ambiguous style that we can discourse of their remedies.

In treating on the subject of education, it must of course be against the instructor, not his pupil, that we must direct our animadversions. The pupil is the clay in the hands of the artificer; I must expostulate with him, not with his materials. Books of education are not written to instruct the young how they are to form their seniors, but to assist the adult in discovering how to fashion the youthful mind.

It would be peculiarly unfortunate, if documents, the object of which is to improve education, and consequently to inspire the adult with new ardour, should be judged to have a discouraging tendency. Instructors indeed, as we now find them, are too often unworthy and unamiable; but instruction is not on that account a less generous and lofty task. It is incident alike to the professors of every art to enumerate difficulties and unfold them; to shew how "Alps on Alps arise*," in opposition to the daring adventurer. Having done so, they must always in a considerable degree leave him to surmount the obstacles for himself. Language is adequate to the first of these objects; it sinks under the delicacy and individualities of the second. The groveling and feeble-hearted are consequently discouraged; they desert the vocation they hastily chose. But the courage of the generously ambitious is by this means elevated to its noblest height.

ESSAY IX.

OF THE COMMUNICATION OF KNOWLEDGE.

In what manner would reason, independently of the received modes and practices of the world, teach us to communicate knowledge?

* Pope.

Liberty is one of the most desirable of all sublunary advantages. I would willingly therefore communicate knowledge, without infringing, or with as little as possible violence to, the volition and individual judgment of the person to be instructed.

Again; I desire to excite a given individual to the acquisition of knowledge. The only possible method in which I can excite a sensitive being to the performance of a voluntary action, is by the exhibition of motive.

Motives are of two sorts, intrinsic and extrinsic. Intrinsic motives are those which arise from the inherent nature of the thing recommended. Extrinsic motives are those which have no constant and unalterable connection with the thing recommended, but are combined with it by accident, or at the pleasure of some individual.

Thus, I may recommend some species of knowledge by a display of the advantages which will necessarily attend upon its acquisition, or flow from its possession. Or, on the other hand, I may recommend it despotically, by allurements or menaces, by shewing that the pursuit of it will be attended with my approbation, and that the neglect of it will be regarded by me with displeasure.

The first of these classes of motives is unquestionably the best. To be governed by such motives is the pure and genuine condition of a rational being. By exercise it strengthens the judgment. It elevates us with a sense of independence. It causes a man to stand alone, and is the only method by which he can be rendered truly an individual, the creature, not of implicit faith, but of his own understanding.

If a thing be really good, it can be shewn to be such. If you cannot demonstrate its excellence, it may well be suspected that you are no proper judge of it. Why should not I be admitted to decide upon that which is to be acquired by the application of my labour?

Is it necessary that a child should learn a thing, before it can have any idea of its value? It is probable that there is no one thing that it is of importance for a child to learn. The true object of juvenile education, is to provide, against the age of five and twenty, a mind well regulated, active, and prepared to learn*. Whatever will inspire habits of industry and observation, will sufficiently answer this purpose. Is it not possible to find something that will fulfil these conditions, the benefit of which a child shall understand, and the acquisition of which he may be taught to desire? Study with desire is real activity: without desire it is but the semblance and mockery of activity. Let us not, in the eagerness of our haste to educate, forget all the ends of education.

* See the close of Essay I.

The most desirable mode of education therefore, in all instances where it shall be found sufficiently practicable, is that which is careful that all the acquisitions of the pupil shall be preceded and accompanied by desire. The best motive to learn, is a perception of the value of the thing learned. The worst motive, without deciding whether or not it be necessary to have recourse to it, may well be affirmed to be constraint and fear. There is a motive between these, less pure than the first, but not so displeasing as the last, which is desire, not springing from the intrinsic excellence of the object, but from the accidental attractions which the teacher may have annexed to it.

According to the received modes of education, the master goes first, and the pupil follows. According to the method here recommended, it is probable that the pupil would go first, and the master follow *. If I learn nothing but what I desire to learn, what should hinder me from being my own preceptor?

* To some persons this expression may be ambiguous. The sort of "going first" and "following" here censured, may be compared to one person's treading over a portion of ground, and another's coming immediately after, treading in his footsteps. The adult must undoubtedly be supposed to have acquired their information before the young; and they may at proper intervals incite and conduct their diligence, but they ought not to do it so as to supersede in them the exercise of their own discretion.

The first object of a system of instructing, is to give the pupil a motive to learn. We have seen how far the established systems fail in this office.

The second object is to smooth the difficulties which present themselves in the acquisition of knowledge.

The method of education here suggested is incomparably the best adapted to the first of these objects. It is sufficiently competent to answer the purposes of the last.

Nothing can be more happily adapted to remove the difficulties of instruction, than that the pupil should first be excited to desire knowledge, and next that his difficulties should be solved for him, and his path cleared, as often and as soon as he thinks proper to desire it.

This plan is calculated entirely to change the face of education. The whole formidable apparatus which has hitherto attended it, is swept away. Strictly speaking, no such characters are left upon the scene as either preceptor or pupil. The boy, like the man, studies, because he desires it. He proceeds upon a plan of his own invention, or which, by adopting, he has made his own. Every thing bespeaks independence and equality. The man, as well as the boy, would be glad in cases of difficulty to consult a person more informed than himself. That the boy is accustomed almost always to consult the man, and not the man the boy, is to be regarded rather as an accident, than any thing essential. Much even of this would be removed, if we remembered that the most inferior judge may often, by the varieties of his apprehension, give valuable information to the most enligtened. The boy however should be consulted by the man unaffectedly, not according to any preconcerted scheme, or for the purpose of persuading him that he is what he is not.

There are three considerable advantages which would attend upon this species of education.

First, liberty. Three fourths of the slavery and restraint that are now imposed upon young persons would be annihilated at a stroke.

Secondly, the judgment would be strengthened by continual exercise. Boys would no longer learn their lessons after the manner of parrots. No one would learn without a reason, satisfactory to himself, why he learned; and it would perhaps be well, if he were frequently prompted to assign his reasons. Boys would then consider for themselves, whether they understood what they read. To know when and how to ask a question is no contemptible part of learning. Sometimes they would pass over difficulties, and neglect essential preliminaries; but then the nature of the thing would speedily recall them, and induce them to return to examine the tracts which before had been overlooked. For this purpose it would be well that the subjects of their juvenile studies should often be discussed, and that one boy should compare his progress and his competence to decide in certain points with those of another. There is nothing that more strongly excites our enquiries, than this mode of detecting our ignorance.

Thirdly, to study for ourselves is the true method of acquiring habits of activity. The horse that goes round in a mill, and the boy that is anticipated and led by the hand in all his acquirements, are not active. I do not call a wheel that turns round fifty times in a minute, active. Activity is a mental quality. If therefore you would generate habits of activity, turn the boy loose in the fields of science. Let him explore the path for himself. Without increasing his difficulties, you may venture to leave him for a moment, and suffer him to ask himself the question before he asks you, or, in other words, to ask the question before he receives the information. Far be it from the system here laid down, to increase the difficulties of youth. No, it diminishes them a hundred fold. Its office is to produce inclination; and a willing temper makes every burthen light.

Lastly, it is the tendency of this system to produce in the young, when they are grown up to the stature of men, a love of literature. The established modes of education produce the opposite effect, unless in a fortunate few, who, by the celerity of their progress, and the distinctions they obtain, perhaps escape from the general influence. But, in the majority of cases, the memory of our slavery becomes associated with the studies we pursued, and it is not till after repeated struggles, that those things can be rendered the objects of our choice, which were for so long a time the themes of compulsion. This is particularly unfortunate, that we should conquer with much labour and application the difficulties that beset the entrance of literature, and then should quit it, when perhaps, but for this unfortunate association, the obstacles were all smoothed, and the improvement to be made would be attended through all its steps with unequivocal delight.

There is but one considerable objection that seems to oppose all these advantages. The preceptor is terrified at the outset, and says, How shall I render the labours of literature an object of desire, and still more how shall I maintain this desire in all its vigour, in spite of the discouragements that will daily occur, and in spite of the quality incident to almost every human passion, that its fervour disappears in proportion as the novelty of the object subsides?

But let us not hastily admit this for an insuperable objection. If the plan here proposed augments the difficulties of the teacher in one particular point, let it be remembered that it relieves him from an insufferable burthen in other respects.

Nothing can be more pitiable than the condition of the instructor in the present modes of education. He is the worst of slaves. He is consigned to the severest of imprisonments. He is condemned to be perpetually engaged in handling and rehandling the foundations of science. Like the unfortunate wretch upon whom the lot has fallen in a city reduced to extremities, he is destroyed, that others may live. Among all the hardships he is compelled to suffer, he endeavours to console himself with the recollection that his office is useful and patriotic. But even this consolation is a slender one. He is regarded as a tyrant by those under his jurisdiction, and he is a tyrant. He mars their pleasures. He appoints to each his portion of loathed labour. He watches their irregularities and their errors. He is accustomed to speak to them in tones of dictation and censure. He is the beadle to chastise their follies. He lives alone in the midst of a multitude. His manners, even when he goes into the world, are spoiled with the precision of pedantry and the insolence of despotism. His usefulness and his patriotism therefore have some resemblance to those of a chimney-sweeper and a scavenger, who, if their existence is of any benefit to mankind, are however rather tolerated in the world, than thought entitled to the testimonies of our gratitude and esteem.

ESSAY X.

OF DOMESTIC OR FAMILY LIFE*.

No subject is of more importance in the morality of private life than that of domestic or family life.

Every man has his ill humours, his fits of peevishness and exacerbation. Is it better that he should spend these upon his fellow beings, or suffer them to subside of themselves?

It seems to be one of the most important of the arts of life, that men should not come too near each other, or touch in too many points. Excessive familiarity is the bane of social happiness.

There is no practice to which the human mind adapts itself with greater facility, than that of apologising to itself for its miscarriages, and giving to its errors the outside and appearance of virtues.

The passionate man, who feels himself continually prompted to knock every one down that seems to him pertinacious and perverse, never fails to

* In the first edition of this work the title of this Essay was Of Cohabitation. It was suggested that there was an unpleasant ambiguity in this word.

expatiate upon the efficacy of this mode of correcting error, and to satirise with great vehemence the Utopian absurdity of him who would set them right by ways of mildness and expostulation.

The dogmatist, who, satisfied of the truth of his own opinions, treats all other modes of thinking as absurd, and can practise no forbearance for the prejudices of his neighbours, can readily inform you of the benefit which the mind receives from a rude shock, and the unceasing duration of errors which are only encountered with kindness and reason.

The man who lives in a state of continual waspishness and bickering, easily alleges in his favour the salutary effects which arise from giving pain, and that men are not to be cured of their follies, but by making them severely feel the ill consequences that attend on them.

The only method therefore of accurately trying a maxim of private morality, is to put out of the question all personal retrospect, and every inducement to the apologising for our own habits, and to examine the subject purely upon its general merits.

In the education of youth no recource is more frequent than to a harsh tone and a peremptory manner. The child does amiss, and he is rebuked. If he overlook this treatment, and make overtures of kindness, the answer is, No, indeed,

I shall take no notice of you, for you have done wrong.

All this is the excess of familiarity.

The tyrant governor practises this, and applauds himself for his virtue. He reviews his conduct with self-complacence; he sees in fancy the admirable consequences that will result from it; and, if it fails, he congratulates himself at least that he has proceeded with the most exemplary virtue.

He does not know that, through the whole scene, he has been only indulging the most shameful vices. He had merely been accumulating a certain portion of black bile, and in this proceeding he has found a vent for it. There was no atom of virtue or benevolence in his conduct. He was exercising his despotism in security, because its object was unable to resist. He was giving scope to the overflowings of his spite, and the child, who was placed under his direction, was the unfortunate victim.

There is a reverence that we owe to every thing in human shape. I do not say that a child is the image of God. But I do affirm that he is an individual being, with powers of reasoning, with sensations of pleasure and pain, and with principles of morality; and that in this description is contained abundant cause for the exercise of reverence and forbearance. By the system of nature he is placed by himself; he has a claim upon his little sphere of empire and discretion; and he is entitled to his appropriate portion of independence.

Violate not thy own image in the person of thy offspring. That image is sacred. He that does violence to it, is the genuine blasphemer. The most fundamental of all the principles of morality is the consideration and deference that man owes to man; nor is the helplessness of childhood by any means unentitled to the benefit of this principle. The neglect of it among mankind at large, is the principal source of all the injustice, the revenge, the bloodshed and the wars, that have so long stained the face of nature. It is hostile to every generous and expansive sentiment of our dignity; it is incompatible with the delicious transports of self-complacence.

The object of the harshness thus employed, is to bring the delinquent to a sense of his error. It has no such tendency. It simply proves to him, that he has something else to encounter, beside the genuine consequences of his mistake; and that there are men, who, when they cannot convince by reason, will not hesitate to overbear by force. Pertinacious and persuaded as he was before in the proceeding he adopted, he is confirmed in his persuasion, by the tacit confession which he ascribes to your conduct, of the weakness of your cause. He finds nothing so conspicuous in your behaviour as anger and ill humour; and anger and ill humour have very little tendency to impress upon a prejudiced spectator an opinion of the justice of your cause. The direct result of your proceeding, is to fill him with indignation against your despotism, to inspire him with a deep sense of the indignity to which he is subjected, and to perpetuate in his mind a detestation of the lesson that occasioned his pain.

If we would ascertain the true means of conviction, we have only to substitute in our minds, instead of this child placed under our care, a child with whom we have slight acquaintance, and no vicious habits of familiarity. I will suppose that we have no prejudices against this child, but every disposition to benefit him. I would then ask any man of urbane manners and a kind temper, whether he would endeavour to correct the error of this stranger child, by forbidding looks, harsh tones and severe language?

No; he would treat the child in this respect as he would an adult of either sex. He would know that to inspire hatred to himself and distaste to his lessons, was not the most promising road to instruction. He would endeavour to do justice to his views of the subject in discussion; he would communicate his ideas with all practicable perspicuity; but he would communicate them with every mark of conciliation and friendly attention. He would not mix them with tones of acrimony, and airs of lofty command. He would perceive that such a proceeding had a direct tendency to defeat his purpose. He would deliver them as hints for consideration, not as so many unappealable decisions from a chair of infallibility. But we treat adults of either sex, when upon a footing of undue familiarity, our wife or our comrade, in a great degree as we do children. We lay aside the arts of ingenuous persuasion; we forsake the mildness of expostulation; and we expect them to bow to the despotism of command or the impatience of anger. No sooner have we adopted this conduct, than in this case, as in the case of education, we we are perfectly ready to prove that it has every feature of wisdom, profound judgment and liberal virtue.

The ill humour which is so prevalent through all the different walks of life, is the result of familiarity, and consequently of cohabitation. If we did not see each other too frequently, we should accustom ourselves to act reasonably and with urbanity. But, according to a well known maxim, familiarity breeds contempt. The first and most fundamental principle in the intercourse of man with man, is reverence; but we soon cease to reverence what is always before our eyes. Reverence is a certain collectedness of the mind, a pause during which we voluntarily impress ourselves with the importance of circumstances and the dignity of persons. In order that we may properly exercise this sentiment, the occasions for calling it forth towards any particular individual, should be economised and rare. It is true, that genuine virtue requires of us a certain frankness and unreserve. But it is not less true, that it requires of us a quality in some degree contrasted with this, that we set a guard upon the door of our lips, that we carefully watch over our passions, that we never forget what we owe to ourselves, and that we maintain a vigilant consciousness strictly animadverting and commenting upon the whole series of our actions.

These remarks are dictated with all the licence of a sceptical philosophy. Nothing, it will be retorted, is more easy than to raise objections. All that is most ancient and universal among men is liable to attack. It is a vulgar task to destroy; the difficulty is to build.

With this vulgar and humble office however let us rest contented upon the present occasion. Though nothing further should result than hints for other men to pursue, our time perhaps will not have been misemployed.

Every thing human has its advantages and disadvantages. This, which is true as a general maxim, is probably true of family life.

There are two different uses that may flow from these hints. Grant that they prove cohabitation fundamentally an erroneous system. It is then reasonable that they should excite the inquisitive to contemplate and unfold a mode of society, in which it should be superseded. Suppose for a moment that cohabitation is indispensible, or that its benefits outweigh those of an opposite principle. Yet the developing its fundamental evil, is perhaps of all modes of proceeding best calculated to excite us to the reduction and abridgement of this evil, if we cannot annihilate it.

ESSAY XI.

OF REASONING AND CONTENTION.

There is a vice, frequently occurring in our treatment of those who depend upon us, which is ludicrous in its appearance, but attended with the most painful consequences to those who are the objects of it. This is, when we set out with an intention of fairness and equality with respect to them, which we find ourselves afterwards unable to maintain.

Let it be supposed that a parent, accustomed to exercise a high authority over his children, and to require from them the most uncontending submission, has recently been convinced of the impropriety of his conduct. He calls them together, and confesses his error. He has now discovered that they are rational beings as well as himself, that he ought to act the part of their friend, and not of their master; and he encourages them, when they differ in opinion with him as to the conduct they ought to pursue, to state their reasons, and proceed to a fair and equal examination of the subject.

If this mode of proceeding can ever be salutary, it must be to a real discussion that they are invited, and not to the humiliating scene of a mock discussion.

The terms must be just and impartial.

If either party convince the other, there is then no difficulty in the case. The difference of opinion is vanished, and the proceeding to be held will be correspondent.

But it perhaps more frequently happens, in the tangled skein of human affairs, if both parties without indolence or ill faith endeavour to do justice to their respective opinions, that no immediate change of sentiment is produced, and that both seem to leave off where they began. What is to be the result in this case?

If the terms are impartial, the child is then to be victorious. For the conduct to be held is his, and ought therefore, so far as equality is concerned, to be regulated by the dictates of his judgment.

But it is more frequent for the parent to say, No, I have heard you out; you have not convinced me; and therefore nothing remains for you but to submit.

Now in this case, putting myself in the place of the child, I have no hesitation to reply, Upon these terms I cannot enter the lists with you. I had rather a thousand times know at once what it is to which I must submit, and comply with a grace, than have my mind warmed with the discussion, be incited to recollect and to state with force a whole series of arguments, and then be obliged to quit the field with disgrace, and follow at the chariot-wheels of my antagonist.

But the case is in reality worse than this. The child may be unprejudiced and open to conviction. But it is little probable that the parent does not bring a judgment already formed to the discussion, so as to leave a small chance that the arguments of the child will be able to change it. The child will scarcely be able to offer any thing new, and has to contend with an antagonist equally beyond his match in powers of mind and body.

The terms of the debate therefore are, first, If you do not convince me, you must act as if I had convinced you. Secondly, I enter the lists with all the weight of long practice and all the pride of added years, and there is scarcely the shadow of a hope that you will convince me.

The result of such a system of proceeding will be extreme unhappiness.

Where the parent is not prepared to grant a real and *bona fide* equality, it is of the utmost importance that he should avoid the semblance of it. Do not open a treaty as between independent states, when you are both able and willing to treat the neighbour-state as a conquered province.

Place me in the condition of a slave, I shall perhaps be able to endure it. Human nature is capable of accommodating itself to a state of subjection, especially when the authority of the master is exercised with mildness, and seems to be directed in a considerable degree to promote the welfare of the dependent.

The situation I deprecate is that of a slave, who is endowed with the show and appearance of freedom. What I ask at your hand is, that you would not, without a good and solid meaning, waken all the secret springs of my nature, and call forth the swelling ambition of my soul. Do not fill me with the sublime emotions of independence, and teach me to take up my rest among the stars of heaven, if your ultimate purpose be to draw closer my fetters, and pull me down unwilling to the surface of the earth. This is a torture more refined than all that Sicilian tyrants ever invented.

The person who has been thus treated, turns restless upon the bed of his dungeon. He feels every thing that can give poignancy to his fate. He burns with indignation against the hourly events of his life. His sense of suffering, which would otherwise be blunted, is by this refinement, like the vitals of Prometheus, for ever preyed upon, and for ever renewed.

The child, whose education has been thus conducted, will be distinguished by a contentious and mutinous spirit. His activity will at first be excited by the invitation perpetually to debate the commands he receives. He will exercise his ingenuity in the invention of objections, and will take care not to lose his office of deliberating counsellor by any neglect of the functions that characterise it. He will acquire a habit of finding difficulties and disadvantages in every thing. He will be pleased to involve you in perpetual dispute, and to show that the acuteness of his talent is not inferior to yours. He will become indifferent to the question of truth and falsehood, and will exhibit the arts of a practised sophister. In this he will at first find gratification and amusement. But he heaps up for himself hours of bitterness. He will be rugged, harsh, tempestuous and untractable; and he will learn to loath almost the consciousness of existence.

The way to avoid this error in the treatment of youth, is to fix in our mind those points from which we may perceive that we shall not ultimately recede, and, whenever they occur, to prescribe them with mildness of behaviour, but with firmness of decision. It is not necessary that in so doing we should really subtract any thing from the independence of youth. They should no doubt have a large portion of independence; it should be restricted only in cases of extraordinary emergency; but its boundaries should be clear, evident and unequivocal. It is not necessary that, like some foolish parents, we should tenaciously adhere to every thing that we have once laid down, and prefer that heaven should perish rather than we stand convicted of error. We should acknowledge ourselves fallible; we should admit no quackery and false airs of dignity and wisdom into our system of proceeding; we should retract unaffectedly and with grace, whenever we find that we have fallen into mistake. But we should rather shun, than invite, controversy in matters that will probably at last be decided by authority. Thus conducting ourselves, we shall generate no resentful passions in the breasts of our juniors. They will submit themselves to our peremptory decisions, in the same spirit as they submit to the laws of inanimate necessity.

It were to be wished that no human creature were obliged to do any thing but from the dictates of his own understanding. But this seems to be, for the present at least, impracticable in the education of youth. If we cannot avoid some exercise of empire and despotism, all that remains for us is, that we take care that it be not exercised with asperity, and that we do not add an insulting familiarity or unnecessary contention, to the indispensible assertion of superiority.

ESSAY XII.

OF DECEPTION AND FRANKNESS.

There is no conduct in the education of youth more pernicious in its consequences, than the practice of deception.

It cuts off all generous reciprocity between children and persons of mature age. It generates a suspicious temper, which, instead of confiding in your demonstrations and assertions, exercises itself in perpetual watchfulness, expecting continually to detect your insincerity.

It teaches our children the practice of similar arts, and, as they have been overreached by their superiors, to endeavour to overreach them in return. What can be more unjust than the conduct of those parents, who, while they pride themselves in the ingenuity with which they deceive their children, express the utmost severity and displeasure, when their children attempt a reprisal, and are detected in schemes of similar adroitness?

It would be a useful task to enumerate the various sorts of deception which it is the custom of ordinary education successively to impose upon its subjects.

The practice of deception is one of those vices of education that are most early introduced into the treatment of youth.

If the nurse find a difficulty in persuading the child to go to sleep, she will pretend to go to sleep along with it. If the parent wish his youngest son to go to bed before his brothers, he will order the elder ones up stairs, with a permission to return as soon as they can do it unobserved. If the mother is going out for a walk or a visit, she will order the child upon some pretended occasion to a distant part of the house, till she has made her escape.

It is a deception too gross to be insisted on, to threaten children with pretended punishments, that you will cut off their ears; that you will put them into the well; that you will give them to the old man; that there is somebody coming down the chimney to take them away.

There is a passage in the Bible that seems to be of this sort, where it is said, "The eye that mocketh at his father, and despiseth to obey his mother, the ravens of the valley shall pick it out, and the young eagles shall eat it *."

This infantine doctrine respecting the punishment of misdemeanour, is succeeded by another, which, though less gross, is equally pernicious. This is, whenever we utter any lessons of pretended morality, which have been taken up by us upon trust, and not duly considered. There is in the world a long established jargon of this kind, sufficiently adapted to terrify those, who are to be terrified by a repetition of well sounding words. It generally happens however that, after the first stage of human life is concluded, this sort of morality appears sufficiently adapted for every body's use, but our own.

Nothing can be more subversive of true morality, of genuine principle and integrity, than this empty and unmeaning cant. Morality has a foundation in the nature of things, has reasons too strong for sophistry to shake, or any future improvement of human understanding to undermine.

* Proverbs, Ch. xxx. ver. 17.

But this rotten morality will not abide the slightest impartial examination; and when it is removed, the dissipated and thoughtless imagine they have detected the fallacy of every thing that bears the much injured name of morality.

It has been remarked that there is a commonplace sort of consolation for distress, which sounds sufficiently specious in the ears of men at ease, but appears unsatisfactory and almost insulting to those who stand in need of consolation. The like remark might be extended to every branch of morality.

If I would dissuade a man from drunkenness, gaming, or any other vice, nothing can be more incumbent upon me, than to examine carefully its temptations and consequences, and afterwards to describe them with simplicity and truth. I ought not to utter a word upon the subject that is not pregnant with meaning. I should take it for granted that the person with whom I expostulate is a rational being, and that there are strong considerations and reasons that have led him to his present conduct. Morality is nothing more than a calculation of pleasures; nothing therefore which is connected with pleasurable sensation, can be foreign to, or ought to be despised in, a question of morality. If I utter in perspicuous language the genuine deductions of my understanding, and results of my reflection, it is scarcely in human nature that I shall not obtain an attentive hearing. But there is a common-place language upon subjects of morality, vague and undefined in its meaning, embracing some truth, but full of absurd prejudice, which cannot produce much effect upon the hearer. It has been repeated a thousand times; it has been delivered down from age to age; and instead of being, what all morality ought to be, an impressive appeal to the strongest and most unalterable sentiments of the human heart, is the heaviest and most tedious homily that ever insulted human patience.

Nothing tends more effectually to poison morality in its source in the minds of youth, than the practice of holding one language, and laying down one set of precepts, for the observation of the young, and another of the adult. You fall into this error if, for instance, you require your children to go to church and neglect going yourself, if you teach them to say their prayers as a badge of their tender years, if they find that there are certain books which they may not read, and certain conversations they may not hear.

The usual mode of treating young persons, will often be found to suggest to children of ardent fancy and inquisitive remark, a question, a sort of floating and undefined reverie, as to whether the whole scene of things played before them be not a delusion, and whether, in spite of contrary appearances, they are not a species of prisoners, upon whom their keepers have formed some malignant design, which has never yet been properly brought to light. The line which is ordinarily drawn between men and children is so forcible, that they seem to themselves more like birds kept in a cage, or sheep in a pen, than like beings of the same nature. They see what is at present going on respecting them; but they cannot see what it means, or in what it is intended to terminate.

Rousseau, to whom the world is so deeply indebted for the irresistible energy of his writings, and the magnitude and originality of his speculations, has fallen into the common error in the point we are considering. His whole system of education is a series of tricks, a puppet-show exhibition, of which the master holds the wires, and the scholar is never to suspect in what manner they are moved. The scholar is never to imagine that his instructor is wiser than himself. They are to be companions; they are to enter upon their studies together; they are to make a similar progress; if the instructor drop a remark which facilitates their progress, it is to seem the pure effect of accident. While he is conducting a process of the most uncommon philosophical research, and is watching every change and motion of the machine, he is to seem in the utmost degree frank, simple, ignorant and undesigning.

The treatise of Rousseau upon education is a work of the highest value. It contains a series of most important speculations upon the history and structure of the human mind; and many of his hints and remarks upon the direct topic of education, will be found of inestimable value. But in the article here referred to, whatever may be its merit as a vehicle of fundamental truths, as a guide of practice it will be found of the most pernicious tendency. The deception he prescribes would be in hourly danger of discovery, and could not fail of being in a confused and indistinct manner suspected by the pupil; and in all cases of this sort a plot discovered would be of incalculable mischief, while a plot rejected could have little tendency to harm.

If we would have our children frank and sincere in their behaviour, we must take care that frankness and sincerity shall not be a source of evil to them. If there be any justice in the reasonings of a preceding essay*, punishment would find no share in a truly excellent system of education; even angry looks and words of rebuke would be wholly excluded. But upon every system it cannot fail to appear in the highest degree impolitic and mischievous, that young persons

* Essay X.

should have reason given them to repent of their sincerity.

There can be no one thing of higher importance in the education of youth, than the inspiring them with frankness. What sort of an idea must we form to ourselves of a young person, who regards his parent or instructor as a secret enemy or as an austere censor, and who is solicitous, as much as possible, to withdraw all his actions and thoughts from his observation? What sort of education must that be, where the thing pressed by the youth upon his confident with the most earnest importunity is, Do not let my father know any thing about it? It is worthy of observation, how early some children contract a cunning eye, a look of care and reserve, and all the hollow and hypocritical tricks and gestures, by which the persons who have the care of them are to be deceived and put upon a wrong scent.

The child that any reasonable person would wish to call his own or choose for the object of his attachment, is a child whose countenance is open and erect. Upon his front sit fearless confidence and unbroken hilarity. There are no wrinkles in his visage and no untimely cares. His limbs, free and unfettered, move as his heart prompts him, and with a grace and agility infinitely more winning than those of the most skilful dancer. Upon the slightest encouragement, he leaps into the arms of every thing that bears a human form. He welcomes his parent returning from a short absence, with a bounding heart. He is eager to tell the little story of his joys and adventures. There is something in the very sound of his voice, full, firm, mellow, fraught with life and sensibility; at the hearing of which my bosom rises, and my eyes are lighted up. He sympathises with sickness and sorrow, not in a jargon purposely contrived to cajole the sufferer, but in a vein of unaffected tenderness. When he addresses me, it is not with infantine airs and in an undecided style, but in a manner that shews him fearless and collected, full of good sense, of prompt judgment, and appropriate phraseology. All his actions have a meaning; he combines the guilelessness of undesigning innocence with the manliness of maturer years.

It is not necessary to contrast this character with that of a child of an opposite description, to demonstrate its excellence. With how ill a grace do cares and policy sit upon the countenance of an infant? How mortifying a spectacle, to observe his coldness, his timidity, the falseness of his eye and the perfidy of his wiles! It is too much, to drive the newly arrived stranger from human society, to inspire him with a solitary and self-centred spirit, and to teach him to fear an enemy, before he has known a friend!

ESSAY XIII.

OF MANLY TREATMENT AND BEHAVIOUR.

It has sometimes been a question among those who are accustomed to speculate upon the subject of education, whether we should endeavour to diminish or increase the distinction between youth and manhood, whether children should be trained to behave like men, or should be encouraged to the exercise of manners peculiar to themselves.

Pertness and primness are always in some degree ridiculous or disgusting in persons of infant years. There is a kind of premature manhood which we have sometimes occasion to observe in young persons, that is destructive of all honest and spontaneous emotion in its subjects. They seem as if they were robbed of the chief blessing of youth, the foremost consolation of its crosses and mortifications —— a thoughtless, bounding gaiety. Their behaviour is forced and artificial. Their temper is unanimating and frigid. They discuss and assert, but it is with a borrowed judgment. They pride themselves in what is eminently their shame; that they are mere parrots or echoes to repeat the sounds formed by another. They are impertinent, positive and self-sufficient. Without any pretensions to an extraordinary maturity of intellect, they are destitute of the modesty and desire of information that would become their age. They have neither the graces of youth nor age; and are like forced plants, languid, feeble, and, to any just taste, unworthy of the slightest approbation.

On the other hand there is a character opposite to this, with which it is impossible to be greatly delighted. The child is timorous, and bashful, and terrified at the idea of encountering a stranger; or he will accost the stranger with an infantine jargon, destitute alike of discrimination and meaning. There are parents, who receive a kind of sensual pleasure from the lisping and half-formed accents of their children; and who will treasure and re-echo them, for the purpose of adding duration to these imaginary or subordinate charms. Nothing is more common, than to employ a particular dialect to young persons, which has been handed down from generation to generation, and is scarcely inferior in antiquity to the dialect of Wicliffe or Chaucer. The children thus educated, understand dolls, and cock-horses, and beating tables, and riding upon sticks, and every thing but a little common sense. This infancy of soul is but slightly disgusting at first; but, as it grows up with growing stature, becomes glaringly unsuitable and absurd. There are children, who seem as if it were intended that they should always remain children, or at least make no proportionable advances towards manhood. They know nothing of the concerns of men, the state of man, or the reasonings of man. They are totally incapable of all sound and respectable judgment; and you might as well talk to your horse as to them, of any thing that required the genuine exercise of human faculties.

It is desirable that a child should partake of both characters, the child and the man. The hilarity of youth is too valuable a benefit, for any reasonable man to wish to see it driven out of the world. Nor is it merely valuable for the immediate pleasure that attends it; it is also highly conducive to health, to the best and most desirable state both of body and mind. Much of it would be cultivated by adults, which is now neglected; and would be even preserved to old age; were it not for false ideas of decorum, a species of hypocrisy, a supersubtle attention to the supposed minutiæ of character, that lead us to check our spontaneous efforts, and to draw a veil of gravity over the innocent as well as the immoderate, luxuriance and wantonness of our thoughts.

But, if hilarity be a valuable thing, good sense is perhaps still better. A comparison has sometimes been instituted between seriousness and gaiety, and an enquiry started as to which of the two is most excellent. Gaiety has undoubtedly a thousand recommendations; it is not so properly the means of happiness, as one of the different species of which happiness consists. No one would gain attention from a reasonable man, who should offer to advance a word against it. But gaiety must probably in the comparison yield to seriousness. The world in which we are engaged, is after all a serious scene. No man can expect long to retain the means of happiness, if he be not sometimes seriously employed in contemplating and combining them. The man of mere gaiety, passes away life like a dream, has nothing to recollect, and leaves behind no traces that he was. His state is rather a state of vegetation, each day like the day before, than a state worthy of a rational being. All that is grand and sublime, in conception or composition, in eloquence or in poetry, is serious. Nay, gaiety itself, if it be such as a delicate taste would approve, must have been indebted for its rearing and growth to seriousness. All that is sublime in character, all that is generously virtuous, all that extorts our admiration and makes conquest of our most ardent affections, must have been accompanied both in its rise and progress by seriousness. A character may be valuable, a man may be contented and happy, without gaiety; but no being can be worthy the name of a man, if seriousness be not an ingredient in his disposition.

A young person should be educated, as if he

were one day to become a man. He should not arrive at a certain age, and then all at once be launched upon the world. He should not be either wholly ignorant of, or unexercised in, the concerns of men. The world is a momentous and a perilous scene. What wise parent would wish his child to enter it, without preparation, or without being initiated in the spectacle of its practices?

The man should, by incessant degrees, be grafted upon the youth; the process should perhaps commence from the period of birth. There is no age at which something manly, considerate and firm, will not be found graceful. The true point of skill is, not to precipitate this important lesson, but to carry it on with a suitable progress; to shew, to the judicious and well-informed spectator, always somewhat to surprise, never any thing premature; or rather perhaps to shew him a youth, always superior to his years, but yet with so graceful and easy a superiority, as never to produce any sensations, but those of delight.

For this purpose, it is not necessary that we should check the sallies of youth. Nothing is of worse effect in our treatment either of the young or the old, than a continual anxiety, and an ever eager interference with their conduct. Every human being should be permitted, not only from a principle of benevolence, not only from a principle of justice, but because without this there can be no true improvement or excellence, to act from himself.

But it is more necessary that we should tolerate the sallies of youth, than that we should foster them. In our own conduct towards them, it is perhaps desirable that we should always talk to them the language of good sense, and never the jargon of the nursery; that we should be superior to the folly of adopting and repeating their little blunders; that we should pronounce our words with accuracy and propriety, and not echo their imperfect attempts at pronunciation. In thus conducting ourselves there is no need of any thing formal or monotonous. We may be gay; we may be affectionate; our countenance may be dressed in smiles; we may stoop to their capacities; we may adapt ourselves to the quickness and mutability of their tempers. We may do all this; we may win the kindness of their hearts; at the same time that we are lifting them up to our level, not sinking ourselves to theirs.

The whole of this branch of education undoubtedly requires the delicate preserving of a certain medium. We should reason with children, but not to such a degree as to render them parrots or sophists. We should treat them as possessing a certain importance, but not so as to render them fops and coxcombs. We should repose in them a certain confidence, and to a certain extent demand their assistance and advice, but not so as to convey a falsehood to their minds, or make them conceive they have accomplishments which they have not.

In early youth there must perhaps be some subjection of the pupil to the mere will of his superior. But even then the friend need not be altogether lost in the parent. At a certain age the parental character should perhaps be wholly lost. There is no spectacle that more forcibly extorts the approbation of the human mind, than that of a father and child, already arrived at years of discretion, who live together like brethren. There is no more unequivocal exhibition of imbecility, than the behaviour of a parent who, in his son now become a citizen at large, cannot forget the child; and who exercises, or attempts to exercise, an unseemly authority over him. The state of equality, which is the consummation of a just education, should for ever be borne in mind. We should always treat our children with some deference, and make them in some degree the confidents of our affairs and our purposes. We should extract from them some of the benefits of friendship, that they may one day be capable of becoming friends in the utmost extent of the term. We should respect them, that they may respect themselves. We should behold their proceedings with the eyes of men towards men, that they may learn to feel their portion of importance, and regard their actions as the actions of moral and intelligent beings.

ESSAY XIV.

OF THE OBTAINING OF CONFIDENCE.

THERE is no problem in the subject of education more difficult and delicate of solution, than that which relates to the gaining the confidence, and exciting the frankness of youth.

This is a point perhaps that is never to be accomplished by austerity; and which seems frequently to refuse itself to the kindest and most equitable treatment.

There is an essential disparity between youth and age; and the parent or preceptor is perhaps always an old man to the pupil. Their dispositions and their pursuits are different; their characters, their studies and their amusements must always be considerably unlike. This disparity will probably be found, however paradoxical the assertion may appear, to be increased in proportion to the frequency of their intercourse. A parent and a preceptor have of all human beings the least resemblance to children. Convert one young person into a sort of superintendent and director to his junior, and you will see him immediately start up into a species of formalist and pedant. He is watching the conduct of another; that other has no such employment. He is immersed in foresight and care; the other is jocund and careless, and has no thought of to-morrow. But what is most material, he grows hourly more estranged to the liberal sentiments of equality, and inevitably contracts some of the vices that distinguish the master from the slave.

Rousseau has endeavoured to surmount this difficulty by the introduction of a fictitious equality. It is unnecessary perhaps to say more of his system upon the present occasion, than that it is a system of incessant hypocrisy and lying.

The end proposed in the problem we are examining is of inestimable importance.

How shall I form the mind of a young person unless I am acquainted with it? How shall I superintend his ideas, and mould his very soul, if there be a thousand things continually passing there, of which I am ignorant? The first point that a skilful artificer would study, is the power of his tools, and the nature of his materials. Without a considerable degree of knowledge in this respect, nothing will be produced but abortive attempts, and specimens that disgrace the operator.

The thoughts which a young person specially

regards as his personal property, are commonly the very thoughts that he cherishes with the greatest affection. The formal lessons of education pass over without ruffling a fibre of his heart; but his private contemplations cause his heart to leap, and his blood to boil. When he returns to them, he becomes a new creature. He casts the slough of sedentary confinement; he resumes that elasticity of limb which his fetters had suspended. His eye sparkles; he bounds over the sod, as the young roe upon the mountains. His moments of restraint being gone, the boy becomes himself again.

The thoughts of childhood indeed, though to childhood they are interesting, are in themselves idle and of small account. But the period advances, in which the case is extremely altered. As puberty approaches, the turn which the mind of a young person shall then take, may have the most important effects upon his whole character. When his heart beats with a consciousness that he is somewhat, he knows not what; when the impatient soul spurns at that constraint, to which before it submitted without a murmur; when a new existence seems to descend upon him, and to double all that he was before; who then shall watch his thoughts and guide his actions? Happy for him, if this development of his nature is proportioned to the growth of his frame, and not forced on prematurely by some injurious associate.

This is a time when he is indeed in want of a pilot. He is now amidst shoals and quicksands, surrounded with dangers, on every side, and of denominations in the utmost degree varied. Yet this is a time when most of all he shuns the confidence of his superiors. If he were before in the utmost degree open and unreserved, and his thoughts always flowed unadulterated to his tongue, yet now shame suspends the communication, and he dares not commit his unfledged notions to the hearing of a monitor. He lights as a confident, upon a person, not less young, ignorant and inexperienced than himself; or, as it too frequently happens, his confident is of an imagination already debauched and depraved, who, instead of leading him with safety through untried fields, perpetually stimulates and conducts him to measures the most unfortunate.

It has sometimes been questioned whether such a confidence as is here alluded to, ought to be sought by the parent or preceptor, and whether the receiving it will not involve him in difficulties and uncertainties from which the wisest moralist cannot afterwards extricate himself, without injury to the pupil, and disgrace to himself. But surely it cannot reasonably be doubted that, where the pupil stands most in need of a wisdom greater than his own, it should be placed within his reach; and that there must, in the nature of things, be a conduct fitter than any other to be observed by the pupil under these circumstances, which investigation can ascertain, and to which the persons who undertake his education may with propriety guide him. To commit the events of the most important period of his life to accident, because we have not yet been wise enough to determine what they should be, may be the part of selfish policy preferring to all other concerns the artifice of its own reputation, but cannot be the part of enlightened affection and liberal philanthropy.

There is another reason beside that of the advantage to be derived from the assistance of superior age and experience, why the parent or preceptor should desire the confidence of the pupil. If I desire to do much towards cultivating the mind of another, it is necessary that there should exist between us a more than common portion of cordiality and affection. There is no power that has a more extensive operation in the history of the human mind, than sympathy. It is one of the characteristics of our nature, that we incline to weep with those that weep, and to rejoice with those that rejoice. But, if this be the case in our intercourse with an absolute stranger, it is unspeakably increased in proportion to the greatness of our esteem, and the strength of our attachment.

Society in any undertaking, lightens all its difficulties, and beguiles it of its weariness. When my friend accompanies me in my task, and our souls mutually catch and emit animation, I can perform labours that are almost more than human with an undoubting spirit. Where sympathy is strong, imitation easily engrafts itself. Persons who are filled with kindness towards each other, understand each other without asking the aid of voice and words. There is, as it were, a magnetical virtue that fills the space between them: the communication is palpable, the means of communication too subtle and minute to be detected.

If any man desire to possess himself of the most powerful engine that can be applied to the purposes of education, if he would discover the ground upon which he must stand to enable himself to move the whole substance of the mind, he will probably find it in sympathy. Great power is not necessarily a subject of abuse. A wise preceptor would probably desire to be in possession of great power over the mind of his pupil, though he would use it with economy and diffidence. He would therefore seek by all honest arts to be admitted into his confidence, that so the points of contact between them may be more extensively multiplied, that he may not be regarded by the pupil as a stranger of the outer court of the temple, but that his image may mix itself with his pleasures, and be made the companion of his recreations.

The road that a sound understanding would point out to us, as leading most directly to the confidence of another, is, that we should make ourselves as much as possible his equals, that our affection towards him should display itself in the most unambiguous colours, that we should discover a genuine sympathy in his joys and his sorrows, that we should not play the part of the harsh monitor and austere censor, that we should assume no artificial manners, that we should talk in no solemn, prolix and unfeeling jargon, that our words should be spontaneous, our actions simple, and our countenance the mirror to our hearts. Thus conducting ourselves, thus bland and insinuating with no treacherous design, we shall not probably meet a repulse in our well-chosen endeavours to be admitted the confidents of youth. Habit will tend to establish us in the post we have obtained; our ascendancy will every day become confirmed; and it is not likely that we shall lose this most distinguishing badge of friendship, unless through our own misconduct and folly.

The whole however of this branch of education is a point of the extremest delicacy. There is no medium so difficult to hit, as that between a distempered vigilance and an unsuspecting security. By falling into the latter it continually happens that parents and those who undertake the guidance of youth, remain satisfied that the persons under their care have no reserves with them, at the very time that they invent a thousand stratagems to elude their observation. Nothing can exceed the ludicrous effect of this arrogant confidence on the part of the senior, if we except the baseness and degradation which are thus, by his misconduct, perpetually inculcated upon and cultivated in the minds of youth.

In the mean time, it is so apparent that to obtain the voluntary confidence of a young person is a point of the greatest difficulty, that the preceptor ought probably to prepare his mind for the event of a failure, and to ascertain to himself the benefits that may be derived from the other advantages of education, when this is denied. So frail is man, so imperfect are his wisest designs, and so easily are we made the dupes of a love of power, that the most skilful instructor may often be expected to miscarry, in this most arduous of problems, this opprobrium of the art of education. It were better that he should not attempt it, than that he should attempt it by illiberal and forbidden means. If he cannot be the chosen confident, he may at least refrain from acting the spy or inquisitor upon his pupil. Let him not extort, what he cannot frankly and generously win. Let him not lie in wait to surprise from the pupil, what the pupil will not consent to give. Let him not so far debase the integrity of man, as to play the thief and the eaves-dropper. One of the most sacred principles in social life, is honour, the forbearance that man is entitled to claim from man, that a man of worth would as soon steal my purse or forge a title-deed to my estate, as read the letter he sees lying upon my table. One of the greatest errors of education, is that children are not treated enough like men, that they are not supported with sufficient care in the empire of their little peculium, that they are not made to feel their importance and to venerate themselves.

There is much that the preceptor may do for the improvement and advantage of his pupil without becoming his confident. He may communicate to him from day to day the most valuable lessons. He may form his mind to the most liberal sentiments. He may breathe into him the philanthropy of a Fenelon and the elevated soul of a Cato. If he be a man of merit, and duly conscious of his merit, he will not fear that he can miscarry in an attempt to excite the sympathy of his pupil. He will defy him to withhold that sympathy. He will dismiss with generous carelessness the question of an entire confidence and the communication of little cares and little projects. His hold upon the youthful mind will be of a higher and more decisive denomination. It would be strange indeed, if one who was initiated in the true science of the human mind, did not know how to wake the springs of the soul of an infant. And, while the pupil is continually subject to the most auspicious influences in all that is most essential to human welfare, while his mind is impregnated with the most generous sentiments and the purest virtues, it may well be believed that, in incidental and inferior points, he will not disgrace the principles by which he has been formed.

ESSAY XV.

OF CHOICE IN READING.

A DIFFICULTY which frequently presents itself in the private and domestic intercourse of parent and child, is that of determining what books it is proper that children should read, and what books they should not read.

It often happens that there are books read by the parent, which are conceived improper for the child. A collection of books, it may be, is viewed through glass doors, their outsides and labels are visible to the child; but the key is carefully kept, and a single book only at a time, selected by the parent, is put into his hands. A daughter is prohibited from the reading of novels; and in this prohibition will often commence a trial of skill, of quick conveyance on the part of the child, and of suspicious vigilance on the part of the parent.

Ought children to be thus restrained? Is it our duty to digest for our offspring, as the church of Rome has been accustomed to digest for her weaker members, an *Index Expurgatorius*, a catalogue of those books in the reading of which they may be permitted to indulge themselves?

Various are the mischiefs that inevitably flow out of such a precaution.

First, a wall of separation is thus erected between children and adults. They are made prisoners, and subjected to certain arbitrary regulations; and we are constituted their jailors. All generous reciprocity is destroyed between the two parties. I cannot ardently love a person who is continually warning me not to enter his premises, who plants a hedge about my path, and thwarts me in the impulses of my heart. I cannot understand the reasons that dictate his judgments; it is well if he understand them himself. I cannot therefore regard him as my friend. Friendship requires that the man in whose bosom it reigns, should act, and appear to act, for the interest of the object of his friendship. It is essentially hostile to all mystery. What I do not understand, cannot excite my affections. The man who shuts against me the secrets of his heart, cannot be unreservedly beloved by me. Friendship requires that the hearts of the persons should, as it were, be amalgamated into one substance, that their thoughts should be transparent to each other, and their communications entire. This perhaps can never be effected in its utmost extent. But it is of the most unfavourable effect, where the division and reserve pertinaciously force themselves upon observation.

Secondly, the despotism which is thus exercised, is peculiarly grating to a mind of generosity and spirit. Curiosity is one of the strongest impulses of the human heart. To curiosity it is peculiarly incident, to grow and expand itself under difficulties and opposition. The greater are the obstacles to its being gratified, the more it seems to swell, and labour to burst the mounds that confine it. Many an object is passed by with indifference, till it is rendered a subject of prohibition, and then it starts up into a source of inextinguishable passion. It may be alleged, that "this uneasiness and impatience in a young person are capable of being corrected." But is this any thing more than saying in other words, that the finest springs of the human mind may be broken, and the whole reduced to a chaos of dishonourable lumber? As long as the fiery grandeur of the soul remains, that will not be controled, and cannot be moulded by the frigid dictates of another's will, the kind of prohibitions here spoken of, will be felt with exquisite indignation, and, though involuntarily, will be registered as examples of a galling injustice.

Thirdly, the trial of skill thus instituted between the parent and child, is of the most pernicious tendency. The child is employed in doing that, in which it is his endeavour not to be detected. He must listen with anxious attention, lest he should be burst in upon before he is aware. He must break off his reading, and hide his book, a thousand times upon a false alarm. At length, when the interruption really occurs, he must rouse his attention, and compose his features. He imposes imperious silence upon the flutterings of his heart; he pitches to the true key of falshood the tone of his voice; the object of his most anxious effort, is to appear the thing that he is not. It is not possible to imagine a school of more refined hypocrisy.

The great argument in favour of this project of an *Index Expurgatorius*, is derived from the various degrees of moral or immoral tendency that is to be found in literary compositions.

One of the most obvious remarks that offer themselves under this head, is, that authors themselves are continually falling into the grossest mistakes in this respect, and show themselves superlatively ignorant of the tendency of their own writings. Nothing is more futile, than the formal and regular moral frequently annexed to Esop's fables of animals. Examine the fable impartially, and you will find that the lesson set down at the foot of it, is one of the last inferences that would have occurred to you. It is in a very different temper that the book-maker squeezes out what he calls his Use, from that in which the reader becomes acquainted with the circumstances of the fable.

To ascertain the moral of a story, or the genuine tendency of a book, is a science peculiarly abstruse. As many controversies might be raised upon some questions of this sort, as about the number six hundred and sixty six in the book of Revelations.

What is the tendency of Homer's Iliad? The author seems to have designed it, as an example of the fatal consequences of discord among political allies. One of the effects it appears most conspicuously to have produced, is that of enhancing the false lustre of military atchievements, and perpetuating the noxious race of heroes in the world.

What is the tendency of Gulliver's Travels, particularly of that part which relates to the Houyhnmhns and Yahoos? It has frequently been affirmed to be, to inspire us with a loathing aversion to our species, and fill us with a frantic preference for the society of any class of animals, rather than of men. A writer of our own day [Hayley*], as a suitable remuneration for the production of such a work, has placed the author in hell, and consigned him to the eternal torment of devils. On the other hand it has been doubted whether, under the name of Houyhnmhns and Yahoos, Swift has done any thing more than exhibit two different pictures of man, in his highest improvement and lowest degradation; and it has been affirmed that no book breathes more strongly a generous indignation against vice, and an ardent love of every thing that is excellent and honourable to the human heart.

There is no end to an enumeration of controversies of this sort. Authors themselves are no more infallible in this respect, than the men who read them. If the moral be invented first, the author did not then know where the brilliant lights of his story would fall, nor of consequence where its principal power of attraction would be found. If it be extracted afterwards, he is often taken at a disadvantage, and must extricate himself as he can.

Otway seems to have pursued the last method. The moral to his tragedy of the Orphan is thus expressed:

* Triumphs of Temper.

'Tis thus that heaven its empire does maintain;
It may afflict: but man must not complain.

Richardson pursued the opposite method. He has drawn in Lovelace and Grandison models of a debauched and of an elevated character. Neither of them is eminently calculated to produce imitation; but it would not perhaps be adventurous to affirm that more readers have wished to resemble Lovelace, than have wished to resemble Grandison.

Milton has written a sublime poem upon a strange story of the eating an apple, and of the eternal vengeance decreed by the Almighty against the whole human race, because their progenitor was guilty of this detestable offence. The object of his poem, as he tells us, was

To justify the ways of God to men. B. I., ver. 26.

But one of the most memorable remarks that suggest themselves under this branch of the subject, is, that the true moral and fair inference from a composition has often lain concealed for ages from its most diligent readers. Books have been handed down from generation to generation, as the true teachers of piety and the love of God, that represent him as so merciless and tyrannical a despot, that, if they were considered otherwise than through the medium of prejudice, they could inspire nothing but hatred. It seems that the impression we derive from a book, depends much less upon its real contents, than upon the temper of mind and the preparation with which we read it.

An instance of this kind, that perhaps deserves to be mentioned, may be adduced from a strain of pious gratitude and exultation in Dr. Watts's Divine Songs for Children.

Not more than others I deserve,
Yet God has given me more:
For I have food; while others *starve*
And beg from door to door!

Thus far we have considered moral and tendency as if they were two names for the same thing. This is however by no means the case.

The moral of any work may be defined to be, that ethical sentence to the illustration of which the work may most aptly be applied. The tendency is the actual effect it is calculated to produce upon the reader, and cannot be completely ascertained but by the experiment. The selection of the one, and the character of the other, will in a great degree depend upon the previous state of mind of the reader.

Let the example be the tragedy of the Fair Penitent. The moral deduced from this admirable poem by one set of readers will be, the mischievous tendency of unlawful love, and the duty incumbent upon the softer sex to devote themselves in all things to the will of their fathers and husbands. Other readers may perhaps regard it as a powerful satire upon the institutions at present existing in society relative to the female sex, and the wretched consequences of that mode of thinking, by means of which, in a woman, "one false step entirely damns her fame." They will regard Calista as a sublime example of a woman of the most glorious qualities, struggling against the injustice of mankind;—capable, by the greatness of her powers, and the heroism of her temper, of every thing that is excellent; contending with unconquerable fortitude against an accumulation of evils; conquered, yet not in spirit; hurried into the basest actions, yet with a soul congenial to the noblest. It is of no consequence whether the moral contemplated by the author, were different from both of these. The tendency again may be distinct from them all, and will be various according to the various tempers and habits of the persons by whom the work is considered.

From the distinctions here laid down it seems to follow, that the moral of a work is a point of very subordinate consideration, and that the only thing worthy of much attention is the tendency. It appears not unlikely that, in some cases, a work may be fairly susceptible of no moral inference, or none but a bad one, and yet may have a tendency in a high degree salutary and advantageous. The principal tendency of a work, to make use of a well known distinction, may be either intellectual or moral, to increase the powers of the understanding, or to mend the disposition of the heart. These considerations are probably calculated to moderate our censures, against many of the authors whose morality we are accustomed to arraign. A bad moral to a work, is a very equivocal proof of a bad tendency. To ascertain the tendency of any work is a point of great difficulty. The most that the most perfect wisdom can do, is to secure the benefit of the majority of readers. It is by no means impossible, that the books most pernicious in their effects that ever were produced, were written with intentions uncommonly elevated and pure.

The intellectual tendency of any book is perhaps a consideration of much greater importance, than its direct moral tendency. Gilblas is a book not very pure in its moral tendency; its subject is the successes and good fortune of a kind of sharper, at least, of a man not much fettered and burthened with the strictness of his principles; its scenes are a tissue of knavery and profligacy, touched with a light and exquisite pencil. Shakespear is a writer by no means anxious about his moral. He seems almost indifferent concerning virtue and vice, and takes up with either as it falls in his way. It would be an instructive enquiry to consider what sort of devastation we should commit in our libraries, if we were to pronounce upon the volumes by their moral, or even by their direct moral tendency. Hundreds of those works that have been the adoration of ages, upon which the man of genius and taste feeds with an uncloyed appetite, from which he derives sense, and power, and discernment, and refinement, and activity, and vigour, would be consigned to the flames for their transgressions, or to the lumber-room for their neutrality. While our choicest favours and our first attention would often be bestowed upon authors, who have no other characteristic attribute but that of the torpedo, and the principal tendency of whose literature is to drive all literature and talent out of the world.

If we suffer our minds to dwell upon the comparative merit of authors, if we free ourselves from the prejudices of the nursery, and examine the question in the liberal spirit of scholars and philosophers, we shall not long hesitate where to bestow our loudest approbation. The principal praise is certainly due to those authors, who have a talent to "create a soul under the ribs of death *;" whose composition is fraught with irresistible enchantment; who pour their whole souls into mine, and raise me as it were to the seventh heaven; who furnish me with "food for contem-

* Milton.

plation even to madness * ;" who raise my ambition, expand my faculties, invigorate my resolutions, and seem to double my existence. For authors of this sort I am provided with an ample licence; and, so they confer upon me benefits thus inestimable and divine, I will never contend with them about the choice of their vehicle, or the incidental accompaniments of their gift. I can guess very nearly what I should have been, if Epictetus had not bequeathed to us his Morals, or Seneca his Consolations. But I cannot tell what I should have been, if Shakespear or Milton had not written. The poorest peasant in the remotest corner of England, is probably a different man from what he would have been but for these authors. Every man who is changed from what he was by the perusal of their works, communicates a portion of the inspiration all around him. It passes from man to man, till it influences the whole mass. I cannot tell that the wisest mandarin now living in China, is not indebted for part of his energy and sagacity to the writings of Milton and Shakespear, even though it should happen that he never heard of their names.

Books will perhaps be found, in a less degree than is commonly imagined, the corrupters of the morals of mankind. They form an effective sub-

* Rowe.

sidiary to events and the contagion of vicious society: but, taken by themselves, they rarely produce vice and profligacy where virtue existed before. Every thing depends upon the spirit in which they are read. He that would extract poison from them, must for the most part come to them with a mind already debauched. The power of books in generating virtue, is probably much greater than in generating vice. Virtue is an object that we contemplate with a mind at peace with itself. The more we contemplate it, the more we find our fortitude increase, enabling us to contend with obstacles, and even to encounter contempt. But vice is an object of a peculiarly unfavourable sort. The thought of entering into a vicious course, is attended with uneasiness, timidity and shame; it disarms, still more strongly than it excites us; and our reluctance to a life of profligacy can scarcely be overcome but by the stimulus of bold and impudent society.

Another observation of considerable importance in deciding on the subject we are here examining, relates to an error that too often pervades the whole course of an attentive and affectionate education. The regard of a parent to his child will frequently rise to the most extravagant height. He considers him as a prodigy. He thinks no labour too great to be expended on him. He scarcely suffers the idea of him at any time to escape from his recollection. He regards him with the fondness of an enthusiastic lover for his mistress; and treats him as the child himself would treat some precious toy, which he will not suffer to be put out of his sight. He protects him with as much anxiety, as if a rude shock would dash him to pieces, or a rough blast wither the very essence of his frame.

This is essentially wrong. The true end of human existence, is not to serve as a toy and amusement to another. Man can never appear in his genuine dignity, but so far as he is capable of standing alone. A child is not to be reared as that precious thing, that no wind may blow, and no sun may scorch. Let us never forget that our child is a being of the same nature with ourselves; born to have passions and thoughts and sentiments of his own; born to fill a station, and act a part; with difficulties that he ought to surmount, and duties that he is bound to discharge.

Such is the genuine vocation of man. In the remembrance of this vocation he ought to be bred. The man ought to descend upon the child by insensible degrees, till his whole bosom swells with the generous freight. He should begin to stand by himself, and respect his own dignity, as soon as he is able to utter an articulate sound.

For this purpose there is always a portion of confidence which it is our duty to repose in him.

He should neither be bred apart from the world, nor in ignorance of what passes in the world. He should be accustomed to behold the faces of his species. He should know something of the story of their passions, their singularities, and even of their vices. He should be suffered to stand where their inclinations may sometimes interfere and jostle with his. It is much to be feared, if we breed him in indolent effeminacy to a certain age, that his whole life will bear the marks of it. The human mind is never so ductile and pliant as in early youth. Whatever therefore we should wish to find it at years of maturity, we should endeavour to begin in it at the tenderest years.

These remarks are obviously applicable to the subject of choice in reading. As, relative to the question of social intercourse, the child should early begin in some degree to live in the world, that is, with his species; so should he do as to the books he is to read. It is not good, that he should be shut up for ever in imaginary scenes, and that, familiar with the apothegms of philosophers, and the maxims of scientifical and elevated morality, he should be wholly ignorant of the perverseness of the human heart, and the springs that regulate the conduct of mankind. Trust him in a certain degree with himself. Suffer him in some instances to select his own course of reading. There is danger that there should be something too studied and monotonous in the selection we should make for him. Suffer him to wander in the wilds of literature. There is a principle in the human mind by which a man seems to know his own time, and it will sometimes be much better that he should engage in the perusal of books at the period of his own choice, than at the time that you may recollect to put them in his hands. Man is a creature that loves to act from himself; and actions performed in this way, have infinitely more of sound health and vigour in them, than the actions to which he is prompted by a will foreign to his own.

There is only one further remark to be added on this subject. It has ready been shewn that the impression we derive from a book, depends much less upon its real contents, than upon the temper of mind and preparation with which we read it. Hence it should seem to follow that a skilful preceptor need be under little apprehension respecting the books which his pupil should select for his perusal. In this sense a celebrated maxim of the apostle Paul may be admitted for true, To the pure all things are pure. Nothing is more common than to see a man who labours under certain prepossessions, exclaiming upon the most demonstrative arguments as flimsy and superficial, and reading the most incoherent and ridiculous rhapsodies with unmingled reverence. This however is not always to be trusted to. Truth is powerful, and, if not instantly, at least by slow degrees, may make good her possession. Gleams of good sense may penetrate through the thickest clouds of error. But we are supposing in the present case that truth is the object of the preceptor. Upon that assumption it would be strange indeed, if he were not able to triumph over corruption and sophistry, with the advantage of being continually at hand, of watching* every change and symptom as they may arise, and more especially with the advantage of real voice, of accommodated eloquence, and of living sympathies, over a dead letter. These advantages are sufficient; and, as the true object of education is not to render the pupil the mere copy of his preceptor, it is rather to be rejoiced in, than lamented, that various reading should lead him into new trains of thinking; open to him new mines of science and new incentives to virtue; and perhaps, by a blended and compound effect, produce in him an improvement which was out of the limits of his lessons, and raise him to heights the preceptor never knew.

* No reader perhaps can need to be reminded of the difference between this watchfulness, and the disingenuous vigilance spoken of in page 112. A philosophical perspicacity is highly beneficial, but not that sort of observingness which is so sensitive as to subvert our tranquillity, or so unscrupulous as to blast our honour.

ESSAY XVI.

OF EARLY INDICATIONS OF CHARACTER.

A FEW remarks will not be unprofitably set down, on the subject of juvenile character, and the promising and unpromising indications that early display themselves in the manners of youth.

Calumny has long been privileged to stalk the world at large, and to shed its poison upon the fairest flowers. It can show a very ancient title, and will not easily suffer ejectment. Secret resentment often delights to add new malignity to its venom; and often a mere gaiety of humour sporting in thoughtless sallies, will fix a sting that neither time, nor all the healing arts of wisdom and virtue, shall be able to cure. The wound rankles unseen. The grandest efforts of genius, and the purest energies of benevolence, thus become enfeebled, discouraged, annihilated. Nothing more easy than to barb the slander; nothing more difficult than to extract the dart. The whole appearance of the man becomes discoloured and disfigured; all his virtues are transformed into vices; all his actions are misrepresented, misunderstood and vilified. It matters not with how much generosity he sets himself to act: the glass of truth shall never be turned on him; nor shall he in any instance obtain justice.

But calumny is doubly execrable and unmanly, when it attacks the first promising dawnings of youth. A man sufficiently adult, has attained some strength, and can cope with it. He can plead his own cause. He has tried the passions of men, and the magic of undaunted truth; and uses both, as tools with the powers of which he is acquainted. Beside, a man must expect some time or other to encounter adversity: if he be hardly pressed upon, and unjustly dealt with, his case is indeed worthy of regret; but it is the lot of man, and the condition under which he was born. It is worse than this, when a weak and defenceless youth is made the butt of these attacks. It is more worthy of regret, when he is refused the common period of probation; is maimed and dismounted at the very entrance of the course; and sent to languish long years of a baffled existence, with his limbs already withered and shrunk up by the shocks of calumny. That men should be condemned unjustly, is that which ought not to be; that they should be condemned untried, and not for what they have done, but for what we presume to foretel they will do, is an aggravation of the calamity.

The argument against calumny however has been carried too far. It is an erroneous system of morality which would teach us, that we judge not, lest we should be judged; and that we speak evil of no man. Falshood is vice, whether it be uttered to a man's commendation or censure; and to suppress that which is true, is to be regarded as a species of falshood. We ought not to desire for ourselves, not to be judged, but that we may not be judged unjustly; and the like equal measure we ought to deal to others. I feel no exultation in that man's applause, who is not also endowed with a republican boldness to censure. Frankness is perhaps the first of virtues; or, at least, is that without which virtue of a manly and liberal dimension cannot exist. To give to our thoughts their genuine and appropriate language, is one of the most wholsome exercises in which we can be engaged. Without this exercise it is scarcely possible that we should learn to think with precision and correctness. It teaches us to review our thoughts; to blush for their absurdity, their groundless singularities, and their exaggeration. It ripens what at first was merely opinion, into system and science. The fault for the most part, when we speak of the merits of our neighbour, is not, that we say what we think; but that, for want of practice and skill, we say what we do not think; we do not suit our words to the measure of our sentiments; we do not call our minds into operation to compare our opinions with the grounds of our opinions, and our phrases with both. We communicate to our hearers sentiments that we do not entertain. We debauch even our own judgments, while we speak; and instead of analysing, arranging and fashioning our conclusions as we ought, become impassioned by listening to the sound of our own voice, subject our matter to our words, not the words to the matter, and talk ourselves into extravagancies, which we did not think of in the outset, but which we have not afterwards the courage and candour to retract, either to others or to ourselves.

What is to be demanded therefore in behalf of the young, is not, that we should refrain from judging them, or fear to utter our judgments; but that we should indefatigably endeavour to form true principles of judgment, that we should allow ourselves in no hasty conclusions, that, recollecting the mutability of youth, we should be reluctant to pass a final condemnation, and above all, that we should not from the force of a jaundiced imagination, convert the little starts, the idle sallies and the temporary deviations of an unformed mind, into inexpiable errors.

It often happens that irregularities which ought perhaps rather to be regarded as indications of future greatness, are converted into subjects of pitiful lamentation and odious condolence, when the spectator is a man of narrow morals, and of principles of judgment absurdly frigid and severe.

The youth respecting whom I should augur

most favourably, is he, in whom I observe some useless luxuriance, and some qualities, which terrify, while they delight me. The most abundant endowments will one day assume a regularity and arrangement, which endowments in the next degree inferior are unable to attain. Sobriety, constancy, an awful and wide-spreading tranquillity, that might in one point of view be compared with that of the Grand Southern Pacific Ocean, are perhaps in some degree the characteristics of a mind of the first order. It is not ruffled by every puff of air; it holds on its way with a majestic course; it is self-balanced and self-centred; always great, always worthy, and always sublime.

But this is not the case with a mind, in which as yet the hints and capabilities of greatness only exist. A mighty machine, till it is put into order, seems only an inexplicable chaos. The limbs and members of which it consists, are scattered wide. Every thing is unarranged and rude.

A feeble mind is not greatly liable to excess. A powerful mind, when it has not yet essayed its powers, and poised its wings, is the seat, sometimes of ridiculous, sometimes of dangerous, irregularities.

A mind, conscious of its destined strength, but which as yet can scarcely be called strong, is often presumptuous, dogmatical, fierce, hard, unkind, tempestuous, unduly severe in its judgments of character and talent;

> Is ne'er so sure our ardour to create,
> As when it treads the brink of all we hate*.

This proposition however is by no means to be understood universally. A young person destined in the sequel to display uncommon talents, will often at present appear singularly amiable. It will be hard, if a young person of talents should not be in some respects amiable. It is a reasonable subject of fear, when the unamiable qualities above enumerated appear with peculiar strength in early youth, that some vestige of them will become essentially interwoven with the character, and even attend their possessor to the grave.

There are some admirable traits of character, that are almost inseparable from the youth of a person destined hereafter to play an illustrious part upon the theatre of mankind.

The first of these is curiosity. His mind may be expected to be incessantly at work, pursuing enquiries, accumulating knowledge, observing, investigating, combining. His curiosity however may frequently be found to be an obstinate, self-willed principle, opening veins of its own chusing, wasting itself in oblique, unprofitable speculations,

* Pope. These are not his exact words.

and refusing to bring its energies to bear upon a pursuit pointed out to it by another.

A second characteristic of early genius is candour. Often will a young person of uncommon endowments be peremptory, rough, building his conclusions on the most unsatisfactory foundations, and asserting them with the most ungraceful arrogance. But there is a tone of voice and sentiment which, the moment it reaches his ears, will, as it were by enchantment, recal him to himself, and bring forth to view all the honest, fearless, unresisting candour, that till then dwelt, idle and unremarked, in his bosom. To common observers, however, and in ordinary cases, he will appear the reverse of candour. There is an imperious tone in the aged and the adult, presuming on slight grounds, dictatorial, peevish and impotent, which he will be apt to repel with rude and unbecoming indignation.

A third characteristic of early genius is the love of distinction. He burns to be somebody. He cannot endure to be confounded in the crowd. It is the nature of the human mind never to be satisfied with itself, except so far as it can by some means procure to have its own favourable opinion confirmed by the suffrage of others. This characteristic however, like the preceding ones, will frequently disappoint the observer. The pupil has chosen his own favourite field of distinction, and will often be callous to allurements which are to invite him into another. He will perhaps be delicate in his appetite for praise. Gross flattery, and still more the spiritless and tedious eulogium of superannuated kindness, or that is dictated by a left-handed purpose of stratagem and bribery, will tire his impatience, or excite his disgust.

One of the faults which has been too often and too severely censured in young persons, is conceit. This is a fault certainly more incident to a youth with talents, than to a youth without. He is like a person newly appointed to some post of honour; he is not yet familiarized to the exercise of authority, or the splendour of decoration. This is a fault of all others that demands our forbearance, since in the nature of things it is almost certain to be temporary. Familiar with distinction, he will in no long time learn to wear it with ease. A man of talents, from the activity of his mind and his incessant spirit of observation, will necessarily compress ten times as much experience into a given period, as an ordinary man. Each day in his history, will furnish him with a comment on the last. He will so often have detected his mistakes, so frequently contemned his absurdities, and will have felt with so much anguish his misconduct and disgraces, that he can scarcely fail, when the first effervescence of youth is over, to become diffident, self-suspicious and, in the best sense of the term, modest. One thing further is to be remarked under this head of conceit. The conceit of young persons, unless observed with an eye peculiarly candid and discerning, will be more than commonly disgustful. It is a frigid, selfish, unchastised, unpolished sentiment. As they ascend to manhood, it will be modified by the better affections and charities of the human heart, its coldness will be animated, its asperities subdued, and the stiffness that fettered it broken off. An enlightened spectator will not fail to take this circumstance into consideration.

There is one point that remains to be discussed, respecting the supposed unpromising indications which discover themselves in the manners of youth, that is of more serious importance than any of the preceding. I mean, what relates to the excesses of their conduct, and their offences against morality.

Too often, by the adult, the anxious parent, and the cassocked pedant, this subject is considered with an unpardonable severity. Let it be recollected, that it is the characteristic of the strong, and therefore the valuable mind, to mix this strength in its vices, as well as its virtues. It is thus frequently that the most inestimable lessons of experience are amassed. The impetuosity of youth must have time to subside. Of all the characteristics of early life, tameness is the characteristic of most fatal augury. A young man, just arrived at years of puberty, will, like a high-bred, well-mettled horse, champ the bit, and spurn the earth, impatient of restraint. He will have his period of intoxication. Provided its date be short, it seems as if it were scarcely to be regretted. The season of sobriety and reflection will take its turn; and, if then a wise, a considerate and an affectionate friend could lend his assistance to the genuine operations of the mind, the event would be inexpressibly auspicious.

There is nothing more contrary to true justice and enlightened morality, than the unsparing harshness with which the old frequently censure the extravagancies of the young. Enamoured of black forebodings, and gorged with misanthropy, they pour out their ill-omened prophesyings with unpitying cruelty. The sober, the dull, the obedient, lads that have no will and no understanding of their own, are the only themes of their eulogium. They know no touch of candour and liberal justice. They make no allowance for the mutability of youth, and have no generous presentiment of their future recollection and wisdom. They never forgive a single offence. They judge of characters from one accidental failing, and will not deign to turn their attention to those great and admirable qualities, by which this one failing, it may be, is amply redeemed. They may be compared to that tyrant of antiquity who, intending to convey a symbolical lesson upon the principles of despotism, passed through a field of corn, and struck off every ear that had the audacity to rear its head above the dull and insipid level of its fellows.

In the midst however of the candid and liberal indulgence which is so amply due to juvenile years, we must not forget the principles of impartial judgment. It will often be our duty to regret, while we forgive. It too frequently happens that the excesses of youth, not only leave an unfavourable stain upon the reputation, but that they corrupt the disposition, and debase the character. It is not every youthful folly that men shake off when they arrive at years of discretion. The wild and inconsiderate boy will often entail some of the worst features of his character on the man.

Owing to this it is, that we frequently meet with that mixed character in the adult over which humanity weeps. We have often occasion to observe the most admirable talents, and even the most excellent dispositions, in men, whose talents and virtues are nevertheless rendered abortive by some habitual indiscretion. These men a well-formed mind cannot fail to love. Their very weakness causes a peculiar kind of tenderness to mix itself with our love. But they go out of the world, having excited its admiration, not added to the stock of good; or their usefulness, if useful they have been, falls infinitely short of that which their great qualities would have enabled them to produce.

Sometimes however the ill consequence that remains from the impression of youthful follies, is much worse than this. The talents remain, but the character becomes debauched. The men excite our admiration, but we view their powers with less of hope, than terror. The ingenuousness, the simplicity of a good heart, are extinguished. They become crafty and deceitful. Possessed with an unhallowed spirit of ambition, the purity and fervour of benevolence in them are lost. They are launched perhaps upon the ocean of affairs; they mix with the giddy scene of fashion; they are initiated in all the degrading arts, by which extravagance is supported, and sudden fortune is acquired; and they prey upon the unwary and the industrious, unless opportunity and policy should call them to prey upon the vitals of their country.

THE

ENQUIRER.

PART II.

ESSAY I.

OF RICHES AND POVERTY.

THERE is nothing that deserves to be more minutely watched, than what may be styled an intemperate spirit of philosophy.

The sect that carried this spirit to the most ridiculous extreme among the ancients, were the Stoics.

One of the decisions of this spirit is, that riches are no benefit, and poverty no evil.

If this maxim were true, particularly the latter member, in its utmost extent, the chief argument in favour of political reform and amendment would be shewn to be utterly false.

The reverse of this maxim, it should seem, ought to be received. Poverty is an enormous evil. By poverty I understand the state of a man possessing no permanent property, in a country where wealth and luxury have already gained a secure establishment.

He then that is born to poverty, may be said, under another name, to be born a slave.

A boy of a thoughtful and reflecting turn, will frequently look forward in this respect to the state of manhood, with an aching heart. Now, he will exclaim, I am maintained by the industry of others; I am freed from all solicitude about the supply of to-morrow. But hereafter I shall be told, You shall not have the necessaries of the day without the labour of the day; "He that will not work, neither shall he eat*." His state in several respects resembles the prophetic denunciation of Jesus Christ to the apostle Peter: "Verily, verily, I say unto thee, When thou wast young, thou girdedst thyself, and walkedst whither thou wouldest: but when thou shalt be old, thou shalt stretch forth thy hands, and another shall gird thee, and carry thee whither thou wouldest not†." In reality however, the child and the adult are both slaves in different ways: when we put on the manly gown, we only change one species of despot for another.

* II Thess. Chap. iii, ver. 10. † John, Chap. xxi, ver. 18.

But, it will be asked, is not the complaint here recited, unreasonable and unjust? Is any man entitled to claim through life, that he should be maintained by the industry of others?

Certainly not. The injustice I suffer, is not in the actual labour, but in the quantity of that labour. If no man were absolutely compelled to perform a greater share of labour than, multiplied by the number of members in the community, was necessary for the subsistence of the community, he would have no right to complain on that account. But the labour then required, would be diminished to a tenth, perhaps a twentieth part of the labour now imposed upon the husbandman and artificer *.

The evil of poverty principally consists of the following particulars: leaving out of the enumeration the frequently experienced insufficiency of labour to maintain the poor; the usual accident of men's being thrust out of their customary train of industry and resource for bread, by the fluctuations of society; and the want of a suitable provision for sickness, infirmity and age.

We will confine ourselves to points of more universal application.

First, the abridgment of life, and privation of the enjoyments of life.

* Political Justice, Book VIII, Chap. VI, octavo edition.

As to the abridgment of life we are scarcely competent judges, since wealth, expended in sensuality and indulgence, is scarcely less hostile to the protraction of existence. Every one can see however, that inordinate labour produces untimely decrepitude. Every one can conceive the varieties of pain and disease, which accrue from the restraint of our limbs, the intemperate exercise of the muscles, and a continual exposure to the inclemency of the seasons.

That the poor are peculiarly subjected to a privation of the enjoyments of life, and obliged to content themselves for the greater part of their existence with that negative happiness which consists in the absence of pain, is a point too evident to need illustration.

Secondly, the poor are condemned to a want of that leisure which is necessary for the improvement of the mind. They are the predestinated victims of ignorance and prejudice. They are compelled for the most part to rank with those creatures, that exist only for a few years, and then are as if they had never been. They merely vegetate. The whole of the powers they possess, is engaged in the pursuit of miserable expedients to protract their existence. Whatever be the prejudice, the weakness or the superstition of their age and country, they have scarcely any chance to escape from it. It is melancholy to reflect, how few moments they can have of complacence, of exultation, of honest pride, or of joy. Theirs is a neutral existence. They go forward with their heads bowed down to the earth, in a mournful state of inanity and torpor. Yet, like the victims of Circe, they have the understanding left ever and anon to afford them a glimpse of what they might have been. In this respect they are more unfortunate than the beasts.

Thirdly, even those who escape from the general sentence of ignorance, are haunted with the ills of poverty in another shape. Leisure well employed is the most invaluable benefit that can fall to the lot of man. If they have had leisure to accumulate the rudiments of knowledge, they have not the leisure to construct them. Even if their immediate avocation have something in it analogous to the cultivation of intellect, still they are not carried whither they would, but whither they would not. Wherever almost we find the records of talents and genius, we find a man impelled by accident, hurried by necessity, and the noblest conceptions of his mind rendered abortive by the ills of fortune. There is no plant that requires to be so assiduously tended, and so much favoured by every incidental and subordinate circumstance, as the effusions of fancy, and the discoveries of science.

While such appear to me the genuine effects

of poverty, never will I insult the sacred presence of its victims, by telling them that poverty is no evil!

Hence also we may be led to perceive the mistake of those persons who affirm, that the wants which are of the first necessity, are inconsiderable, and are easily supplied.

No; that is not inconsiderable, which cannot be purchased but by the sacrifice of the best part of my time, and the first fruit of my labours.

This is the state of society at the period in which I am born into the world. I cannot remedy the evil, and therefore must submit to it. I ought to work up my mind to endure it with courage; I should yield with a chearful and active temper to the inequality of my burthen; but it is neither necessary nor desirable that I should be insensible to the true state of the case.

Addison ludicrously exclaims in his tragedy of Cato:

> What pity 'tis
> That we can die but once to serve our country!

If the condition of human life corresponded indeed with this patriotic wish, a man might content himself to pass through one of its repetitions under the pressure of great disadvantages. But, when we recollect that we appear but once upon this theatre, that our life is short and precarious, that we rise out of nothing, and that, when we die, we "pass a bourne from which no traveller returns*;" we cannot but deeply regret, that our exertions are so many ways fettered and drawn aside from their true direction, and that the life we would improve for happiness or for honour, is almost inevitably rendered in a great degree abortive.

The genuine wealth of man is leisure, when it meets with a disposition to improve it. All other riches are of petty and inconsiderable value.

Is there not a state of society practicable, in which leisure shall be made the inheritance of every one of its members?

ESSAY II.

OF AVARICE AND PROFUSION.

WHICH character deserves our preference, the man of avaricious habits, or of profuse ones? Which of the two conducts himself in the manner most beneficial to society? Which of the two is actuated by motives the most consonant to justice and virtue?

Riches and poverty are in some degree necessarily incidental to the social existence of man.

* Shakespear.

There is no alternative, but that men must either have their portion of labour assigned them by the society at large, and the produce collected into a common stock; or that each man must be left to exert the portion of industry, and cultivate the habits of economy, to which his mind shall prompt him.

The first of these modes of existence deserves our fixed disapprobation*. It is a state of slavery and imbecility. It reduces the exertions of a human being to the level of a piece of mechanism, prompted by no personal motives, compensated and alleviated by no genuine passions. It puts an end to that independence and individuality, which are the genuine characteristics of an intellectual existence, and without which nothing eminently honourable, generous or delightful can in any degree subsist.

Inequality therefore being to a certain extent unavoidable, it is the province of justice and virtue to counteract the practical evils which inequality has a tendency to produce. It is certain that men will differ from each other in their degrees of industry and economy. But it is not less certain, that the wants of one man are similar to the wants of another, and that the same things will conduce to the improvement and happiness of

* Political Justice, Book VIII, Chap. II, octavo edition.

each, except so far as either is corrupted by the oppressive and tyrannical condition of the society in which he is born. The nature of man requires, that each man should be trusted with a discretionary power. The principles of virtue require, that the advantages existing in any community should be equally administered; or that the inequalities which inevitably arise, should be repressed, and kept down within as narrow limits as possible.

Does the conduct of the avaricious man, or of the man of profusion, best contribute to this end?

That we may try the question in the most impartial manner, we will set out of the view the man who subjects himself to expences which he is unable to discharge. We will suppose it admitted, that the conduct of the man, whose proceedings tend to a continual accumulation of debt, is eminently pernicious. It does not contribute to his own happiness. It drives him to the perpetual practice of subterfuges. It obliges him to treat men, not according to their wants or their merits, but according to their importunity. It fixes on him an ever gnawing anxiety that poisons all his pleasures. He is altogether a stranger to that genuine lightness of heart, which characterises the man at ease, and the man of virtue. Care has placed her brand conspicuous on his brow. He is subject to occasional paroxysms of anguish which no luxuries or splendour can compensate. He accuses the system of nature of poisonous infection, but the evil is in his own system of conduct.

The pains he suffers in himself are the obvious counterpart of the evils he inflicts upon others. He might have foreseen the effects of his own conduct, and that foresight might have taught him to avoid it. But foresight was in many instances to them impracticable. They suffer, not in consequence of their own extravagance. They cannot take to themselves the miserable consolation, that, if now they are distressed, they have at least lavished their money themselves, and had their period of profusion and riot.

There is no reason to be found in the code of impartial justice, why one man should work, while another man is idle. Mechanical and daily labour is the deadliest foe to all that is great and admirable in the human mind. But the spendthrift is not merely content that other men should labour, while he is idle. They have reconciled themselves to that. They have found that, though unjust in itself, they cannot change the system of political society; and they submit to their lot. They console themselves with recollecting the stipulated compensation of their labours. But he is not satisfied that they should labour for his gratification: he obliges them to do this gratuitously; he trifles with their expectations; he baffles their hopes; he subjects them to a long succession of tormenting uncertainties. They labour indeed; but they do not consume the commodities they produce, nor derive the smallest advantage from their industry. "We have laboured; and other men have entered into the fruits of our labours *."

Setting therefore out of the question the man who subjects himself to expences which he is unable to discharge, it may prove instructive to us to enquire into the propriety of the maxim so currently established in human society, that it is the duty of the rich man to live up to his fortune.

Industry has been thought a pleasing spectacle. What more delightful than to see our provinces covered with corn, and our ports crowded with vessels? What more admirable than the products of human ingenuity? magnificent buildings, plentiful markets, immense cities? How innumerable the arts of the less favoured members of society to extort from the wealthy some portion of their riches? How many paths have been struck out for the acquisition of money? How various are the channels of our trade? How costly and curious the different classes of our manufactures? Is not this much better, than that the great mass of society should wear out a miserable existence in idleness and want?

* John, Chap. iv. ver. 38.

It is thus that superficial observers have reasoned, and these have been termed the elements of political wisdom. It has been inferred, that the most commendable proceeding in a man of wealth, is to encourage the manufacture of his country, and to spend as large a portion of his property as possible in generating this beautifnl spectacle of a multitude of human beings, industriously employed, well fed, warmly clothed, cleanly and contented.

Another view of the subject which has led to the same conclusion is, that the wealth any man possesses is so much of pleasure and happiness, capable of being enjoyed, partly by himself, partly by others; that it is his duty to scatter the seeds of pleasure and happiness as widely as possible; and that it is more useful that he should exchange his superfluity for their labour, than that he should maintain them in idleness and dependence.

These views of the subject are both of them erroneous. Money is the representative and the means of exchange to real commodities; it is no real commodity itself. The wages of the labourer and the artisan have always been small; and, as long as the extreme inequality of conditions subsists, will always remain so. If the rich man would substantially relieve the burthens of the poor, exclusive of the improvement he may communicate to their understandings or their temper, it must be by taking upon himself a part of their labour, and not by setting them tasks. All other relief is partial and temporary.

Three or four hundred years ago in England, there was little of manufacture, and little comparatively of manual labour. Yet the great proprietors found then, as they find now, that they could not centre the employment of their wealth entirely in themselves; they could not devour to their own share all the corn and oxen and sheep they were pleased to call their property. There were not then commodities, decorations of their persons, their wives and their houses, sufficient to consume their superfluity. Those which existed, were cumbrous and durable, a legacy handed down from one generation to another; not as now, a perpetual drain for wealth and spur to industry. They generously therefore gave away what they could not expend, that it might not rot upon their hands. It was equitable however in their idea, that they should receive some compensation for their benefits. What they required of their beneficiaries, was that they should wear their liveries, and by their personal attendance contribute to the splendour of their lords.

It happened then, as it must always happen, that the lower orders of the community could not be entirely starved out of the world.

The commodities that substantially contribute to the subsistence of the human species, form a very short catalogue. They demand from us but a slender portion of industry. If these only were produced, and sufficiently produced, the species of man would be continued. If the labour necessarily required to produce them were equitably divided among the poor, and still more, if it were equitably divided among all, each man's share of labour would be light, and his portion of leisure would be ample. There was a time, when this leisure would have been of small comparative value. It is to be hoped that the time will come, when it will be applied to the most important purposes. Those hours which are not required for the production of the necessaries of life, may be devoted to the cultivation of the understanding, the enlarging our stock of knowledge, the refining our taste, and thus opening to us new and more exquisite sources of enjoyment. It is not necessary that all our hours of leisure should be dedicated to intellectual pursuits; it is probable that the well-being of man would be best promoted by the production of some superfluities and luxuries, though certainly not of such as an ill-imagined and exclusive vanity now teaches us to admire; but there is no reason in the system of the universe or the nature of man, why any individual should be deprived of the means of intellectual cultivation.

It was perhaps necessary that a period of monopoly and oppression should subsist, before a period of cultivated equality could subsist. Savages perhaps would never have been excited to the discovery of truth and the invention of art, but by the narrow motives which such a period affords. But surely, after the savage state has ceased, and men have set out in the glorious career of discovery and invention, monopoly and oppression cannot be necessary to prevent them from returning to a state of barbarism. Thus much is certain, that a state of cultivated equality, is that state which, in speculation and theory, appears most consonant to the nature of man, and most conducive to the extensive diffusion of felicity.

It is reasonable therefore to take this state as a sort of polar star, in our speculations upon the tendency of human actions. Without entering into the question whether such a state can be realised in its utmost extent, we may venture to pronounce that mode of society best, which most nearly approaches this state. It is desirable that there should be, in any rank of society, as little as may be of that luxury, the object of which is to contribute to the spurious gratifications of vanity; that those who are least favoured with the gifts of fortune, should be condemned to the smallest practicable portion of compulsory labour; and that no man should be obliged to devote his life to the servitude of a galley-slave, and the ignorance of a beast.

How far does the conduct of the rich man who lives up to his fortune on the one hand, and of the avaricious man on the other, contribute to the placing of human beings in the condition in which they ought to be placed?

Every man who invents a new luxury, adds so much to the quantity of labour entailed on the lower orders of society. The same may be affirmed of every man who adds a new dish to his table, or who imposes a new tax upon the inhabitants of his country. It is a gross and ridiculous error to suppose that the rich pay for any thing. There is no wealth in the world except this, the labour of man *. What is misnamed wealth, is merely a power vested in certain individuals by the institutions of society, to compel others to labour for their benefit. So much labour is requisite to produce the necessaries of life; so much more to produce those superfluities which at present exist in any country. Every new luxury is a new weight thrown into the scale. The poor are scarcely ever benefited by this. It adds a certain portion to the mass of their labour; but it adds nothing to their conveniences *. Their wages are not changed. They are paid no more now for the work of ten

* Political Justice, Book VIII, Chap. II, octavo edition.

hours, than before for the work of eight. They support the burthen; but they come in for no share of the fruit. If a rich man employ the poor in breaking up land and cultivating its useful productions, he may be their benefactor. But, if he employ them in erecting palaces, in sinking canals, in laying out his parks, and modelling his pleasure-grounds, he will be found, when rightly considered, their enemy. He is adding to the weight of oppression, and the vast accumulation of labour, by which they are already sunk beneath the level of the brutes. His mistaken munificence spreads its baleful effects on every side; and he is entailing curses on men he never saw, and posterity yet unborn.

Such is the real tendency of the conduct of that so frequently applauded character, the rich man who lives up to his fortune. His houses, his gardens, his equipages, his horses, the luxury of his table, and the number of his servants, are so many articles that may assume the name of munificence, but that in reality are but added expedients for grinding the poor, and filling up the measure of human calamity. Let us see what is the tendency of the conduct of the avaricious man in this respect.

He recognises, in his proceedings at least, if not as an article of his creed, that great principle of austere and immutable justice, that the claims of the rich man are no more extensive than those of the poor, to the sumptuousness and pamperings of human existence. He watches over his expenditure with unintermitted scrupulosity; and, though enabled to indulge himself in luxuries, he has the courage to practise an entire self-denial.

It may be alleged indeed that, if he do not consume his wealth upon himself, neither does he impart it to another; he carefully locks it up, and pertinaciously withholds it from general use. But this point does not seem to have been rightly understood. The true development and definition of the nature of wealth have not been applied to illustrate it. Wealth consists in this only, the commodities raised and fostered by human labour. But he locks up neither corn, nor oxen, nor clothes, nor houses. These things are used and consumed by his contemporaries, as truly and to as great an extent, as if he were a beggar. He is the lineal successor of those religious fanatics of former ages, who conveyed to their heirs all that they had, and took themselves an oath of voluntary poverty. If he mean to act as the enemy of mankind, he is wretchedly deceived. Like the dotard in Esop's fables, when he examines his hoard, he will find that he has locked up nothing but pebbles and dirt.

His conduct is much less pernicious to mankind, and much more nearly conformable to the unalterable principles of justice, than that of the man who disburses his income in what has been termed, a liberal and spirited style. It remains to compare their motives, and to consider which of them has familiarised himself most truly with the principles of morality.

It is not to be supposed, when a man, like the person of splendour and magnificence, is found continually offending against the rights, and adding to the miseries, of mankind; and when it appears, in addition to this, that all his expences are directed to the pampering his debauched appetites, or the indulging an ostentatious and arrogant temper;——It is not, I say, to be supposed in this case, that the man is actuated by very virtuous and commendable motives.

It would be idle to hold up the miser as a pattern of benevolence. But it will not perhaps be found an untenable position to say, that his mind is in the habit of frequently recurring to the best principles of morality. He strips the world of its gaudy plumage, and views it in its genuine colours. He estimates splendid equipages and costly attire, exactly, or nearly, at their true value. He feels with acute sensibility the folly of wasting the wealth of a province upon a meal. He knows that a man may be as alert, as vigorous, and as happy, whose food is the roots of the earth, and whose drink the running stream. He understands all this in the same sense and with the same perspicuity, as the profoundest philosopher.

It is true indeed that he exaggerates his principles, and applies them to points to which upon better examination they would not be found applicable. His system would not only drive out of the world that luxury, which unnerves and debases the men that practise it, and is the principal source of all the oppression, ignorance and guilt which infest the face of the earth: it is also hostile to those arts, by which life is improved, the understanding cultivated, and the taste refined. It would destroy painting, and music, and the splendour of public exhibitions. Literature itself would languish under its frigid empire. But our censure would be extensive indeed, if we condemned every enthusiast of any science or principle, who exaggerated its maxims.

After every deduction, it will still be found that the miser considers himself as a man, entitled to expend upon himself only what the wants of man require. He sees, and truly sees, the folly of profusion. It is this perception of the genuine principles of morality, it is this consciousness of unassailable truth, that support him in the system of conduct he has chosen. He perceives, when you endeavour to persuade him to alter his system, that your arguments are the arguments of sophistry and misrepresentation. Were it not for this, he would not be able constantly to resist the force of expostulation and the shafts of ridicule. Were it not for this, he could not submit to the uniform practice of self-denial, and the general obloquy he encounters from a world of which he is comparatively the benefactor.

Such appears to be the genuine result of the comparison between the votary of avarice and the man of profusion. It by no means follows from the preference we feel compelled to cede to the former, that he is not fairly chargeable with enormous mistakes. Money, though in itself destitute of any real value, is an engine enabling us to vest the actual commodities of life in such persons and objects, as our understandings may point out to us. This engine, which might be applied to most admirable purposes, the miser constantly refuses to employ. The use of wealth is no doubt a science attended with uncommon difficulties. But it is not less evident that, by a master in the science, it might be applied, to chear the miserable, to relieve the oppressed, to assist the manly adventurer, to advance science, and to encourage art. A rich man, guided by the genuine principles of virtue, would be munificent, though not with that spurious munificence that has so often usurped the name. It may however almost be doubted whether the conduct of the miser, who wholly abstains from the use of riches, be not more advantageous to mankind, than the conduct of the man who, with honourable intentions, is continually misapplying his wealth to what he calls public benefits and charitable uses.

It deserves to be remarked that the prejudice and folly of the world has frequently bestowed the epithet of miser upon a man, merely for the parsimony and simplicity of his style of living, who has been found, whenever a real and unquestionable occasion occurred, to be actuated by the best charities and the most liberal spirit in his treatment of others. Such a man might answer his calumniators in the words of Louis the twelfth of France, I had rather my countrymen should laugh at my parsimony, than weep for my injustice and oppression.

This speculation upon the comparative merits of avarice and profusion, may perhaps be found to be of greater importance than at first sight might be imagined. It includes in it the first principles of morality, and of justice between man and man. It strikes at the root of a deception that has long been continued, and long proved a curse to all the civilised nations of the earth. It tends to familiarise the mind to those strict and severe principles of judging, without which our energy, as well as our usefulness, will lie in a very narrow compass. It contains the germs of a code of political science, and may perhaps be found intimately connected with the extensive diffusion of liberty and happiness.

ESSAY III.

OF BEGGARS.

THE use of wealth is a science attended with uncommon difficulties.

This is a proposition that would prove extremely revolting to those whom fortune has placed under no very urgent necessity of studying this science. The poor imagine they can very easily tell in what manner a rich man ought to dispose of his wealth. They scarcely ever impute to him ignorance, scruples or difficulties. If he do not act as they would have him, they ascribe it to the want of will to perform his duty, not to the want of knowledge as to what duty prescribes.

The first observation that offers itself, is, that he cannot give to all that ask, nor even to all that want, for his faculty in this respect is limited. There must therefore be a selection.

The limitation of his faculties is however by no means the only difficulty that presents itself to a rich man in the employment of his riches.

Knotty points, uncertainties, and a balance of good and evil as to almost every case that can occur, present themselves on every side.

This may be illustrated from the trite question respecting the relief of common beggars. Much has been written and remarked upon this subject, but perhaps it is not yet exhausted.

The case in their favour is an obvious one. What they appear to stand in need of, is food and shelter, articles of the first necessity. I can scarcely look at them without imagining their wants to be urgent. It is past dispute that their situation is unfortunate, worthy of interference and pity. What they ask is of very trivial value. No man can be so dead to the first feelings of the heart, so hardened by long practice of the world and the frequent sight of calamity, as not to know that the first impulse of the mind is to direct us to comply. If an angelic being were to descend from a superior sphere, ignorant of the modes of human life and the nature of human character, and were to see a poor, half-naked, shivering creature, entreating in the most doleful accents the gift of the smallest coin, while another creature, with all the exterior of ease and comfort, passed by, and turned a deaf ear to the complaint, he would pronounce this man corrupt, cruel, and unfeeling, the disgrace of a rational nature.

Yet there are men that do honour to our nature, who regard it as a duty to conduct themselves in this manner.

Riches is a relative term. Many men who are enabled to maintain an appearance of ease and comfort, and have something to spare, if they have daily occasion to traverse the streets of this metropolis, would find their purse exhausted, and themselves unable to support the drain, if they were to give, to every beggar they met, no more than the precise sum which custom has taught him to demand. The richest nobleman would find a liberal relief of common beggars amount to so serious a sum, as would oblige him, if he were prudent and conscientious, to consider maturely whether this were the most useful mode in which it could be expended. It was the multiplicity of common beggars, that first taught men at ease in their circumstances to hesitate respecting the propriety of indiscriminately relieving them.

Another circumstance which was calculated to suggest doubts, is the impudence and importunity which are frequently practised by those who pursue the trade of a common beggar. It is sufficiently evident respecting many that infest the streets of London, that they depend upon this as their principal resource. Their cry is loud; their demand is incessantly repeated; they obstinately attach themselves to your steps; and it is only by a manner as resolute as theirs that you can shake them off. There is something in the human mind that lends its aid to their project. We are at least not sure but that we shall do right in relieving them. A suspicion of duty joins itself with the desire to rid ourselves of a troublesome intrusion, and we yield to their demand. This is not however an action that we review with much complacency; and it inevitably communicates a sentiment of scepticism to the whole system.

A third circumstance which produces a similar effect, is the impostures which we frequently discover in this species of suitors. The whole avocation seems reduced to an art. They cannot be always in that paroxysm of sorrow, the expression of which so many of them endeavour to throw into their voice. If we observe them from a distance, we frequently perceive that they are talking tranquilly and at their ease, and we discover that a part of their misery is made for other persons to see, not for themselves to feel. They are careful to expose the parts of their bodies that are diseased; they affect an appearance of being more wretched than they are; not seldom they assume the guise of infirmities to which they are really strangers.

Beggars are of two classes. Those who practice the vocation for a time only, driven by the pressure of some overwhelming calamity; and those who regard it as the regular source of their subsistence.

The first of these are principally entitled to our kindness. Yet there may be danger of some ill consequences to arise from an indiscriminate relief to be extended to these. It is good that men should be taught to depend upon their own exertions. That cowardice, which induces us willingly to suppose that the mischief we experience is beyond their reach, is a pernicious vice. It induces us to look to a precarious, instead of a certain remedy. It robs us of half our energy, and all our independence. It steals from us those eminent sources of happiness, self-complacence and the exultation of conscious rectitude.

But the principal danger attending the relief of the first class of beggars, is that it should induce them to enlist themselves in the second. The relief they venture to solicit from any individual, is by no means adequate to their supply. Their story therefore must be often repeated, before the pressure which drove them to this expedient can be adequately removed. Each repetition renders the practice easier, and invites the sufferer to repeat it oftener than he originally purposed. It is no wonder, that even the miserable trade of a common beggar should have its allurements, to persons who find themselves condemned by the condition of their birth to incessant labour, a labour which, however iniquitous in its magnitude, is insufficient to rescue them from hunger and misery, and which, odious and oppressive as it is, they are frequently compelled to regard as a blessing, and are frequently deprived of the occasion to perform. The trade of a common beggar has the temptation of idleness, and is often found to produce considerably more than the amount of the wages of an industrious workman.

Let us turn from the beggar who exercises the vocation for a time only, driven by the pressure of some overwhelming calamity, to the beggar who regards it as the regular source of his subsistence.

Of all the characters in which human nature is depraved, there is not perhaps one that a man of true virtue and discernment will regard with more pain than this species of beggar.

Look through the catalogue of vices, of moral defect and deformities, that are incident to the heart of man! If you ask me to point out which are worst, there are two that I will cover with my hand, as being those that I cannot think of, or advert to, but with the most poignant regret; insincerity, and a temper abject and servile.

The employment of him who has taken up for life the trade of a beggar, is one routine of hypocrisy. If he were to tell the truth it would be of no use to him. It would not extort a farthing from the tenderest hearted man that lives. But his tongue and truth have taken a lasting leave of each other. He scarcely so much as knows what it means. He is all a counterfeit. The melancholy tone of his voice, the forlornness of his gestures, the tale that he tells, are so many constituent parts of one infamous drama. He is the outcast of mankind.

Nor is his servility less than his falshood. There is no vile trick of fawning and flattery in which he is not an adept. You would think him the humblest creature that lives. Trample upon him, and he would express no resentment. He seems to look up to his petty benefactor, or the man he hopes to render such, as to a height that it makes the eyes ache to contemplate. He pours forth his blessings and prayers for you in so copious a stream, that the powers of speech seem to labour beneath the vastness of his gratitude. The baseness imputed to the spaniel, is put to shame by the vileness of this man. He is the most abject thing upon the face of the earth.

The true element of man is to utter what he thinks. He is indeed a man, who willingly exposes his whole soul to my observation. He is not subject to the continual necessity of weighing his words; for he has an unvarnished story to tell, and the story itself supplies him with eloquence.

He expresses his genuine feelings. If he is depressed, he describes his misfortune in the way that he sees it. If he is rejoiced, he does not attempt to conceal his joy. He does not endeavour to appear any thing but what he is.

He walks erect, an equal among his equals. He asks of you nothing but what you ought to grant him, and he asks it with a firm tone, and an unembarrassed countenance. He is no man's slave. He is full of kindness to all, but he cannot stoop to practise suppleness and flattery to any. He derives his resources from himself, and therefore cannot be a dependent.

Such a man cannot fail to be of some use in the world. He shews an example inexpressibly useful. He is active, and therefore at once derives benefits, and confers them. Every day that he lives counts for something; and for every day that he lives mankind, through some of their ramifications, are the better.

There is no man, with an understanding and a heart, that would not make considerable exertions and considerable sacrifices to preserve a being like this.

It is contrary to the true interest and policy of the human species to destroy a man, because he is useless, or even perhaps because he is noxious. But there are men whom, if we would not destroy, we ought to rejoice to hear that some casualty had destroyed. For man to be destroyed by the hands of man, is a proceeding fraught with alarming consequences. But men who are worse than an incumbrance upon the face of the earth, it would be well, to speak in the jargon of the vulgar, if God would be pleased to take to himself. Such men, it is to be feared, if they should be found incorrigible in their habits, are common beggars. They are the opprobrium of human nature, and the earth would feel itself lightened by their removal. We may sympathise with them as creatures susceptible of pleasure and pain, but we cannot reasonably desire a protraction of their existence*.

* What is here said, requires perhaps to be guarded against misconstruction. For this purpose let two things be recollected.

First, beggars in themselves considered, do not deserve to be made the subjects of pain, or to be abridged of pleasure; for no man deserves this. If in any instance there be a congruity between a given character, and an assignable degree of suffering, negative or affirmative, this congruity is founded in a recollection of what is due to others, not of what is due to him. Add to this, that no class of men ought to be regarded as incorrigible. We are speaking here of a certain description as applicable to common beggars; but it cannot perhaps be affirmed of any man, though now a common beggar, that he may not be made a valuable member of the community.

Secondly, it is here affirmed of common beggars, that, while they remain such, they are useless, and injurious to so-

To contribute by our alms to retain a man a day longer in such a profession, instead of removing him out of it, is not an act that we can regard with much complacence. To incite by our alms a man to embrace this profession, who is not yet fallen into that state of degradation, is an act that a man of virtue would look back upon with the severest regret.

Such are the objections and difficulties that occur as to the relief of beggars. They are certainly of very serious importance. Yet they are scarcely of such weight, as to induce a man of feeling and humanity uniformly to withhold his interference.

We must not be too severe in our judgment of men, when it is certain, or even probable, that they are under the pressure of uncommon distress. We ought to be just; but a severity of this sort is at war with justice. A virtuous man will feel himself strongly prompted to do an action, even when there is only a probability that it may alle-

ciety. It is of common beggars only that we are here called upon to speak. But of how many other orders of men might the same thing be affirmed? How few comparatively are those, that might not be struck out of the roll of existence, and never be missed? How few, of whom it might not justly be decided, that they are nugatory and neutral, if not hostile, to the cause of mankind? Let not then the common beggar be held up as the exclusive object of our disapprobation! Political Justice, Vol. I. p. 273, octavo edition.

viate great misery, or produce exquisite enjoyment. Nothing is more suspicious than a system of conduct, which, forming itself inflexibly on general rules, refuses to take the impression, and yield to the dictates, of circumstances as they may arise.

It is said that men that are idle, may, if they please, procure themselves employment. This is easily said by men at ease. But do we not often see, by some vicissitude in the manufactures of a country for example, multitudes of men at once thrust out of employment? Can all these procure themselves employment of another sort?

"They can procure themselves employment," we are told. Be it so! But when? Does not the substitution of one manufacture or industry for another require time? Does it not require time for an individual, thrust out of one avocation, to gain admittance to another? But in the mean while he is in need of clothing and shelter; in the mean while he is without bread to eat. This is the particular aggravation of human calamities: not that we must maintain ourselves by our own industry; but that we cannot gain time for deliberation, for expedients, for prudence, and for preparation.

Let us not treat the adversities of men with a spirit of levity. It is a serious hardship, after having devoted myself to one profession, and accomplished myself with one species of skill, to be driven forth in pursuit of another. This is a situation that requires kindness and soothing. Who art thou, that assumest to deck thy brows in frowns, and to drive away the sorrows of thy brother by imperious tones and stern rebuke?

The very prejudices and weaknesses of mankind have a claim upon our indulgence. The whole end of virtue, all that is to be desired for man, is the procuring of pleasure and the averting of pain. Those evils, which in a different temper of mind would appear to be no evils, but which through the medium of prejudice wake up agony in my bosom, are under my present circumstances real and important evils, and ought to be treated as such. It would therefore be a real evil to many, to be obliged to change the functions of a clerk in a public office, for those of a scavenger who sweeps the streets, though perhaps in themselves considered, the one may be no more eligible than the other.

No spectacle is more worthy of regret, than that of virtuous intention assuming to itself all the hardness, the morose and unkind demeanour, that can belong to the most odious vice. There are men possessing such intentions, who too often shew themselves void of consideration for the feelings of others, and can be content to inflict on them the most agonising sensations with an unaltered temper. Wherever they come, they diffuse frowns and severity. They assume to be the censors of mankind. And, which is worst, it generally happens that men, who view the errors of their neighbours with this implacable temper, dispense a measure of sufficient indulgence to their own.

It is a mistake however to suppose that the austerely virtuous, are commonly persons endowed with a small portion of feeling. It will perhaps be found that they are frequently imbued with feelings the most uneasy and irrepressible. The master, to whom probably I ought to be least willing to be a slave, is rather the passionate, than the impenetrable man. The persons here spoken of, are usually little subject to apathy and insensibility. While they inflict evil upon others, or refuse their succour and interference, they are by no means conscious of inward complacence. They are in reality anxious to do justice; their minds are full of secret tumult and contradiction; and it is to this cause we are to ascribe it, if the asperity, fermenting in their own bosoms, overflow upon others. When therefore we recollect their errors, we shall recollect them, if we are impartial, with sentiments of the most poignant regret and sympathy.

The rule that ought to govern us in our treatment of mankind in general, seems to be best understood in the case of kindred and relations.

Here men are commonly sufficiently aware that, though it is possible to dispense assistance with too lavish a hand, yet assistance may often be given, in proportion to my capacity to assist, with much advantage and little chance of injury. The true mode of benefiting others, is not through the medium of anguish and torture. I cannot be sure that I distinguish rightly between virtue and defect; I cannot be sure that my efforts to remove defects will be crowned with success: I am nevertheless contented to endeavour their removal by expedients of affection and kindness, but not by the intervention of rigour and austerity. It becomes me to seek, to the extent of my power, to add to men's virtue, as well as happiness; I may allow myself, to a certain degree, in expostulation and sorrow; but I ought perhaps never, of my own mere good-pleasure, to incarcerate them in the house of correction, that they may learn wisdom.

One further consideration that is of great importance on this subject, is, that the case of the man who demands my charity in the streets, is often of the most pressing nature, and is therefore no proper field for experiments. I have sometimes been told, that the existence of beggars is a reproach to the government, and that the evil must be suffered to gain its proper height to force a remedy. But I cannot consent to lending even my passive assistance to the starving men to death, that the laws may be reformed. The police of most countries reasonably suspends the penalties ordinarily commanded, when the case is that of a starving man stealing a morsel of bread that he may eat. In the same manner, there are some sufferings, so great and so urgent, that a sound morality will teach us to dispense with our general maxims, and, for no possible calculation of distant evils, to turn a deaf ear to the cries of humanity.

One further observation occurs to me on this subject, and I will put it down. Among the persons who demand our charity in great towns there are various classes. One of these classes is of persons, who cannot earn a subsistence by labour, or who on account of some bodily imperfection will always be refused employment. I remember a man that I saw for twenty years in the streets of London, who was the mere trunk of a man, wanting all the lower members of the human body. His name was Samuel Horsley. Some accident had reduced him to this. He was almost irreversibly cut off from the world of those that labour. He was in good case, with a fresh colour, and a contented aspect. It was almost impossible to look upon him, and be angry. He scarcely ever asked an alms; only there he sat, constantly at his post. He at least did not degrade himself by an abject demeanour. Add to this, if you relieved him, there could be little chance of your doing much harm, for such a man is almost unique. By and by I heard that this man was seized by the vigilance of the police, and sent to the House of Correction. For what was he to be corrected? Of what vice was he to be cured? Was he not entitled equally with myself, to look upon the blue heavens, and to feel the healthful and invigorating breeze play on his cheek?—There are others from whom we must withhold the censure to which common beggars are for the most part entitled, for they are disturbed in their minds, and therefore cannot be kept to labour. They are maniacs, who hurt nobody, and are therefore indulged in the privilege to go free. They also in this resemble the preceding: they do not degrade themselves by an abject demeanour.

It is desirable that the number of common beggars should be diminished. But I do not altogether approve the method of discouraging them by a notice that has often met my eye in entering a country-town, Whoever is found begging in this town shall be whipped, or thrust into prison. Wherever there is great inequality, it is natural there should be some beggary; and to trample upon and maltreat persons indiscriminately, merely because they are wretched, must certainly be wrong. They have crossed with difficulty a long tract of country, they have proceeded along a hot and weary road, where they saw none to help them; at length they arrive at the habitations of men, and are cheered. Must they be forbidden to enter this street; or, entering, must they be required to shroud their griefs and their wants in silence?

To conclude; one of the worst schemes of conduct I can adopt is that which breeds moroseness and misanthropy. It is my duty not altogether to shut my ears to the person who addresses me: and, if his tale appears, not to my imbecility, but to a fair and upright humanity, to be a sad and a moving one, why should I not act as if I felt it to be such?

ESSAY IV.

OF SERVANTS.

One of the most considerable difficulties that present themselves in the execution of a plan of domestic education, relates to the degrees of intercourse which is to be allowed to take place between children and servants.

The parent and the preceptor may be in the utmost degree judicious in their conduct, and delicate in their treatment and communications. But servants will inevitably counteract the salutary results. The friends of our infancy may conduct themselves towards us with an even hand and a prudent rule; but servants will sometimes be despotic and unreasonable, and perhaps oftener prompt to injurious indulgencies, infusing into the youthful bosom the passions of empire and command. They will initiate us in low maxims, and coarse and vulgar modes of thinking. They will instruct us in the practice of cunning, and the arts of deceit. They will teach us to exhibit a studied countenance to those who preside over us, and to triumph in the success of our duplicity as soon as they are withdrawn. They will make us the confidents of their vices. They will accustom us to the spectacle of falshood and imposture. They will terrify us with false fears, threaten us with fictitious evils, and inspire us with the groveling cowardice of a prevailing superstition.

Such are the evils to be apprehended from an intercourse of children and servants. Yet how, in domestic education, are they to be prevented? We cannot make our children prisoners. We have other concerns and other business in human life, which must occasionally draw us off from attention to them. In fact, it would be a strange perversion of the system of nature and the world, for the adult to devote themselves to a perpetual attendance on the young; for the trees of the forest to be sacrificed, that their slips and offsets may take their growth in the most advantageous manner.

A resource frequently employed in this case, is for parents to caution their offspring against the intercourse of menials, and explicitly tell them that the company of servants is by no means a suitable relaxation for the children of a family.

We are afraid of the improper lessons which our children should learn from our servants: what sort of lesson is it that we teach them, when we hold to them such language as this?

It is a lesson of the most insufferable insolence and magisterial aristocracy, that it is possible for any language to convey. We teach them that they are themselves a precious species of creatures, that must not be touched too rudely, and that are to be fenced round and defended from the common accidents of nature. We shew them other human creatures, upon whose forehead the system of the universe has written the appellation of man, whose limbs outwardly seem to have been formed in the same mold, but upon whom we think proper to fix a brand and attach a label with this inscription, Come not near me! In the exuberance of our humanity perhaps, we inform our children, that these creatures are to be tenderly treated, that we must neither scratch nor bite them, and that, poisonous and degraded as they are, we must rather soothe than aggravate their calamity. We may shake our heads in arrogant compassion of their lot; but we must think of them as of the puppy-dog in the hall, who is not to be touched, because he has got the mange.—This lesson of separation, mixing with the unformed notions of childhood, will almost necessarily produce the most injurious effects.

The dangers above enumerated as likely to attend upon the intercourse of children and servants, are undoubtedly real. It is somewhat surprising that the perception of them should not have led men to reason more deeply and generally upon the condition of servants.

A rich man has in his house various apartments. The lower tier of the dwelling is inhabited by a species of beings in whom we apprehend the most sordid defects. If they are not in an emphatical degree criminal, at least their ignorance makes them dangerous, and their subjection renders them narrow. The only safety to persons of a generous station, is to avoid their society. Adults are usually wise enough to be aware of this, but the thoughtlessness of childhood renders our offspring perpetually in danger of falling a prey.

If we were told of a man who appropriated a considerable portion of his house to the habitation of rats and pole-cats, and serpents, and wolves, we certainly should not applaud either his taste or his judgment. . . . .

To a man who had studied philosophy in the school of science and retirement, who had drawn his lessons from the storehouse of reason, and was unacquainted with the practices of mankind, the house of a rich man would undoubtedly afford an impressive spectacle.

This house is inhabited by two classes of beings, or, more accurately speaking, by two sets of men drawn from two distant stages of barbarism and refinement. The rich man himself, we will suppose, with the members of his family, are persons accomplished with elegance, taste and a variety of useful and agreeable information. The servants below stairs, can some of them perhaps read without spelling, and some even write a legible hand.

> But knowledge, to their eyes, her ample page,
> Rich with the spoils of time, did ne'er unrol. GRAY.

Their ignorance is thick and gross. Their mistakes are of the most palpable sort. So far as relates to any species of intellectual inprovement, they might as well have been born in Otaheite. But this disturbs not the tranquillity of their masters. They pass them with as little consciousness of true equality, and as little sense of unrestrained sympathy, as they pass the mandarins upon their chimney-pieces.

The fortune of the rich man is expended between two different classes of beings, the inmates of the same mansion. The first class consists of the members of the family, the second of the servants. The individuals of the first class have each a purse well furnished. There is scarcely a luxury in which they are not at liberty to indulge. There is scarcely a caprice which crosses their fancy, that they cannot gratify. They are attired with every thing that fashion or taste can prescribe, and all in its finest texture and its newest gloss. They are incensed with the most costly perfumes. They are enabled to call into play every expedient that can contribute to health, the freshness of their complexion, and the sleekness of their skin. They are masters of their time, can pass from one voluntary labour to another, and resort, as their fancy prompts, to every splendid and costly amusement.

The wealth of the servant amounts perhaps to ten or fifteen pounds a year; and it is not unfrequent to hear persons of ten or fifteen thousand a year exclaim upon the enormousness of wages. With this he is to purchase many articles of his apparel, coarse in their texture, or already tarnished, the ape of finery and wealth. His utmost economy is necessary to provide himself with these. He can scarcely obtain for himself an occasional amusement, or, if he were smitten with the desire of knowledge, the means of instruction. If he be put upon board-wages, his first enquiry is at how humble a price he can procure a sordid meal. The purchase of his food for a whole week, would not furnish out the most insignificant dish for his master's table.

This monstrous association and union of wealth and poverty together, is one of the most astonishing exhibitions that the human imagination can figure to itself. It is voluntary however, at least on the part of the master. If it were compulsorily imposed upon him, there is no chearfulness and gaiety of mind, that could stand up against the melancholy scene. It would be a revival of the barbarity of Mezentius, the linking a living body and a dead one together. It would cure the most obdurate heart of its partiality for the distinction of ranks in society. But, as it is, and as the human mind is constituted, there is nothing, however intolerable to sober and impartial reason, to which custom does not render us callous.

There is one other circumstance, the object of the senses, characteristic of this distinction of classes in the same house, which, though inferior to the preceding, deserves to be mentioned. I amuse myself, suppose, with viewing the mansion of a man of rank. I admire the splendour of the apartments, and the costliness of their decorations. I pass from room to room, and find them all spacious, lofty and magnificent. From their appearance my mind catches a sensation of tranquil grandeur. They are so carefully polished, so airy, so perfectly light, that I feel as if it were impossible to be melancholy in them. I am even fatigued with their variety.

I will imagine that, after having surveyed the rest of the house, the fancy strikes me of viewing the servants' offices. I descend by a narrow staircase. I creep cautiously along dark passages. I pass from room to room, but every where is gloom. The light of day never fully enters the apartments. The breath of heaven cannot freely play among them. There is something in the very air that feels musty and stagnant to my sense. The furniture is frugal, unexceptionable perhaps in itself, but strangely contrasted with the splendour of the rest of the house. If I enter the apartment which each servant considers as his own, or, it may be, is compelled to share with another, I perceive a general air of slovenliness and negligence, that amply represents to me the depression and humiliated state of mind of its tenant.

I escape from this place, as I would escape from the spectacle of a jail. I cannot return again to the splendid apartments I have left. Their furniture has lost its beauty, and the pictures their charms. I plunge in the depth of groves and the bosom of nature, and weep over the madness of artificial society.

Yet, notwithstanding these things, the rich pretend to wonder at the depravity and vices of their servants. They are astonished that they should enter into a confederacy of robbers, and strip the houses of their masters, even at the risk of the gallows.

Servants have only the choice of an alternative. They must either cherish a burning envy in their bosoms, an inextinguishable abhorrence against the injustice of society; or, guided by the hopelessness of their condition, they must blunt every finer feeling of the mind, and sit down in their obscure retreat, having for the constant habits of their reflections, slavery and contentment. They can scarcely expect to emerge from their depression. They must look to spend the best years of their existence in a miserable dependence. It is incompatible with their ignorance, that they should be able to look down upon these misfortunes with philosophical tranquillity.

We have been considering the condition of servants in the houses of the great. But it is not materially different in the middle classes of society. The evil is incurable. It is a radical defect in the present system of human intercourse. Those persons are to be commended who endeavour to diminish the evil; but they will excite in an enlightened observer a smile of pity for their simplicity, when they pretend that they can totally extract the sting.

Treat a servant as you will, he will be a servant still. His time is not his own. His condition is infinitely more pitiable, than that of the day-labourer who reasons upon his functions, and ascertains the utility of his efforts. He has nothing to do, but to obey; you have nothing to do, but to command. At every moment he is to be called this way, to be sent that, to run, to ride, to be the vehicle and conduit-pipe to affairs of which he has neither participation nor knowledge. His great standing rule is to conform himself to the will of his master. His finishing perfection is to change himself into a mere machine. He has no plan of life, adding the improvement of to-day to the progress of the day before. He is destitute of the best characteristics of a rational being.

It is absurd in us for the most part to reason with them, and endeavour to explain to them the grounds of our commands, unless indeed we can make them our companions, the partakers of our counsels, the coadvisers of our undertakings. To attempt it any other way, is the mockery of equality. We may make them surly and mutinous, but we cannot make them free. All that we can perform with success, is to exercise a mild empire over them, to make our commands few, simple and unoppressive, and to excite them, if possible, to adopt for their leisure hours pursuits and a business which shall be properly their own.

It has sometimes been alleged, that servants cannot be considered as slaves, because the engagement into which they enter is a voluntary compact. Suppose I could compel a man, by the pressure of a complication of circumstances, to sell himself for a slave, and authorise him to spend the purchase-money in decorating his own person, would he not nevertheless be a slave? It is the condition under which he exists, not the way in which he came into it, that constitutes the difference between a freeman and a slave. It must be acknowledged that the slavery of an English servant has its mitigations, and is, in several intelligible and distinct particulars, preferable to that of a West-Indian Negro.

ESSAY V.

OF TRADES AND PROFESSIONS.

In the world of which man is an inhabitant, there are some who, by the established distribution of property, are provided with the means of subsistence, from the period of their birth, without the intervention of any industry of theirs; and others who have no prospect of obtaining even the necessaries of life, but through the medium of their own exertions.

The numbers in this latter class are so great, and in the former so insignificant, that the latter, whether the question to be considered relate to freedom, virtue or happiness, may well pass for all, and the former be regarded as nothing.

The class of the unprovided, comprehensive as it is, is somewhat swelled, by the addition of those persons who, though provided for by the condition of their birth as to the necessaries of life, are yet dissatisfied, covet something more, and resort to some species of industry or occupation that they may fill up the imaginary deficiency.

From this survey of the human species it appears that there cannot be a question of greater importance, than that which every anxious parent asks concerning his child, which the child, if endowed with foresight and an active mind, asks perhaps with still greater anxiety and a nicer perception, what is the calling or profession to which his future life shall be destined?

This is probably the question of all others, that irresistibly dispels the illusion which causes human life to appear in such gaudy colours, and compels the miserable fabric of civil society to exhibit itself in all its deformity.

To what calling or profession shall the future life of my child be devoted?—Alas! I survey them all; I cause each successively to pass in review before me: but my mind can rest upon none: there is not one that a virtuous mind can regard with complacency, or select with any genuine eagerness of choice! What sort of a scene then is that in the midst of which we live; where all is blank, repulsive, odious; where every business and employment is found contagious and fatal to all the best characteristics of man, and proves the fruitful parent of a thousand hateful vices?

Trade in some form or other is the destination of the majority of those, to whom industry is either in part or in whole made the source of pecuniary income. Let us analyse the principles of trade.

The earth is the sufficient means, either by the fruits it produces, or the animals it breeds, of the subsistence of man. A small quantity of human labour, when mixed and incorporated with the bounties of nature, is found perfectly adequate to the purposes of subsistence. This small quantity it is, in the strictness of moral obligation, every man's duty to contribute; unless perhaps, in rare instances, it can be shewn that the labour of some, directed to a higher species of usefulness, would be injuriously interrupted by the intervention of this trivial portion of mechanical and subordinate labour.

This is the simple and undebauched view of man in, what we may call, his state of innocence.

In the experiment of human society it is found that the division of labour tends considerably to diminish the burthen to which it would otherwise amount, and to forward the improvement of human skill and ingenuity. This variation does not necessarily produce any defalcation from the purity of human motives and actions. Were the members of any community sufficiently upright and disinterested, I might supply my neighbour with the corn he wanted, and he supply me with the cloth of which I was in need, without having recourse to the groveling and ungenerous methods of barter and sale. We might supply each other for this reason only, because one party had a superfluity and the other a want, without in the smallest degree adverting to a reciprocal bounty to be by this method engendered; and we might depend upon the corresponding upright and disinterested affections of the other members of the community, for the being in like manner supplied with the commodities of which we were in want*.

Liberal and generous habits of thinking and acting, are the growth only of a high degree of civilisation and refinement. It was to be expected therefore that, in the coarse and narrow state of human society, in which the division of labour was first introduced, the illiberal ideas of barter and sale would speedily follow.

* Political Justice, Book VIII, Chap. VIII, octavo edition.

The persons who first had recourse to these ideas, undoubtedly were not aware what a complication of vices and misery they were preparing for mankind. Barter and sale being once introduced, the invention of a circulating medium in the precious metals gave solidity to the evil, and afforded a field upon which for the rapacity and selfishness of man to develop all their refinements.

It is from this point that the inequality of fortunes took their commencement. Here began to be exhibited the senseless profusion of some and the insatiable avarice of others. It is an old remark, that there is no avarice so great and so destitute of shame, as that of the licentious prodigal.

Avarice is not so thoroughly displayed in the preservation, as in the accumulation, of wealth. The chief method by which wealth can be begun to be accumulated by him who is destitute of it, is trade, the transactions of barter and sale.

The trader or merchant is a man the grand effort of whose life is directed to the pursuit of gain. This is true to a certain degree of the lawyer, the soldier, and the divine, of every man who proposes by some species of industry to acquire for himself a pecuniary income. But there is a great difference in this respect. Other men, though, it may be, their first purpose in choosing their calling was the acquisition of income, yet have their attention frequently diverted from this object, by the progress of reputation, or the improvements of which they have a prospect in the art they pursue. The trader begins, proceeds and concludes with this one end constantly in view, the desire of gain. This thought rises with him every morning, and accompanies him at the close of every day. Ideas of reputation can scarcely occur to give dignity to his pursuit; and he rarely hopes to give new improvement to the arts of existence, or has the notion of improvement mixing itself with his thoughts. His whole mind is buried in the sordid care of adding another guinea to his income.

The ideas of the division of labour, and even of barter and sale, first presented themselves, as conducive to mutual accommodation, not as the means of enabling one of the parties to impose an unequal share of labour or a disproportionate bargain upon the other. But they did not long remain in this degree of purity. The sagacity of the human mind was soon whetted to employ these ideas, as the instruments of fraud and injustice.

Is it to be expected that any man will constantly resist the temptations to injustice, which the exercise of a trade hourly suggests?

The buying and selling price of a commodity will always be different. If we purchase it of the manufacturer, he must not only be paid for the raw material, but for his industry and skill. If we buy it of the trader strictly so called, he must be paid for his time, for the rent of his house, and for the subsistence of himself and his family. This difference of price must be left to his deliberation to adjust, and there is thus vested in him a large discretionary power. Will he always use this discretion with perfect integrity?

Let us suppose that the price fixed by the trader is always an equitable one, for of that the generality of his customers are incompetent to judge. There is one thing that stands out grossly to the eye, and respecting which there can be no dispute: I mean, the servile and contemptible arts which we so frequently see played off by the tradesman. He is so much in the habit of exhibiting a bended body, that he scarcely knows how to stand upright. Every word he utters is graced with a simper or a smile. He exhibits all the arts of the male coquette; not that he wishes his fair visitor to fall in love with his person, but that he may induce her to take off his goods. An American savage, who should witness the spectacle of a genteel and well frequented shop, would conceive its master to be the kindest creature in the world, overflowing with affection to all, and eager to contribute to every one's accommodation and happiness. Alas, it is no such thing! There is not a being on the face of the earth, with a heart more thoroughly purged from every remnant of the weakness of benevolence and sympathy. The sole principle of all this fair outside, is the consideration how to make the most of every one that enters his shop.

Yet this being, this supple, fawning, cringing creature, this systematic, cold-hearted liar, this being, every moment of whose existence is centred in the sordid consideration of petty gains, has the audacity to call himself a man. One half of all the human beings we meet, belong, in a higher or lower degree, to the class here delineated. In how perverted a state of society have we been destined to exist?

Nothing is more striking than the eagerness with which tradesmen endeavour to supplant each other. The hatred of courtiers, the jealousy of artists, the rivalship of lovers attached to a common mistress, scarcely go beyond the fierceness of their passions. The bitterness of their hatred, the impatience with which they think and speak of each other, the innumerable arts by which they undermine a brother, constitute a memorable spectacle. There is nothing in which they so much rejoice, as in the ruin of an antagonist. They will sell their goods at a loss, and sometimes ruin themselves, in the attempt to accomplish this wished-for event.

And for what is all this mighty contention, this unintermitted and unrelenting war? For the most poisonous and soul-corrupting object, that can possibly engross a man's persevering attention. For gain.

Shall I destine my child to the exercise of a trade? Shall I not rather almost wish that the custom of antiquity were revived, and that I were permitted to expose my new-born infant to perish with hunger, sooner than reserve him, that he may afterwards exhibit a spectacle that I cannot think of without moral loathing, and appear in a character that is the opprobrium of a rational nature?

From trades let us proceed to a review of professions.

There is scarcely any profession that obtains for a man a higher degree of consideration in civil society, than the profession of the law.

Law, we are told, is that by which one man is secured against the injustice and the passions of others. It is an inflexible and impartial principle, holding out one standard of right and wrong to all mankind. It has been devised by sages, in the tranquillity of the closet, not to accommodate particular interests, but to provide for the welfare of the whole. Its view is sublime and universal. It cannot be warped to suit temporary and personal objects. It teaches every man what he has to depend upon, not suffering him to be condemned at the caprice of his judges, but by maxims previously promulgated and made known to all. It gives fair warning to one party, of the punishment which a certain conduct will incur. It affords to the other party, a remedy against the usurpation of his neighbour, known, definite, and universally accessible.

If law be, to this eminent extent, the benefactor and preserver of mankind, must it not reflect some of its own lustre upon its professors? What character can be more venerable than an expounder of law, whether we apply this appellation to the judge who authoritatively declares its meaning from the bench, to the pleader who takes care to do justice to the case of a man who is unable to do justice to it himself, or to the less brilliant, but not less useful, functions of him, who from his chamber communicates the result of the researches of years, to the client, who would otherwise be unable to find his way amidst the complexities of statutes, glosses and precedents?

We will not here enquire into the soundness of the panegyric which has so often been pronounced upon the institution of law. All that our present subject requires of us, is, to ascertain what sort of character the study of law is likely to entail upon its professors.

The business of a man is to enquire into the dictates of reason and the principles of justice. The business of a lawyer is of a very different sort. He has nothing to do with general and impartial reason; his concern is with edicts and acts of parliament. He is to consider these as the standards of right and wrong to mankind. He must either wholly expel from his mind all notions of independent investigation; or he must submit to the necessity of maintaining that to be right, because it is conformable to law, which he knows to be wrong, because it is irreconcilable to justice. What may be the general merits of law as an institution would be a proper topic of separate investigation*. But thus much is too plain to need any profound elucidation: that laws, in their great outline, are usually the prejudices of a barbarous age artificially kept alive and entailed upon a civilised one; that such of them as are of long standing, derive their character from principles and systems that have since been wholly exploded and brought into disuse; that such of them as are of recent date, have too often originated in temporary objects, in antisocial passions, in the intemperate desire of giving strength to monopoly, and firmness to the usurpation of the few over the many. From this immense and heterogeneous mass the lawyer extracts his code of ethics; and nothing is more usual among persons of this pro-

* See this question considered, in Political Justice, Book VII, Chap. VIII, octavo edition.

fession, than to see them expressing their sensations by a look of astonishment and contempt, if they hear a man arraigning the infallibility of law, and calling into question the justice of its decisions.

The salutary condition of the human mind, is that in which it is prepared to bring every principle upon which it proceeds, within the scope of its own examination; to derive assistance from every means of information, oral or scriptory; but to admit nothing, upon the score of authority, to limit or supersede the touchstone of reason. If I would understand what is justice, if I would estimate the means of human happiness, if I would judge truly of the conduct of my neighbour, or know rightly how to fashion my own, I must enquire deeply, not superficially: I must enter into the principles of things, and not suffer conclusions to steal upon me unawares. I must proceed step by step; and then there will be some chance that the notions I form, will be sound in themselves, and harmonious with each other.

But, when, instead of adopting my opinions with this degree of caution and deliberation, I am induced to admit at a stroke whole volumes of propositions as unappealable and decisive, I resign the most beneficial prerogative of human understanding.

This expedient, instead of shortening my course,

multiplies my difficulties a thousand fold. When I proposed only to consult the volume of nature, I knew to a certain degree what was the task I undertook. All the evidence I collected, bore immediately upon the point under consideration. But now the principal point becomes involved with innumerable subordinate ones. I have no longer merely to be satisfied, by a long or a compendious course, what it is that is absolutely right. I am concerned with the construction of phrases; the removal of ambiguities; the reconciling contradictions; the ascertaining the mind of the composer; and for this purpose the consulting history, the ascertaining the occasion of institutions, and even the collecting as far as possible every anecdote that relates to their origin. I am concerned with commentators, as I am concerned with the text, not merely to assist my own deductions, but because they have a certain authority fettering and enchaining my deductions. I sought, it may be, repose for my indolence; but I have found an eternal labour. I have exchanged a task comparatively easy, for difficulties unconquerable and endless.

Such is the mode in which a lawyer forms his creed. It is necessarily captious and technical, pregnant with petty subtleties and unmeaning distinctions. But the evil does not stop here. It would be a mistake peculiarly glaring and gross to suppose that a lawyer studies the law principally that he may understand it. No; his great object is to puzzle and perplex. His chief attention is given to the enquiry, how he may distort the law so as to suit the cause in which he is engaged. This is a necessary consequence of one man's being hired to tell another man's story for him. The principal, however erroneous, may be expected to express himself with good faith. The agent is careless himself about the merits of the cause. It is totally indifferent to him whether his client be right or wrong. He will plead for the plaintiff to-day, and, if properly applied to, will plead on the opposite side in another court to-morrow. He stands up before a judge and jury in the most important questions, upon which the peace of families, and the lives and liberties of individuals depend. If he have an honest tale to deliver, it is well. But, if he have the weaker side, what he undertakes is, by a solemn and public argument, to mislead and confound, if he is able, the court and the jury. He justifies this to himself; for, if men are to have their cause pleaded by others, the greatest delinquent is entitled to the same privilege; to reject his application would be to prejudge his cause, and to withhold from him that to which all men are entitled, a solemn and public hearing. The lawyer is weak enough not to see the consequences of his practice: he does not know that, by this serious trifling, pleading indifferently on either side or on both, he brings all professions and integrity into discredit, and totally subverts the firmness and discernment of his own understanding.

Another circumstance common to the lawyer with all those professions which subsist upon the misfortunes of mankind, is that he labours under a perpetual temptation to increase those misfortunes. The glorious uncertainty of the law is his daily boast. Nothing so much conduces to his happiness, as that his neighbours should be perpetually engaged in broils and contention. Innumerable are the disputes that would soon terminate in an amicable adjustment, were it not for the lawyer, who, like an evil genius, broods over the mischief and hatches it into a suit. There may be instances in which he adopts an opposite conduct. But no father would wish for a child, no prudent man would choose for himself, a situation in which he was perpetually exposed to such enticements. Where such is the character of a profession, it cannot fail to happen, that the majority of its adherents will be seduced from their integrity.

The concluding part of these observations will apply also to the physician. Pain, sickness and anguish are his harvest. He rejoices to hear that they have fallen upon any of his acquaintance. He looks blank and disconsolate, when all men are at their ease. The fantastic valetudinarian is particularly his prey. He listens to his frivolous tale of symptoms with inflexible gravity. He pretends to be most wise, when he is most ignorant. No matter whether he understand any thing of the disease; there is one thing in which his visit must inevitably terminate, a prescription. How many arts have been invented to extract ore from the credulity of mankind? The regular and the quack have each their several schemes of imposition, and they differ in nothing so much as in the name.

Let us pass from the physician to the divine.

I am almost tempted to dismiss this part of my subject with the exclamation of Cato, *De Carthagine satius est silere quam parcius dicere:* It is better to be silent on this head, than to treat it in a slight and inadequate manner. We will not however pass it over without a remark.

A clergyman is a man educated for a certain profession; and, having been so educated, he cannot, without much inconvenience, exchange it for another. This is a circumstance indeed to which his pursuit is exposed in common with every other walk and distribution of human life. But the evil that results to him from this circumstance, has its peculiar aggravations.

It is the singularity of his office, that its duties principally consist in the inculcating certain opinions. These duties cannot properly be discharged, without an education, and, in some degree, a life of study. It is surely a strange and anomalous species of existence, where a man's days are to be spent in study, with this condition annexed, that he must abstain from enquiry. Yet abstain he must, for he has entered into a previous engagement, express or implied, what his opinions shall be through the course of his life. This is incompatible with any thing that deserves the name of enquiry. He that really enquires, can by no means foresee in what conclusions his enquiry shall terminate.

One of two consequences is especially to be apprehended by a man under these circumstances.

He will perhaps arrive at sceptical or incredulous conclusions, in spite of all the bias impressed upon him, at once by pecuniary considerations, and by the fear of losing the friendship and admiration of those to whom his habits perhaps had chiefly attached him, and who were the principal solace of his existence. In that case he must determine for the rest of his life, either to play a solemn farce of hypocrisy, or, unless his talents be considerable, to maintain his integrity at the expence of an obscure and solitary existence.

The infidelity however of a studious and conscientious clergyman is perhaps a rare circumstance. It more frequently happens, that he lives in the midst of evidence, and is insensible to it.

He is in the daily contemplation of contradictions, and finds them consistent. He reads stories the most fabulous and absurd, and is filled with the profoundest reverence. He listens to arguments that would impress conviction upon every impartial hearer, and is astonished at their futility. He receives a system with the most perfect satisfaction, that a reflecting savage would infallibly scoff at for its grossness and impertinence. He never dares trust himself to one unprejudiced contemplation. He starts with impatience and terror from its possible result. By long habits of intellectual slavery, he has learned to bear the yoke without a murmur. His thoughts are under such perfect discipline that not a doubt ever ventures to intrude itself. That such should be the character of an ignorant and a weak man, need not surprise us; but that it should equally suit men of the profoundest learning and the most elevated talents, is indeed a matter of surprise and regret.

A second disadvantage incident to the clerical profession is the constant appearance of sanctity, which a clergyman, ambitious of professional character, is obliged to maintain. His sanctity does not rise immediately from spiritual motives and the sentiments of the heart; it is a certain exterior which he finds himself compelled to preserve. His devotion is not the result of devout feelings; he is obliged equally to affect them, when he experiences them least. Hence there is always something formal and uncouth in the manners of a reputable clergyman. It cannot be otherwise. His continual attention to a pious exterior, necessarily gives a constrained and artificial seeming to his carriage.

A third circumstance disadvantageously affecting the character of a clergyman, arises from his situation as a guide and teacher to others. He harangues his auditory at stated periods, and no one is allowed to contradict him. He occupies the most eminent situation in the building appropriated to public worship. He pronounces the prayers of the congregation, and seems to act the mediator between the Creator and his creatures. It is his office to visit the sick, and to officiate as an oracle to such as are in distress. The task principally incumbent upon him, is to govern the thoughts of his parishioners, and to restrain the irregular sallies of their understandings. He is placed as a champion to resist the encroachments of heresy and infidelity. Upon his success in this respect depends the prosperity of the church of which he is a pillar. He warns his flock against innovation and intrepidity of thinking. The adversary is silent before him. With other men I may argue; but, if I attempt to discuss a subject freely and impartially with him, it is construed a personal insult. I ought to have known that all his schemes and prospects depended upon the perennial stationariness of his understanding. Thus the circumstances of every day tend to confirm in him a dogmatical, imperious, illiberal, and intolerant character.

Such are the leading features of the character which, in most instances, we must expect to find in a reputable clergyman. He will be timid in enquiry, prejudiced in opinion, cold, formal, the slave of what other men may think of him, rude, dictatorial, impatient of contradiction, harsh in his censures, and illiberal in his judgments. Every man may remark in him study rendered abortive, artificial manners, infantine prejudices, and a sort of arrogant infallibility.

It is not unfrequent indeed to find clergymen of a character different from this. Men go into the church from convenience, and because a living lies within their reach to obtain. These men are often dissipated and ignorant. They pretend to no extraordinary orthodoxy or devotion. They discharge the functions of their office in a slight and careless manner, merely because they must be discharged. They are devoted to the sports of the field, or the concerns of ordinary life.

These men will probably appear to a just observer less respectable than the class previously described. They are conscious of assuming a description to which they do not belong, and the delicacy of their mind is evidently blunted. There is a sort of coarseness in their character, arising from the attempt to laugh away a stigma, the existence of which they can never entirely forget. Nothing is more contemptible than a man who is only known by his adherence to a profession, of which he has none of the virtues, the industry, the skill, and the generous ambition. He belongs properly to no class of beings, and is a mere abortion and blot upon the face of the earth.

Another profession which has been thought not less honourable than that of the lawyer or the divine, is that of the soldier.

A distinction has sometimes been made between those lawyers, who take up the profession *bona fide*, and pretend never to engage in a cause but so far as it is conformable to their own sentiments; and the lawyers who reason themselves into the propriety of dismissing their personal feelings and opinions when they come into a court of justice, and, in consequence, of pleading any cause, indifferent as to their own idea of its soundness. A similar distinction may be applied to the soldier.

A soldier who will never fight but in a cause that he shall conscientiously and scrupulously judge to be good, can scarcely be a soldier by profession.

But, to dismiss this consideration, it is no enviable circumstance that a man should be destined to maintain the good cause by blows and fighting. In this respect, assuming the propriety of corporal punishments, he is upon a par with the beadle and the executioner. To employ murder as the means of justice, is an idea that a man of enlightened mind will not dwell upon with pleasure. To march forth in rank and file, with all the pomp of streamers and trumpets, for the purpose of shooting at our fellow-men as at a mark, to inflict upon them all the variety of wounds and anguish, to leave them weltering in their blood, to wander over the field of desolation, and count the number of the dying and the dead, are employments which in thesis we may maintain to be necessary, but which no good man will contemplate with gratulation and delight. A battle, we will suppose, is won. Thus truth is established; thus the cause of justice is confirmed! It surely requires no common sagacity, to discern the connection between this immense heap of calamities, and the assertion of truth, or the maintenance of justice.

It is worse where the soldier hires himself, not for the service of any portion or distribution of mankind, but for the mere purpose of fighting. He leaves it to his employer and his king to determine the justice of the cause; his business is to obey. He has no duty but that of murder; and this duty he is careful amply to discharge. This he regards as the means of his subsistence, or as the path that leads to an illustrious name.

A soldier, upon every supposition, must learn ferocity. When he would assert the cause of truth, he thinks not of arguments, but of blows. His mind is familiarised to the most dreadful spectacles. He is totally ignorant of the principles of human nature; and is ridiculous enough to suppose that a man can be in the right, who is attempted to be made so through the medium of compulsion.

But, though it could be imagined that coercion was the means of making men wise and good, this assumption, large as it is, would not serve to establish the morality of war. War strikes not at the offender, but the innocent.

*Quicquid delirant reges, plectuntur Achivi**. HOR.

Kings and ministers of state, the real authors of the calamity, sit unmolested in their cabinet, while those against whom the fury of the storm is directed, are, for the most part, persons who have been trepanned into the service, or who are dragged unwillingly from their peaceful homes into the field of battle. A soldier is a man whose business it is to kill those who never offended him,

* When doating Monarchs urge
Unsound Resolves, their Subjects feel the Scourge.
FRANCIS

and who are the innocent martyrs of other men's iniquities. Whatever may become of the abstract question of the justifiableness of war, it seems impossible that a soldier should not be a depraved and unnatural being.

To these more serious and momentous considerations, it may be proper to add a recollection of the ridiculousness of the military character. Its first constituent is obedience. A soldier is of all descriptions of men the most completely a machine. Yet his profession inevitably teaches him something of dogmatism, swaggering, and self-consequence. He is like the puppet of a showman, who, at the very time he is made to strut, and swell, and display the most farcical airs, we perfectly know cannot assume the most insignificant gesture, advance either to the right or the left, but as he is moved by the exhibitor. This singular situation gives to the military a correspondent singularity of manner. The lofty port of a generous spirit, flowing from a consciousness of merit and independence, has always something in it of grand and impressive. But the swagger of a soldier, which it costs him an incessant effort to support, is better calculated, in a discerning spectator, to produce laughter, than to excite awe.

The sailor, if he is to come into the list of professions, so far as his character is warlike, falls under the same objections as the soldier, with this aggravation of the nature of his pursuits, that they usurp an element which, by itself, man is scarcely able to subdue, and compound a scene still more infernal, than that of a battle to be decided by land.

Where the sailor is not a military character, he is frequently a mercantile one, and the merits of mercantile pursuits have already been estimated.

But he labours under one disadvantage peculiar to himself. He passes his existence in a state of banishment from his species. The man who is sentenced to reside in New Holland or Siberia, may improve his faculties, and unfold his affections. Not so the man who passes his life in a coop, like a fowl set apart to be fatted. Men accustomed to speculate upon the varieties of human nature, can have no conception, previous to the experiment, of the ignorance of a sailor. Of the concerns of men, their pursuits, their passions, all that agitates their mind and engrosses their attention, he is almost as uninformed, as an inhabitant of the remotest planet. Those expansive affections, that open the human soul, and cause one man to identify himself with the pleasure and pains of his fellows, are to him like the dialects of Nineveh or Carthage. And what renders the abortiveness of his character the more glaring, is that he has visited all countries, and has seen none. He goes on shore for half an hour at a time, and advances half a mile up the province upon which he anchors. If he return in the close of life to his native village, he finds himself unspeakably outstripped in sagacity and knowledge, by the poor peasant, whose remotest researches have never led him further, than to a country-wake or a neighbouring fair.

It is to be remembered that, through this whole disquisition, we have been examining different professions and employments, under the notion of their being objects for the contemplation of a man, who would choose a destination for himself or his child. Our business therefore lay entirely with their general tendency. If there be any extraordinary characters, that have escaped the prevailing contagion it has been our purpose to detect, they have no right to be offended. Let not truth however be sacrificed to a wish to conciliate. If a man have escaped, he must be of a character truly extraordinary and memorable. And even such a man will not have passed entirely uncontaminated. He will bear upon him the stamp of his occupation, some remnants of the reigning obliquity, though he shall be fortunate enough to have redeemed them by virtues illustrious and sublime.

Thus then we have successively reviewed the manners of the trader, the lawyer, the physician, and the divine, together with the military and naval professions. We proposed to ascertain which of these avocations a wise man would adopt for a regular employment for himself or his child; and, though the result may be found perhaps to contribute little to the enlightening his choice, but rather to have cast the gloom of strong disapprobation upon all, we may however console ourselves at least with this reflection, that, while engaged in the enquiry, we have surveyed a considerable portion of the occupations and characters of men in society, and put together materials which may assist our judgment respecting the economy of human life.

ESSAY VI.

OF SELF-DENIAL.

THE greatest of all human benefits, that at least without which no other benefit can be truly enjoyed, is independence.

He who lives upon the kindness of another, must always have a greater or less portion of a servile spirit. He has not yet come to feel what man is. He has not yet essayed the muscles of his mind, and observed the sublimity of his nature. True energy, the self-conscious dignity of the man, who thinks not of himself otherwise than he ought to think, but enjoys in sober perception the certainty of his faculties, are sentiments to which he is a stranger. He knows not what shall happen to-morrow, for his resources are out of himself. But the man that is not provided for to-morrow, cannot enjoy to-day. He must either have a trembling apprehension of sublunary vicissitude, or he must be indebted for his repose to the lethargy of his soul.

The question relative to the establishment and maintenance of independence, is intimately connected with the question relative to our taste for, and indulgence in, the luxuries of human life.

Various are the opinions that have been held upon the latter of these topics.

One of these opinions has been carried to its furthest extreme by certain sects of religionists.

Their doctrine is commonly known by the appellation of self-denial. The postulate upon which it principally proceeds, is that of the superiority of the mind to the body. There is an obvious distinction between intellectual pleasures and sensible ones. Either of them taken in any great degree, tends to exclude the other. The man who is engrossed in contemplation, will, without expressly intending it, somewhat macerate his body. The man who studies without restraint the gratifications of appetite, will be in danger of losing the activity of his mind, the delicacy of his intellectual tact, and the generosity of his spirit.

There must be a superiority in favour, either of intellectual pleasures, or of sensible ones. But that man's mind must surely be of an unfortunate construction, who can hesitate to prefer the former to the latter. That which we possess in common with the brutes, is not of so great value, as that which we possess distinctively to ourselves. That man must possess the surest, the most extensive, and the most refined sources of happiness, whose intellect is cultivated with science, and purified by taste, is warmed with the ardour of genius, and exalted by a spirit of liberality and benevolence. There can be no comparison between this man and the glutton, the epicure or the debauchee*.

The inference drawn from these premises by the persons whose system we are here considering, is as follows. Sensible pleasures are to be avoided, when they tend to impair the corporeal faculties. They are to be avoided when they tend to the injury of our neighbours, or are calculated to produce in ourselves habits of stratagem and deceit. Thus far all systems of morality and rational conduct are agreed. But the preachers of self-denial add to these limitations, a prohibition to the frequent indulgence of sensible pleasures, from the danger of suffering ourselves, to set too great a

* Political Justice, Book IV, Chap. XI, octavo edition.

value upon them, and to postpone the best and most elevated, to the meanest, part of our natures.

Having assumed this new principle of limitation, there is no visionary and repulsive extreme to which these sectaries have not in some instances proceeded. They have regarded all sensible pleasure as a deduction from the purity and dignity of the mind, and they have not abstained from invective against intellectual pleasure itself. They have taught men to court persecution and calamity. They have delighted to plant thorns in the path of human life. They have represented sorrow, anguish, and mortification as the ornaments and honour of our existence. They have preached the vanity and emptiness of all earthly things, and have maintained that it was unworthy of a good man and a wise to feel complacency in any of the sensations they can afford.

These notions may sufficiently accord with the system of those who are willing to part with all the benefits of the present scene of existence, in exchange for certain speculations upon the chances of a world to come. But they cannot enter into any liberal and enlightened system of morality. Pleasure or happiness is the sole end of morality. A less pleasure is not to be bartered but for a greater, either to ourselves or others, nor a scheme attended with the certainty or probability of considerable pleasure for an air-built speculation.

Dismissing therefore these extravagant dogmas, it remains to enquire how far we ought to sacrifice or restrain the empire of sensible pleasures, for the sake of contributing to the substantial improvement of the better part of our nature.

There are obvious reasons why this restraint is not to be severely imposed.

It is a mistake to suppose that sensible pleasures and intellectual ones are by any means incompatible. He that would have great energy, cannot perhaps do better than to busy himself in various directions, and to cultivate every part of his nature. Man is a little world within himself, and every portion of that world is entitled to attention. A wise man would wish to have a sound body, as well as a sound mind. He would wish to be a man at all points. For this purpose he would exercise and strengthen the muscles of every part of his frame. He would prepare his body to endure hardship and vicissitude. He would exercise his digestic powers. He would cultivate the delicacy of the organs of taste. He would not neglect the sensations, the associations, and the involuntary processes and animal economy annexed to the commerce of the sexes. There is a harmony and a sympathy through every part of the human machine. A vigorous and animated tone of body contributes to the advantage of the intellect, and an improved state of intellect heightens and refines our sensible pleasures. A modern physician of great character *, has maintained life to be an unnatural state, and death the genuine condition of man. If this thesis is to be admitted, it seems to follow, that true wisdom would direct us to that proceeding, which tended most to inform with life, and to maintain in activity, every portion of our frame and every branch of our nature. It is thus that we shall most effectually counterwork an enemy who is ever in wait for us.

Another argument in favour of a certain degree of attention to be paid to, and cultivation to be bestowed upon, sensible pleasures, is, that the sensations of our animal frame make an important part of the materials of our knowledge. It is from sense that we must derive those images which so eminently elucidate every department of science. One of the great objects both of natural science and morality, is to judge of our sensible impressions. The man who had not yielded a due attention to them, would in vain attempt to form an enlightened judgment in the very question we are here attempting to discuss. There is a vast variety of topics that he would be disqualified to treat of or to estimate.

Add to this, that all our refined and abstracted

* Brown.

notions are compounded from ideas of sense. There is nothing so elevated and pure, but it was indebted to this source for its materials. He therefore who would possess vividness in his ideas of intellect, ought probably to maintain with care the freshness and vigour of his ideas of sense.

It seems to be owing to this that we find, for the most part, the rustic, slow of apprehension, and unsusceptible of discernment; while it is only from the man who keeps alive not only the health of his body, but the delicacy and vividness of his corporeal tact, that we ordinarily expect delicacy of taste, brilliancy of imagination, or profoundness of intellectual discussion.

Having endeavoured to ascertain the benefits to be derived from delicacy and activity in our external senses, let us recur to the direct part of the question, how far the improvement of the better part of our nature, demands from us a sacrifice of, or a restraint to be imposed on, sensible pleasure.

In the first place, if, as we have already endeavoured to prove, intellectual pleasures are entitled to a preference over sensible ones, they are of course also entitled to be first considered in the arrangement of our time, and to occupy the choicest part of our life. Nothing can be more contemptible, than the man who dedicates all the energies of his mind to the indulgence of his appetites. They may, comparatively speaking, if we may be allowed the expression, be thrust up in a corner, and yet enjoy scope enough for every valuable purpose. It is more necessary that we should not proscribe them, than that we should make them one of the eminent pursuits of our lives.

Secondly, we ought not only to confine them within limits considerably narrow, as to the time they should occupy, but should also be careful that they do not confound and inebriate our understandings. This is indeed necessary, in order to the keeping them in due subordination in the respect last mentioned. If they be not held in subjection as to their place in our thoughts, they will speedily usurp upon all other subjects, and convert the mind into a scene of tumult and confusion. Intellectual and elevated pursuits demand from us a certain calmness of temper; that the mind should rest upon its proper centre, that it should look round with steadiness and freedom, that it should be undisturbed by the intrusion of thoughts foreign to the present object of its attention, and that it should be capable of a severe and obstinate investigation of the point under review.

A further reason for moderation in our appetite for sensible pleasure, not less important than any other that can possibly be assigned, is that which was alluded to in the commencement of this essay, the preservation of our independence.

The man who is anxious to maintain his independence, ought steadily to bear in mind how few are the wants of a human being. It is by our wants that we are held down, and linked in a thousand ways, to human society. They render the man who is devoted to them, the slave of every creature that breathes. They make all the difference between the hero and the coward. The man of true courage is he who, when duty and public good demand it, can chearfully dispense with innumerable gratifications. The coward is he who, wedded to particular indulgences and a certain mode of life, is not able so much as to think with equanimity of the being deprived of them.

Hunc solem, et stellas, et decedentia certis
Tempora momentis, sunt qui, formidine nulla
Imbuti, spectent *. HOR.

Such undoubtedly is the characteristic of genuine virtue. It teaches us to look upon events, not absolutely with indifference, but at least with tranquillity. It instructs us to enjoy the benefits which we have, and prepares us for what is to follow. It smiles upon us in the midst of poverty and adverse

* This vault of air, this congregated ball,
Self-centred sun, and stars that rise and fall,
There are, my friend! whose philosophic eyes
Look thro',
And view this dreadful All without a fear. POPE.

circumstances. It enables us to collect and combine the comforts which a just observer may extract from the most untoward situation, and to be content.

The weakness which too many are subject to in regard to the goods of fortune, puts such persons to a certain degree in every man's power. It is of little consequence how virtuous may be a man's habitual inclinations, if he be inordinately sensible to the presence or absence of the accommodations and luxuries of life. This man is not his own master. If he have not been seduced to the commission of base and dishonourable actions, he may thank accident for his escape, not the strength of his virtue. He is truly a slave. Any man, possessing the command of a certain portion of the goods of life, may order him this way or that at his pleasure. He is like those brute animals, that are allured to the learning innumerable postures and ridiculous tricks, by the attraction of a morsel of meat. He knows not whether he shall end his life with a virtue, plausible, hollow, and ever on the brink of dissolution; or whether, on the contrary, his character shall be hated and contemned, as long as his story endures.

He that desires to be virtuous, and to remain so, must learn to be content with a little; to use the recreations of sense for the purposes of living, and not to live for the sake of these recreations.

Summum credet nefas animam præferre pudori,
*Et propter vitam vivendi perdere causas**. JUV.

How far then is it requisite that he, who would not be the slave of appetite, should rigidly restrain himself in the indulgence of appetite?

There have been men who, living in the midst of luxury and inordinate indulgence, have yet, when an adequate occasion presented itself to rouse their virtue, shewn that they were superior to these trivial accessories of human life, and that they could stoop with a chearful spirit to calamity and penury.

He however, who would desire to have reason to depend upon his fortitude, ought not probably to expose himself to so doubtful an experiment. It has often happened that those who, in the outset of their career, have been full of a gallant spirit, have been insensibly subdued by a course of unexpected gratification. There is something particularly dangerous in this situation. The man remembers with how much chearfulness he formerly submitted to inconvenience, and he does not feel, and cannot persuade himself, that he is worse than he was. He does not advert to the

* He'd chuse
To guard his Honour, and his Life to lose,
Rather than let his Virtue be betrayed;
Virtue, the Noble Cause for which he's made.
STEPNEY.

way in which luxury is undermining all the energies of his soul. He does not see that it is twining itself about his heart, and will not be torn away but with life. This is unfortunately one of the peculiar characteristics of degeneracy, that it invades us in a secret and crafty manner, and is less easily perceived by its victim, than by the least sagacious of the bystanders.

ESSAY VII.

OF INDIVIDUAL REPUTATION.

SECT. I.

SOURCES OF POPULAR APPLAUSE.

Few speculations can be more interesting than that which relates to the truth or falshood of the ordinary standard of morality.

The just and sound standard of morality is easily assigned. The first object of virtue is to contribute to the welfare of mankind. The most essential attribute of right conduct therefore is, that it shall have a beneficent and salutary tendency. One further characteristic it is usual to add. Men, in the exercise of their rational faculties, are influenced by motives and inducements apprehended by the intellect. The more a man is incited to an action by reflecting on the absolute nature of that action, the more ground of expectation he affords of a repetition of such actions. We do not therefore consider ourselves as authorised to denominate an action virtuous, unless it spring from kind and beneficent intentions *.

These two circumstances taken together, constitute every thing that can reasonably be included in the term virtue. A beneficent action to which a man is incited by a knowledge of its beneficent tendency, is an act of virtue. The man who is in the frequent practice of such actions, is a worthy, virtuous and excellent man.

The ordinary standard of morality is different from that which is here assigned.

Common observers divide the whole human species into two classes, the honest and the dishonest.

Honesty, according to their idea, consists in the following particulars.

First, a certain regularity of conduct not deviating into any thing too questionable for vulgar understandings to explain, nor into any thing notoriously mean and abject. Vulgar and undiscriminating judges of morality, love those things that preserve a certain level, and abhor every thing that

* Political Justice, Book II, Chap. IV, octavo edition.

ference; and, provided that which he calls right be maintained, he is unmoved by the slighter consideration, of the misery of his species, or the destruction of a world. This idea, when stripped of the ranting and pompous words in which it has been enveloped, seems to be that of an exclusive regard to one's own integrity and consistency, to the utter neglect of every generous sentiment, and of all those things, to a connection with which integrity and consistency are indebted for their value.

A certain coldness of character seems indeed to be essential to that species of honesty which is most applauded in the world. The alliance which subsists between a sober and vigilant plausibility on the one hand, and an impenetrable temper on the other, is plainly to be discerned. Honesty, taken in this sense, is a sort of non-conductor to all the sympathies of the human heart. The men, whose character we are here attempting to describe, are not subject to the fervours and the shocks of humanity. A smile of self-complacency for the most part sits enthroned upon their visage. To ordinary observers indeed they frequently appear uncommonly in earnest; but their zeal, such as it is, is distinguished rather by verbosity than animation, and impresses us rather by weight of phrase, than by that glowing and happy diction which feeling is prone to inspire.

The habitual motive therefore of the man to

whom the world exclusively awards the praise of common honesty, may be emphatically selfish.

It may be vanity, conducing indeed in some degree to the good of others, but unmixed with almost any discernible portion of sympathy or kindness. The regularity which constitutes its characteristical feature, may be principally owing to a sort of pride of soul, which, while its regards are exclusively centred at home, will not permit the person in whom it exists, to do any thing that might afford materials for ridicule, or opportunity for censure.

The motive may be ambition, cautious of admitting any thing that should operate as a bar to its claims. The object of its unremitted attention may be to exhibit its most smooth and glossy surface, desirous either of being mistaken for somewhat more excellent than it is; or, which is more probable, confused and doubtful in its judgment of itself, it seeks the suffrage of the world, to confirm it in its propensity to inordinate self-admiration.

Lastly, the motive may be the mere desire of wealth. Avarice is for obvious reasons closely connected with regularity of proceeding. A very ordinary degree of experience and observation will teach us, that honesty, particularly that vulgar and moderated species of honesty of which we are here treating, is "the best policy." In the majority of cases at least, a fair character seems essential to eminent success in the world. What degree of scrupulosity of conduct, and delicacy of proceeding, is required for the maintenanee of a fair character, is a topic of separate consideration.

In the mean time nothing can be clearer, than that common honesty is not prone to allow itself in any peculiar refinements. It acts as if it considered morality, rather as a necessity to be submitted to, than as a business to be entered upon with eagerness and passion. It therefore willingly takes morality as it finds it. It readily indulges in all those things which, the world has agreed, constitute no impeachment upon the character of an honest man. It carefully draws the line in this respect, and is little fearful of being induced to trespass by the vehemence of its passions. What the majority of mankind has determined to be essential to a moral character, it submits to with the most edifying resignation; those things, which a severe and inflexible examination might pronounce to be dishonest, but which the world has agreed to tolerate, it can practise in all instances without the visitings of compunction.

But, of all the characteristics by which common honesty is distinguished, there is none more infallible than a certain mediocrity. It is impossible that any thing great, magnanimous and ardent, can be allied to it. Qualities of this unusual dimension would disturb its composure, and interfere with the even, phlegmatic, procession pace by which it is distinguished. When it is warm, it is warm by rule. Its fervour never oversteps an assigned limit; and it is produced in the first instance, by a deliberate judgment that fervour, under the circumstances, will be of good effect.

If common honesty be justly pourtrayed in the preceding observations, it is certainly to be regretted, that the applause of the world, and all general moral reputation, should be confined to characters of this description. He that would proceed by the most certain way to obtain an honest fame among mankind, must discard every thing that is most illustrious in his nature, as that which will, almost infallibly, sooner or later bring his reputation into hazard. He on the contrary, that would adorn himself with the most elevated qualities of a human being, ought to come prepared for the encounter of obloquy and misrepresentation. He ought not to expect to unite things so incompatible, as exalted virtue and general favour. He should cultivate the same temper with respect to morality, that Horace imputes to himself as a poet.

Men' moveat cimex Pantilius? aut cruciet, quod
Vellicet absentem, Demetrius? aut quod ineptus
Fannius Hermogenis lædat conviva Tigelli?
Plotius et Varius, Mæcenas, Virgiliusque,

Valgius, et probet hæc Octavius;——
————Demetri, teque, Tigelli,
Discipularum inter jubeo plorare cathedras.*

Nor did Horace perhaps expect that his verses should be praised by all men of talents. At least certain it is in life, that such men frequently join the herd, are governed in their judgment of men's characters by the weakest prejudices, and senselessly apply those rules to others, which shall soon afterwards be employed for the condemnation of themselves.

* Let Budgel charge low Grub-street on my quill,
And write whate'er he please, except my will!
Let the two Curls of town and court, abuse
My father, mother, body, soul and muse!—
But why then publish? Granville the polite,
And knowing Walsh, would tell me I could write;
Well-natur'd Garth inflam'd with early praise,
And Congreve lov'd, and Swift endur'd my lays;
The courtly Talbot, Somers, Sheffield read,
Even mitred Rochester would nod the head,
And St. John's self (great Dryden's friends before)
With open arms receiv'd one poet more.
Happy my studies, when by these approv'd!
Happier their author, when by these belov'd!

POPE.

SECT. II.

SOURCES OF POPULAR DISAPPROBATION.

It may be useful to enumerate some of those circumstances, by one or other of which, men in some respects of uncommon moral endowments, are usually found to forfeit, in the judgment of the mass of mankind, the most ordinary degree of moral reputation.

First, men of uncommon moral endowments, may be expected to be men of uncommon intellectual powers. But such men, in some points at least, will be apt to think for themselves, to meditate profoundly, and, by an almost necessary consequence, to embrace some opinions that are not embraced by the multitude. This is an obvious disqualification in a candidate for common fame. No man can, it may be added, no man ought, to think quite as favourably of the man who differs from him in opinion, as of the man with whom he agrees. To say that the opinions which any man entertains, appear to him to be true, is an identical proposition. Add to which, that he must be a weak man indeed, who does not perceive the connection between opinion and practice, or who, while he respects the virtues of his friend, does not regret, as a serious disadvantage, the error of his sentiments. But this privilege, or this duty, of blaming the dissent of our neighbours, the vulgar abuse. Nor does it seldom happen, that the opinions they regard as most sacred and momentous, whether in religion, in politics, or morals, are the most ridiculously absurd, or flagrantly indefensible.

Secondly, the man, whose opinions are the result of his own reflection, will often have an individual mode of acting, as well as of thinking. The cheapest plan for acquiring reputation will be found to consist in the conforming ourselves to the prejudices of others. He that acts in unison with other men's sentiments and expectations, will be easily understood; they will find nothing ambiguous in the interpretation of his conduct, and nothing revolting in its tenour. The mass of mankind do not love, in the practice of human affairs at least, any thing that surprises or puzzles them. They are partial to things trite and plain; and no man is in more danger of missing their applause, than the man who takes extraordinary pains to deserve it. Upon uncommon flights of virtue they usually put a sinister interpretation. Great delicacy of sentiment is, in their apprehension, affectation and artifice. And they do not incline to yield much to those comprehensive and disinterested sentiments of which they have no experience in their own bosoms.

But a mistake, still more general than those yet enumerated, as well as more fatal to every impartial decision respecting men's virtue or vice, is the propensity we have every day occasion to observe among mankind, to magnify some quality or action that is really worthy of regret, into a vice altogether destructive of every pretension to moral excellence.

This general propensity is, of course, in the highest degree favourable to ordinary and feeble characters, and threatens with all its hostility characters of energy, of grand and decisive features.

Characters, endowed with great excellencies, will, unfortunately, frequently stand in need of great allowances. Men cannot perhaps be equally attentive to minutiæ and to matters of lofty import. Ordinary characters are generally safe in this respect. They venture upon no untried paths. They attempt no sublime and unusual virtues. They have no other care incumbent upon them in this respect, but that of keeping within a certain beaten road, never straying after peculiar beauties, never compelled to have recourse to doubtful expedients.

Want of punctuality, particularly in the mercantile concerns of life, is one of those defects which, for time immemorial, have supplied materials for invective against eminent and extraordinary men.

Punctuality is no doubt a quality of high importance. That man's virtue deserves to be regarded with some suspicion, who can readily be induced to trifle with the time, and perhaps still more with the property, of his neighbours.

But we must always be peculiarly exposed to error in our judgment of the conduct of men, when we judge it indiscriminately in the mass, without taking into account the circumstances that attend them.

There are no persons so vehement in their condemnation of pecuniary breach of contract, as many of those who, coming early into the possession of an income fully commensurate to their wants, never felt the pressure of difficulties.

One of the circumstances often omitted in the estimation, is the spirit in which perhaps the pecuniary supply was granted. It is often the speculation of a tradesman, who thought the concern worth accepting, at the same time that he fully took into account the uncertainty of payment. It is often the kindness of a friend, who says to himself, If the debt never be discharged, I am content; and who afterwards perhaps leaves the claim among his heirs. These circumstances by no means cancel the pecuniary obligation; but they ought not in justice to be forgotten.

People in general accustom themselves to forget the anguish of the insolvent debtor, and the unwearied struggles he has perhaps made to appear in a different character. Nothing can be more strongly marked with folly and injustice, than the tone of voice with which we frequently hear persons say, He should satisfy the demands against him: Shewing plainly that the feeling of their mind is, as if he had the money in his desk, or could satisfy these demands as easily as lift his finger. We are never authorised to say of a poor man, He ought to pay his debts; but, He ought to exert himself for their liquidation.

A strict and inflexible morality is no doubt worthy of commendation. But strict and inflexible morality does not require, that we should totally damn a man's character for a few faults, and still less for what perhaps it was not in his power to do. It is not morality, but insanity, that would teach us to say, Every debtor confined in the King's-Bench-Prison, is a knave.

Laying prejudice therefore aside, let us consider how much of moral and essential defect the character of an insolvent debtor necessarily implies.

He that can with an indifferent temper, consider himself as preying on the labour of others surprised from them by a sort of fraud, or as violating the fundamental principle, upon the preservation of which the whole fabric of civil society depends, must have a mind callous to all that is most important in morality. Nor will the man less deserve our censure, who visibly indulges in luxuries, and glaringly pampers his appetites, at the cost, but without the consent, of his neighbour.

M

In the mean time, how many ways are there, in which a man may innocently fall into the condition of an insolvent debtor? The present state of society, by a most odious and accursed contrivance, is continually stimulating one man to make himself responsible for the eventual vice or miscalculation of another. One of the wretched consequences of a state of debt is, that the debtor is not permitted to make an election among his creditors; and that, at the penalty of the loss of liberty and capacity for future exertions, he is compelled to grant to unjust and unmanly importunity, what he is by the same means compelled to deny to merit.

The poor man who is endowed with active virtue, will be, in a higher degree than his indolent neighbour, a man of experiments. He ought not to make experiments singularly hazardous, at another man's expence. He ought to be upon all occasions explicit and unreserved. But human life, in every one of its parts, is a calculation of probabilities. Any man may be deceived in his calculations. He that is determined never to expose himself to error, must never expose himself to action.

Let us suppose however that the debtor is clearly in the wrong; that he drank a bottle of wine, or solaced himself with a public amusement, at a time when his pecuniary affairs were unquestionably worse than nothing. Let us suppose that these are vices that will admit of no explanation. Yet how great and eminent virtues may exist in this man's bosom! He may be the most generous and philanthropical of mortals. He may be the greatest benefactor the human species ever knew. Every man probably is inconsistent. Every man probably, be he in whatever degree virtuous, has some point to which unaccountably he has not applied those principles by which he is ordinarily governed. We ought to be rigid in laying down maxims of conduct, when the degree in which those maxims shall be realised depends upon their existence; but; in judging the past conduct, particularly of others, he that is not liberal and indulgent, is not just.

There are other qualities of the same general description, which are in like manner fatal, in vulgar apprehension, to the character in which they exist. Such are a neglect of the established modes of religion, swearing, loose conversation, gaming, excessive drinking, and incontinence.

The question respecting these heads of conduct may be divided into two; first, what degree of disrepute justly attaches itself to every single instance of this kind; and secondly, how much ought be imputed, in cases where the instance has enlarged itself into a habit.

No fair and unprejudiced man will condemn a

character, and least of all a character in which high promise discloses itself, for any single instance of this kind.

Where the habit exists, there is certainly much matter for regret; with this reserve with respect to the first head of enumeration, in the mind of every man who duly considers the extreme uncertainty and innumerable errors to which we are liable, that, if religion may be true, it certainly may also be false.

Excessive drinking usually leads men into debauched company and unprofitable conversation. It inevitably impairs, in a greater or less degree, the intellectual faculties; and probably always shortens the life of the person addicted to it, a circumstance particularly to be regretted when that life is eminently a useful one.

Gaming, beside the execrable company to which it inures a man, of persons who can scarcely be said to redeem their guilt in this respect by one virtue, accustoms him to the worst habits of mind, induces him to seek, and to rejoice in, the misfortunes of others. In games where chance most presides, it commits fortune, a thing for the right administration of which we are no doubt accountable, to the hazard of a die. Whichever party loses a considerable sum, his mind is unhinged, his reputation is tarnished, and his usefulness suffers considerable injury. In games in which skill is concerned, which is more or less the case with almost all games, the gamester for the most part proposes to take advantage of his superior knowledge and to overreach his antagonist.

Promiscuous venery seems to argue a depraved appetite. It encourages, by becoming the customer to, a trade, all of whose members perhaps are finally reserved for want, disease and misery, not to mention the low and odious depravity to which they are almost inevitably subject.

Customary swearing seems to be the mark of a passionate man, and certainly proves the absence of delicacy of taste.

Loose conversation, in those persons with whom it becomes a habit, is ordinarily very disgustful. It is singular enough, that the sallies of persons who indulge themselves in this way, are commonly more remarkable for ordure and a repulsive grossness, than for voluptuousness. The censure however against loose conversation, has probably been carried too far. There seems to be no reason why knowledge should not as unreservedly be communicated on the topic here alluded to, as on any other affair of human life. With respect to persons who, like Sterne, may have chosen this subject as the theme of a wit, pleasant, elegant and sportive, it is not easy to decide the exact degree of reprimand that is to be awarded against them.

Such appears to be the sum of what is to be alleged against these habits.

Nothing can be less reasonably a subject of controversy than that, if the injury and unhappiness of which a man is the author, outweigh the contrary effects, he is to be regarded as a bad member of society. No splendour of talents, no grandeur and generosity of sentiment, can redeem this one plain proposition, in any case where it can be fairly asserted. Men who have practically proved themselves the greatest pests and enemies of their species, have frequently been distinguished by eminent talents and uncommon generosity *.

But, if this proposition is to be rigidly applied to the condemnation of men, for whom, even while he condemns them, a well formed mind will not fail to experience sympathy, it ought on the other hand to be as rigidly applied to the benefit of men whom the world is accustomed to censure.

Nothing can be less defensible than that we should overwhelm with our censure, men, in whom usefulness will perhaps be found greatly to preponderate, and whose minds overflow with the most disinterested kindness and philanthropy.

* Political Justice, Book II, Chap. IV, octavo edition.

SECT. III.

USES OF POPULARITY.

HAVING endeavoured to ascertain the rules according to which reputation is ordinarily distributed, it may be a matter of just curiosity to enquire into the value of that, the acquisition of which is thus capricious and uncertain.

The value of reputation is unquestionably great, whether we consider it as the instrument of personal happiness, or as an ally whose office it is to render efficacious our services to others.

As the instrument of personal happiness. Man in society is to be regarded, in all the most fundamental questions of moral or intellectual science, as an individual. There are points of view however in which he is scarcely an individual. The seats of contact and sympathy between any one human being and his fellows are numerous. The magnetism of sentiment propagates itself instantaneously and with great force. It is scarcely possible for a man to adhere to an opinion or a body of opinions, which all other men agree to condemn. It is scarcely possible for a man to experience complacency and satisfaction in a conduct, in which he is utterly unsupported by the suffrage of his neighbours. Every one seeks to gain partisans, and upon them he rests as his securities. Failing in this, he takes refuge in imaginary suffrages, drawn from the recorded past, from the supposition of generations yet unborn, or from the doctrines of an invisible world. With these he is obliged to content himself; but they are usually feeble, cold and insufficient.

Nor is reputation more necessary as a security for the permanence of our own good opinion, than it is as an ally communicating efficacy to our services to others. Men will not allow force to the advice, they will not listen to the arguments, often they will even decline the practical good offices, of a person they disesteem. If I would do good to others, it is for the most part requisite that they should not be vehemently prejudiced against me. Though I spoke with the tongue of an angel, if they hate me, I shall scarcely convince them. To have a chance of convincing them, or in other words truly to gain from them a hearing, I must first counterbalance their prejudices. A powerful and happy mode of enunciating truth will effect this with some; but there are others, and it is to be feared very many, whose prejudices of a personal sort, when once they have taken deep root, no powers of enunciation, at this time existing in the world, will be able to conquer. He whom obloquy hunts in his terrestrial course, is like a man whose hands are tied, or whose mouth is gagged. He would serve mankind, but his exertions are nerveless; he would convince them, but they are deaf: he would animate them to generous action, but they are impenetrable to his exhortations.

If I am to do good to my fellow man, it is necessary, not only that I should act, but that he should co-operate with me. It is little that I can do for the man who sits with his arms folded, and in supine indifference. He must sympathise with my passions, melt with my regrets, and pant with my enthusiasm. To hear justly the ideas imparted to him, to read adequately the arguments I have digested and committed to writing, is an active service. In proportion to the activity which this implies, it is not merely desirable that he should feel no revulsion against me; it is to be wished that he should set out with some degree of favourable opinion. Undoubtedly the validity of my positions should be ascertained solely by the strength of my arguments; but he should prepare himself with a sentiment already conceived, that I am an advocate worth hearing. The most impartial investigator wishes only to read the best books that have been written on each side of a given question, not to abuse his time with the lucubrations of every miserable scribbler. If for some accidental purpose he take up a book that he expects to be bad, but finds to be able, the first thing he thinks of, is to turn back again the pages he has read, and re-enter upon the perusal with an attentive and respectful temper.

What species of reputation will best answer the purposes here described, of security to our own happiness, and efficacy to our services to others?

Undoubtedly the most extensive: that which includes the favourable judgment of the vulgar, along with the suffrage of all the instructed and all the wise.

It has appeared however that this is for the most part unattainable. He that would conduct himself with uncommon excellence, must in all probability expect to lose the kindness of a large portion of the vulgar, whether in an obscure, or a more conspicuous station.

In the mean time there is a species of reputation, which, though not so effectual as that above mentioned, will in an important degree answer the purposes of complacency and usefulness.

If we have reference only to the first of these objects, it will be sufficiently secured by the approbation of the acute and the excellent. So far as relates to a personal satisfaction in my opinions, I can dispense with the suffrage of the vulgar, provided they be confirmed to me by the consenting judgment of impartial thinkers and profound reasoners. So far as relates to my conduct, I shall have great reason to be contented, if I find myself honoured by numbers of those whom, upon mature investigation, I perceive reason to honour.

With respect to the reputation that is connected with usefulness, a distinction is to be made between that which is to be desired for the man who is only to communicate his ideas to others, and the man whose purpose it is to act in their behalf.

In both cases a more extensive degree of reputation is necessary, to co-operate with my usefulness, than to secure my contentment. The last of these purposes may be effected by the approbation of the discerning few; the former demands an approbation of a more extensive sort.

To give effect to exertions in speaking or writing, it is exceedingly to be desired that the speaker or writer should be regarded, in the first place, as a man of ability. In the next, it is for the most part necessary that he should not be supposed to speak or write with any malevolent or sinister design; for the majority of readers tacitly exhibit in this case a diffidence in their own understandings, and prefer stopping their ears against the persuasions of such a man, to the task of fairly investigating the proofs he exhibits.

These are the principal points. A reasoner of acknowledged ability, and who is accounted passably honest, may gain perhaps the indulgence to be heard. Some discredit he must inevitably labour under with those he would convince; for it is impossible for any man not to think the worse of another for differing with him in opinion. He may be contented to be accounted wrong-headed and paradoxical. He will of course be regarded more or less as a visionary, absurdly deserting the plain road of his interest for the sake of gratifying his vanity. He will be considered as dangerous; for every serious thinker conceives that opinion upon any important subject, which for the present he apprehends to be false, to be also attended with pernicious consequences.

The reputation that is necessary to secure an adequate advantage to the man who is to act in the behalf of others, is of greater extent, than is required for the man who only desires to be heard by them. It is not enough that he should be regarded as able, and free from all sinister design. He must be esteemed prudent, judicious, uniform in his activity, sound in his calculations, and constant in his vigilance. He must be supposed to have that acuteness which may prevent him from being deceived by others, and that sobriety which may defend him from being duped by himself. It is also to be desired that he should be supposed faithful to his trust, and actuated by an earnest desire for the prosperity of the interests committed to him. Perhaps no man ought to seek or accept a delegation, who is unpopular with, or distrusted by, those whom it concerns.

Such is the value of, and such the benefits arising from, reputation. No reasonable man will feel himself indifferent to the character he bears. To be in want of the sanction derived from the good opinion of others, is an evil greatly to be deprecated.

Yet on the other hand it is an error, to be acutely anxious about reputation, or, more accurately speaking, to suffer our conduct to be influenced in essential particulars by a consideration of the opinion of others.

The world is in this respect like certain individuals of the female sex, whom, if a man would gain to favour his addresses, he must not seem too anxious to please. No sooner do they find him completely in their power, than they delight to treat him with harshness and tyranny. The world appears to be imbued with a secret persuasion, that its opinion is too little discerning to be worth the courting, and that an habitual regard to this opinion is a motive that degrades the man that submits to it.

An erect and dignified virtue leads us to consider chiefly the intrinsic and direct nature of our actions, and to pay a very subordinate attention to the accidents that may attend upon them. An elevated temper will induce us to act from our own reflections, and not from the judgment of others. He that suffers himself to be governed by public opinion, substitutes the unsteadiness of a weather-cock, instead of the firmness of wisdom and justice.

If a degree of reputation is sometimes secured by this servility, it cannot however be a solid and lasting one. It may answer the purpose of him who desires to impose upon others a temporary delusion, but a man of generous ambition will spurn it from him with contempt. Nothing is more mortifying than that species of reputation, which the least discernment would show us was immediately to be succeeded by infamy or oblivion.

He that would gain in any valuable sense the suffrage of the world, must show himself in a certain degree superior to this suffrage.

But, though reputation will never constitute, with a man of wisdom and virtue, the first and leading motive of his actions, it will certainly enter into his consideration. Virtue is a calculation of consequences, is a means to an end, is a balance carefully adjusted between opposing evils and benefits. Perhaps there is no action, in a state of civilisation and refinement, that is not influenced by innumerable motives; and there is no reason to believe that virtue will tend to diminish the subtlety and delicacy of intellectual sensation. Reputation is valuable; and whatever is of value ought to enter into our estimates. A just and reasonable man will be anxious so to conduct himself as that he may not be misunderstood. He will be patient in explaining, where his motives have been misapprehended and misconstrued. It is a spirit of false bravado that will not descend to vindicate itself from misrepresentation. It is the refuge of indolence; is is an unmanly pride that prefers a mistaken superiority to the promotion of truth and usefulness. Real integrity ought not indeed to be sore and exasperated at every petty attack. Some things will explain themselves; and in that case defence appears idle and injudicious. A defence of this sort is an exhibition of mental disease, not an act of virtue. But, wherever explanation will set right a single individual, and cannot be attended with mischief, there explanation appears to be true dignity and true wisdom.

ESSAY VIII.

OF POSTHUMOUS FAME.

THE distribution of individual reputation is determined by principles in a striking degree capricious and absurd. Those who undertake to be the benefactors of mankind from views of this sort, are too often made in the close of their career to devour all the bitterness of disappointment, and are ready to exclaim, as Brutus is falsely represented to have done, " Oh, virtue! I followed thee as a substantial good, but I find thee to be no more than a delusive shadow!" *

It is common however for persons, overwhelmed with this sort of disappointment, to console themselves with an appeal to posterity, and to observe that future generations, when the venom of party has subsided, when their friendships and animo-

* The only historian by whom this infamous story is told, is Dion Cassius, the professed flatterer of tyrants, the bitter enemy of liberty and virtue. It is curious to observe how the tale was manufactured. Plutarch relates that, a short time before his death, Brutus repeated two scraps of poetry, of which Volumnius, the philosopher, his friend, remembered one, and forgot the other. The first was an imprecation against the successful wickedness of Antony. This hint was enough for the malignity of Dion to work upon. Dion lived more than one hundred years after Plutarch. He sought in Euripides, Brutus's favourite poet, for a passage that might serve to fix a stain on the illustrious patriot, and he found one to his purpose. The last words that Plutarch relates of Brutus are: "I do not complaine of my fortune, but onely for my countries sake: for, as for me, I thinke my selfe happier then they that have ouercome, considering that I haue a perpetuall fame of our courage and manhood, the which our enemies the conquerors shall neuer attaine vnto." Plutarch, by Sir Thomas North.

Another silly story has been propagated for the purpose of injuring Brutus's character, that he was the son of Cæsar. This will be sufficiently refuted by the bare statement that there was but fourteen years' difference between their ages. Middleton, life of Cicero, Section VIII. Middleton by mistake sets down the difference as fifteen years.

sities are forgotten, when misrepresentation shall no longer disfigure their actions, will not fail to do them justice.

Let us enquire into the soundness of this opinion. The more we consider it, the more perhaps we shall find this last prop of what may be styled, a generous vanity, yielding a very uncertain support.

To posterity we may apply what Montaigne has remarked of antiquity, " It is an object of a peculiar sort; distance magnifies it." If we are to judge from experience, it does not appear that that posterity upon which the great men of former ages rested their hopes, has displayed all that virtue, that inflexible soundness of judgment, and that marvellous perspicacity of discernment, which were prognosticated of it before it came into existence.

Let us take the case of literary reputation.

It is a well-known remark that the reputation of philosophers, natural historians, and writers of science is intrinsically and unalterably of a perishable nature. Science is progressive; one man builds upon the discoveries of another; one writer drives another off the stage of literature; that which was laudable and excellent when first produced, as mankind advance, necessarily appears childish, inept, garrulous, and full of error and absurdity.

Art affords a more permanent title to fame than science. The poets and fine writers of antiquity still appear to us excellent; while the visions of Plato, and the arrangements of Aristotle, have no longer a place but in the brains of a few dreaming and obscure individuals.

Poetry itself however affords but an uncertain reputation. Is Pope a poet? Is Boileau a poet? These are questions still vehemently contested. The French despise the tragic poetry of England, and the English repay their scorn with scorn. A few scholars, who are disposed to rest much of their reputation on their Greek, affirm Sophocles to be the greatest dramatic author that ever existed, while the generality of readers exclaim upon him as feeble in passion and barren in interest. The unlearned are astonished what we can find to be so greatly charmed with, in the imitative genius of Virgil, and the sententious rambles of Horace. The reputation of Shakespear endures every day a new ordeal; while some find in him nothing but perfection, and others are unable to forgive the occasional obscurity of his style, pedantry of his language, meanness of his expressions, and disproportion of his images. Homer has stood the test of more than two thousand years; yet there are hundreds of no contemptible judges who regard his fame as ill-grounded and usurping. They are mortally offended with the ridiculousness of his mythology, the barbarism of his ethics, and the incoherence of an ill-constructed tale, told, for the most part, in a series of tedious, prosaic verses. From these instances it appears, that the most which a successful author can pretend to, is to deliver up his works as a subject for eternal contention.

The aspirant to literary fame must however be uncommonly fortunate, if he is permitted to look as high as this. If a man could go through the island of Great Britain, and discover the secrets of every heart, as the Lame Devil of Le Sage discovers the secrets of every house in Madrid, how much genius, what a profusion of talent, would offer themselves to his observation? In one place he would discover an embryo politician, in another a philosopher, in a third a poet. There is no benefit that can be conferred upon the human race, the seeds and materials of which would not present themselves to his view. Yet an infinite majority of these are destined to be swept away by the remorseless hand of oblivion, and to remain to all future ages as if they had never been. They will either confer no benefit upon mankind, or none in any degree proportioned to the promise they exhibited. Centuries will glide away, and pine in want of those benefits, which seemed ready to burst from their bud and gladden the human race. Genius perhaps is indebted for its earliest birth to the occurrence of favourable circumstances. But, be this as it will, certain it is that it stands in need of every advantage to nurse it to perfection, and that for this reason, it is almost constantly frost-nipped, or stunted, or distorted in its proportions, and scarcely in any instance arrives at what genius is capable of being.

After all however, reputation for talents is not the ultimate object which a generous mind would desire. I am not contented to be admired as something strange and out of the common road; if I desire any thing of posthumous honour, it is that I may be regarded with affection and esteem by ages yet unborn. "I had rather," says a generous and amiable author of antiquity, "it should be affirmed of me, there never was such a man as Plutarch, than that Plutarch was ill-humoured, morose, and odious in his manners."

Moral fame is subject to a variety of disadvantages, which are not incident to the fame of literature. In the latter instance posterity has the whole subject fairly before them. We may dispute about the merits of Homer and Shakespear, but they have at least this benefit, that the entire evidence is in court. Whoever will, may read their works; and it needs only a firm, unbiassed and cultivated judgment to decide upon their excellencies.

A story of sir Walter Raleigh has often been repeated; but its peculiar aptness to the illustration of the present subject, may apologise for its being mentioned here. When sir Walter Raleigh wrote his History of the World, he was a prisoner in the Tower of London. One morning he heard the noise of a vehement contention under his window, but he could neither see the combatants, nor distinguish exactly what was said. One person after another came into his apartment, and he enquired of them the nature of the affray; but their accounts were so inconsistent, that he found himself wholly unable to arrive at the truth of the story. Sir Walter's reflection on this was obvious, yet acute. What, said he, can I not make myself master of an incident that happened an hour ago under my window, and shall I imagine I can truly understand the history of Hannibal and Cæsar?

History is in reality a tissue of fables. There is no reason to believe that any one page in any one history extant, exhibits the unmixed truth. The story is disfigured by the vanity of the actors, the interested misrepresentations of spectators, and the fictions, probable or improbable, with which every historian is instigated to piece out his imperfect tale. Human affairs are so entangled, motives are so subtle and variously compounded, that the truth cannot be told. What reasonable man then can consign his reputation to the Proteus-like uncertainty of historical record, with any sanguineness of expectation?

We are perpetually told, Time will clear up the obscurity of evidence, and posterity judge truly of our merits and demerits. There cannot be a grosser imposition than this. Where is the instance in which a character once disputed, has ceased to be disputed? We are bid to look forward patiently to the time when party and prejudice shall be stripped of their influence. There is no such time. The feuds and animosities of party contention are eternal. The vulgar indeed cease to interest themselves in a question, when it ceases to be generally discussed. But, of those who curiously enquire into its merits, there is not one in a thousand that escapes the contagion. He finds by unobserved degrees insinuated into him all the exclusive attachments, sometimes all the polemical fierceness, that ever fell to the lot of contemporaries and actors.

A few years before the commencement of the Christian æra, Cicero and Cæsar entered into a paper-war respecting the real worth of the character of Cato. Is this controversy yet decided? Do there not still exist, on the one hand, men who look upon Cato with all the enthusiastic veneration expressed by Cicero; and, on the other, men who, like Cæsar, treat him as a hypocritical snarler, and affirm that he was only indulging his pride and ill-humour, when he pretended to be indulging his love of virtue?

Perhaps there never was a man that loved fame so much as Cicero himself. When he found himself ill-treated by the asperity of Cato and the impatience of Brutus, when he was assailed with a torrent of abuse by the partisans of Antony, he also comforted himself that this was a transitory injustice. While he stretched out his neck to the sword of the assassin, he said within himself, In a little time the purity of my motives will be universally understood. Ignorant, misjudging man! Do we not hear at this hour the character of this illustrious ornament of the human race, defamed by every upstart school-boy? When is there a day that passes over our heads, without a repetition of the tale of his vain-gloriousness, his cowardice, the imbecility of his temper, and the hollowness of his patriotism?

There is another curious controversy strikingly illustrative of the present subject. What sort of men were the ancient Romans? It was not to be wondered at, that, amidst the dregs of monarchical government, great pains should be taken to dishonour them, and to bring them down to the miserable level of the men of modern times. One would have thought that no man could have perused the history of Rome and the history of England, without seeing that in the one was presented the substance of men, and in the other the shadow. I might as well have called up into the rivalship the histories of Bilidulgerid or Senegambia. But, no: the received maxim was, Men in all ages are the same. In France, since her revolution, the venerable shade seems about to be avenged of her calumniators. But there are many, even among professed republicans, that join the cry, and affirm that the supposed elevation of the Roman character is merely a delusion. This is so extensively the case, that a man diffident in his opinions, and sceptical in his enquiries, dares scarcely pronounce how the controversy may terminate, if indeed it shall have any termination.

This uncertainty it is illiberal and unjust to impute to the mere perverseness of the human mind: It is owing, however paradoxical that may seem, to the want of facts. Decisive evidence could not fail to produce a decisive effect. We should have lived first with the ancient Romans, and then with the men of the present day, to be able to institute a demonstrative comparison between them. This want of facts is a misfortune much more general than is ordinarily imagined. A man may live for years next door to a person of the most generous and admirable temper, Mr. Fox for instance, and may, by the force of prejudice merely, transform him into a monster. A given portion of familiar intercourse would render this mistake impossible. The evil however does not stop here. It has been found for example that two persons of opposite sexes may be lovers for half their lives, and afterwards a month of unrestrained, domestic, matrimonial intercourse shall bring qualities to light in each, that neither previously suspected. No one man ever completely understood the character of any other man. My most familiar friend exaggerates perhaps some virtues in me; but there are others which I know I possess, to which he is totally blind. For this reason I should lay it down as a maxim, never to take the report of a man's zealous and undoubted advocate against him. Let every thing be examined, as far as circumstances will possibly admit, before it is assumed for true.

All these considerations however tend to check our ardour for fame, which is built upon so uncertain a tenure.

There is another circumstance of considerable moment in this subject, and that is the fickleness of reputation and popularity. I hear one man praise another to-day; what security does that afford for his opinion a twelvemonth hence? Often the changes are sudden and abrupt; and he has scarcely put a period to the exuberance of his eulogium, before he passes to the bitterness of invective. Consistency is one of the virtues most applauded in society, and as to his reputation for which every man is most anxious; yet no quality is more rare. Nor ought it to be frequent: there is scarcely any proposition, as to which a man of an active and reflecting mind, may not recollect to have changed his sentiments at least once in his life. But, though inconsistency is no serious imputation, levity undoubtedly is. If I am right in changing my opinion, at least I was wrong in the hasty manner in which I formerly adopted it. Particularly in the case of reputation, no man can without pain realise as to himself, the facility with which partialities are discarded, friendships dissolved, and the man who was your warmest advocate, subsides into indifference or worse.

Before we take our leave of this subject, it may be amusing, perhaps instructive, to add a few more instances to those already cited, of the doubtfulness and obscurity of historical fame.

There is scarcely any controversy that has been agitated within the last twenty years, which has been distinguished by more fierceness of assertion, than that respecting Mary Queen of Scots and the English Elizabeth. If I ask the two first inquisitive persons I meet, what is become of this controversy? they will each of them tell me, that the question is completely decided, but one will affirm that the issue is in favour of Mary, and the other of Elizabeth. How shall I determine between their opposite assertions? A few incidental points have been cleared, but the main question is where it was. Was Mary accessory to the murder of her husband? After his death, is she to be regarded as a chaste and noble-minded woman in the hands of an audacious free-booter (Bothwel), or must she be considered as an abandoned slave to the grossest passions, and classed with the Messalinas and the Julias? Was Elizabeth incited to consent to her death, from low motives of rivalship and jealousy, or because she conceived the public safety would allow no longer delay? Was her reluctance to consent real, or only a well concerted fiction? Was she a party to the execrable intrigue of which Davison was the tool; and were her subsequent indignation and grief merely a scene that she played to impose upon the understandings of mankind? All these are questions in a suit not yet determined. While some are influenced in their judgment by the talents of Elizabeth, by the prosperity and happiness of her reign, and by certain instances of the moderation and rectitude of her domestic counsels, others find themselves unable to devise terms of abhorence and infamy to express their aversion against her. Such a thing is fame! There are even some, ridiculous as it may appear, that are bribed by personal charms which more than two centuries ago were consigned to putrefaction and dust, and would feel it as an imputation on their gallantry, if they could side with a woman so little attractive as Elizabeth, against the most accomplished beauty of her age.

The character of Charles the first is in like manner a subject of eternal contention, and he is treated as a model of intellectual grace and integrity, or as frigid, austere and perfidious, according as his judges shall happen to be tories or whigs, monarchical or republican.

Henry lord Bolingbroke was one of the great ornaments of the beginning of the present century. He has been admired as a statesman, an orator, a man of letters and a philosopher. Pope, in the eagerness of his reverence and devotion, foresaw the time when his merits would be universally acknowledged, and assured the world that the "sons" of his personal adversaries, would "blush" for the malignity and injustice of "their fathers *." But Pope, though a poet, was no prophet. We every day hear Bolingbroke spoken of by one man or another, with as much contempt as could have been expressed by the most rancorous of his political rivals.

The late doctor Johnson is a memorable instance in support of our position. Never have so many volumes been filled with the anecdotes of any private individual. If the character of any

* Essay on Man.

man can be decided by a record of facts, certainly his ought to be decided. But the case is otherwise. Each man has an opinion of his own respecting it; but, if the subject be started in conversation, it would be totally impossible to predict whether the favourers or the enemies would prove the greater number; were it not that the mass of mankind are generally ready to combine against excellence, real or presumed, because we can never adequately understand that, of which we have no experience in ourselves. Nor will it be any arrogance to foretel, that, unless the improvement of the human species shall prove rapid beyond all former example, the same dispute about the character of Johnson will remain a century hence, and the posterity will be still unborn that are to pass an unanimous verdict upon his merits.

ESSAY IX.

OF DIFFERENCE IN OPINION.

SECT. I.

PRINCIPLES OF EQUITABLE INTERPRETATION.

One of the best practical rules of morality that ever was delivered, is that of putting ourselves in the place of another, before we act or decide any thing respecting him.

It is by this means only that we can form an adequate idea of his pleasures and pains. The nature of a being, the first principle of whose existence is sensation, necessarily obliges us to refer every thing to ourselves; and, but for the practice here recommended, we should be in danger of looking upon the concerns of others with inadvertence, consequently with indifference.

Nor is this voluntary transmigration less necessary, to enable us to do justice to other men's motives and opinions, than to their feelings.

We observe one mode of conduct to be that which, under certain given circumstances, as mere spectators, we should determine to be most consistent with our notions of propriety. The first impulse of every human being, is, to regard a different conduct with impatience and resentment, and to ascribe it, when pursued by our neighbour, to a wilful perverseness, choosing, with open eyes and an enlightened judgment, the proceeding least compatible with reason.

The most effectual method for avoiding this misinterpretation of our neighbour's conduct, is to put ourselves in his place, to recollect his former habits and prejudices, and to conjure up in our minds the allurements, the impulses and the difficulties to which he was subject.

Perhaps it is more easy for us to make due allowances for, or, more accurately speaking, to form a just notion of, our neighbour's motives and actions, than of his opinions.

In actions it is not difficult to understand, that a man may be hurried away by the pressure of circumstances. The passion may be strong; the temptation may be great; there may be no time for deliberation.

These considerations do not apply, or apply with a greatly diminished force, to the case of a man's forming his judgment upon a speculative question. Time for deliberation may, sooner or later, always be obtained. Passion indeed may incline him to one side rather than the other; but not with the impetuosity, with which from time to time it incites us to action. Temptation there may be; but of so sober and methodical a sort, that we do not easily believe, that its march can go un-undetected, or that the mind of the man who does not surmount it, can possess any considerable share of integrity or good faith.

No sentiment therefore is more prevalent, than that which leads men to ascribe the variations of opinion which subsist in the world, to dishonesty and perverseness. It is thus that a Papist judges of a Protestant, and a Protestant of a Papist; such is the decision of the Hanoverian upon the Jacobite, and the Jacobite upon the Hanoverian;

such the notion formed by the friend of establishments concerning the republican, and by the republican concerning the friend of establishments. The chain of evidence by which every one of these parties is determined, appears, to the adherent of that party, so clear and satisfactory, that he hesitates not to pronounce, that perverseness of will only could resist it.

This sort of uncharitableness was to be expected under the present condition of human intellect. No character is more rare than that of a man who can do justice to his antagonist's argument; and, till this is done, it must be equally difficult to do justice to an antagonist's integrity. Ask a man, who has been the auditor of an argument, or who has recently read a book, adverse to his own habits of thinking, to restate the reasonings of the adversary. You will find him betraying the cause he undertakes to explain, in every point. He exhibits nothing but a miserable deformity, in which the most vigilant adversary could scarcely recognise his image. Nor is there any dishonesty in this. He tells you as much as he understood. Since therefore he understands nothing of the adversary but his opposition, it is no wonder that he is virulent in his invective against him.

The ordinary strain of partisans, are like the two knights, of whom we are told that, in coming in opposite directions to a head fixed on a pole in a cross-way, of which one side was gold, and the other silver, they immediately fell to tilting; the right-hand champion stoutly maintaining that the head was gold, and the other as indignantly rejoining that it was silver. Not one disputant in ten ever gives himself the trouble to pass over to his adversary's position; and, of those that do, many take so short and timid a glance, and with an organ so clouded with prejudice, that, for any benefit they receive, they might as well have remained eternally upon the same spot.

There is scarcely a question in the world, that does not admit of two plausible statements. There is scarcely a story that can be told, of which one side is not good, till the other is related. When both sides have been heard, the ordinary result to a careful and strict observer, is, much contention of evidence, much obscurity, and much scepticism. He that is smitten with so ardent a love of truth, as continually to fear lest error should pass upon him under some specious disguise, will find himself ultimately reduced to a nice weighing of evidence, and a subtle observation as to which scale preponderates upon almost every important question. Such a man will express neither astonishment nor unbelief, when he is told that another person, of uncommon purity of motives, has been led to draw a different conclusion.

It would be difficult to confer a greater benefit upon mankind, than would be conferred by him, who should persuade them to a discarding of mutual bigotry, and induce them to give credit to each other for their common differences of opinion. Such a persuasion would effect an almost universal rout of the angry passions. Persecution and prosecution for opinion would rarely venture abroad in the world. Much of family dissension, much of that which generates alienation in the kindest bosoms, much even of the wars which have hitherto desolated mankind, would be swept away for ever from the face of the earth. There is nothing about which men quarrel more obstinately and irreconcilably, than difference of opinion. There is nothing that engenders a profounder and more inveterate hate.

If this subject were once understood, we should then look only to the consequences of opinions. We should no more think of hating a man for being an atheist or a republican, though these opinions were exactly opposite to our own, than for having the plague. We should pity him; and regret the necessity, if necessity there were, for taking precautions against him. In the mean time there is this difference between a man holding erroneous opinions, and a man infected with contagious distemper. Wrong opinions are perhaps never a source of tumult and disorder, unless the persons who hold them are persecuted *, or placed under circumstances of iniquitous oppression †. The remedy therefore in this case, is to remove unjustifiable restraints; and then leave the question to be fairly decided in the lists of argument and reason.

The opinions men espouse are of two sorts; those of which they cannot recollect the commencement, but that have been entertained by them ever since they had an idea of the subjects to which they relate; and those that belong to subjects, respecting which they have by some means been induced to reverse their first judgments, and embrace tenets different from those to which they formerly professed an adherence.

In the beginning of the present Essay, we had occasion to recommend the rule of morality which directs us, to put ourselves in the place of another, before we act or decide any thing respecting him.

There is another rule, the observation of which would be scarcely less salutary in the subject of which we are treating: the rule which enjoins us, to retire into ourselves, and examine the motives of our own characters and proceeding, before we

* As at the period of the Reformation.

† As in the period preceding the French revolution, where the general oppression of all orders of men, gave a tumultuous activity to the principle of innovation.

hold ourselves competent to decide upon those of others.

Self-examination is well calculated to teach us indulgence towards those opinions of others, of which the holder is unable to recollect the commencement. Where is the man presumptuous enough to affirm that, in all his opinions, religious, moral and political, in science and art, of decorum, of pleasure and prudence, he is wholly uninfluenced by education and early habits, and holds his sentiments from deduction alone, entirely independent of his parents, his companions, his age and his country? Beyond doubt, there is no man thus independent. One man has done a little more, and another a little less. But in the wisest of us, if I may be allowed the expression, the mother still lurks about the heart *. Arrogant assertions of independence indeed are frequent enough; but they only prove the folly and supineness of the man that makes them. It will presently appear from the very nature of the human mind, that nothing is more easy than a deception of this sort.

In those errors which a man derives from his education, it is obvious to remark, that at least there was nothing designing or dishonest on his part in the first receiving them. The only blame that can be imputed to him, is, that he has not

* Persius, Sat. V. ver. 92.

yielded an impartial attention to the evidence by which they are refuted. Alas! impartiality is a virtue hung too high, to be almost ever within the reach of man!

How many men are there, that have had this evidence exhibited to them, or possessed an opportunity of examining it? Thousands of Papists, Jacobites, and republicans, as well as of persons holding an opposite sentiment, have gone out of the world, without ever attaining a fair and adequate occasion of bringing their tenets to the test.

But what is perhaps chiefly worthy of observation under this head, is, the feeble and insufficient manner in which almost every tenet, however unquestionably true, is usually maintained. The rigid logician or philosopher, if he admit the principle intended to be supported, is frequently obliged to throw away and discard the whole edifice upon which it rested. To the majority of the world, this circumstance is unknown.

Every argument is liable to be exposed to the inspection of two sets of hearers or readers; the first friendly, the second hostile, to the doctrine intended to be supported. To the former of these, in general at least, every argument is satisfactory, every evidence conclusive. No man can have been much conversant in matters of debate, without having had occasion to hear, from men otherwise of great sagacity and talent, the most extravagant encomiums of the vilest compositions, without any other assignable cause, than that they were written on their own side of the question. This single circumstance blinded them to every defect.

On the other hand, those hearers or readers, who are hostile to the doctrine intended to be supported, can discover nothing but defects. Every argument, however skilfully treated, has perhaps its weak and vulnerable part. Upon this part they obstinately fix. They never recur to the equitable rule, of separating a doctrine from its champion, and remembering that the first may be sound, while the last may be feeble; but absurdly construe every mistake of the champion, into a defect in the cause. He that would seek truth with inflexible zeal, must himself become counsel for the adversary, must reconstruct his arguments, remove the dross, supply the omissions, and give consistency and combination to the whole. He must not confound the question, which is a portion struck off from the mass of eternal science, with the character of him that agitates it, the creature of a day. But where is the man who will undertake this persevering and laborious task?

Both the sets of hearers or readers here described, are honest after their different modes. But it is the furthest in the world from being wonderful, that men, who read in so different a spirit, should rise from the perusal with opposite impressions.

Reasons like these sufficiently shew how easy it is to account for the obstinacy with which men adhere to first impressions, and how little ground there is for imputing it to them as an enormous offence. The causes of this pertinacity are closely interwoven with the nature of man; and, instead of conceiving, as we are apt to do, that the persons in whom it betrays itself fall below the standard of humanity, we ought, on the contrary, to regard those who conquer it as having lifted themselves above the level of almost the whole mass of their species.

But the world, even when it is prevailed on to forgive an adherence to the impressions of education, does not fail to regard with particular severity those changes of sentiment in which a man embraces any new error, or any tenet which his censors regard as an error *. Their invective acquires double bitterness, when the change of opinion appears to coincide in time with certain cir-

* Since this passage was written, many of my early friends have undergone the sort of change here referred to. I have for the most part retained the opinions we then held in common. Their change then appears to me to be from truth to error: and in what follows I have been unconsciously penning their apology for what they were afterwards to do.

cumstances of interest rendering the new opinion particularly convenient to the convert.

It would constitute perhaps the most curious chapter in the history of the human mind, if any person sufficiently competent to the task, were to undertake to detect the various causes which generate change of opinion among men. It happens in most cases that the person who undergoes this change, is himself unable to assign the period at which it took place. He only knows that he was of one opinion in January, and holds another in June. This circumstance alone is sufficiently suspicious.

It will probably be found that every man who undergoes a change of opinion, imagines he has obtained a new accession of evidence. But was this the only cause of the change?

Undoubtedly argument is in its own nature capable of effecting a change of opinion. But there are other causes which have a similar influence, and that unconsciously to the person in whom they operate.

Man has not only an understanding to reason, but a heart to feel. Interest, as has been already remarked, can do much; and there are many kinds of interest, beside that which is expressly pecuniary.

I was of one opinion in January, and am of another in June. If I gain a pension, or a rich church-living by the change, this circumstance may well be supposed to have some weight with me. If it recommend me to a wealthy relative or patron, this is not indifferent. It perhaps only tends to introduce me into good company. Perhaps I am influenced by an apprehension of something beautiful, generous and becoming in the sentiment to be embraced, instead of being under the mere influence of argument. Men are rarely inclined to stop short in a business of this sort; and, having detected one error in the party to which they formerly adhered, they are gradually propelled to go over completely to the opposite party. A candid mind will frequently feel itself impressed with the difficulties which bear upon its sentiments, especially if they are forcibly brought forward in argument; and will hastily discard its own system for another, when that other, if fairly considered, was liable to objections not less cogent than the former.

But, what is most material to the subject of which we are treating, all these influencess are liable, in a greater or less degree, to escape the man who is most rigid in scrutinising the motives by which he is influenced. Indeed we have spoken of them as changes of opinion; which implies a certain degree of sincerity. The vulgar, it is true, where they suspect any sinister motive, regard the man as holding the same opinion still, and only pretending to have undergone a change. But this is a phenomenon much more rare than is commonly imagined. The human mind is exceedingly pliable in this respect; and he that earnestly wishes to entertain an opinion, will usually in no long time become its serious adherent. We even frequently are in this respect the dupes of our own devices. A man who habitually defends a sentiment, commonly ends with becoming a convert. Pride and shame fix him in his new faith. It is a circumstance by no means without a precedent, for a man to become the enthusiastic advocate of a paradox, which he at first defended by way of bravado, or as an affair of amusement.

Undoubtedly the man who embraces a tenet from avarice, ambition, or the love of pleasure, even though he should not be aware of the influence exerted by these motives, is so far an imbecil character. The censure to which he is exposed, would however be in some degree mitigated, if we recollected that he fell into this weakness in common with every individual of his species, and that there is not a man that lives, of whom it can be affirmed that any one of his opinions was formed with impartiality.

There is nothing more memorable in the analysis of intellectual operations, than the subtlety of motives *. Every thing in the phenomena of the

* Political Justice, Vol. I, Chap. V, §. 2, octavo edition.

human mind, is connected together. At first sight one would suppose nothing was easier, than for the man himself to assign the motive of any one of his actions. Strictly speaking this is absolutely impossible. He can never do it accurately; and we often find him committing the absurdest and most glaring mistakes. Every incident of our lives contributes to form our temper, our character, and our understanding; and the mass thus formed modifies every one of our actions. All in man is association and habit.

It may be objected indeed that our voluntary actions are thus influenced, but not our judgments, which are purely an affair of the understanding. But this is a groundless distinction. Volition and understanding, in the structure of the human mind, do not possess provinces thus separate and independent. Every volition is accompanied by a judgment; and we cannot perform one voluntary action, till we have first enlightened, or imposed upon, as the case may require, the reasoning faculty. It is true to a proverb, that what a man wishes to believe, he is in the most direct road to regard as a branch of his creed.

How ridiculous then and dull of apprehension is the man, who affirms of himself, in any imaginable instance, that he is under no sinister influence, and loudly asserts his own impartiality? Yet no spectacle more frequent than this. Let us take the first example that offers.

A letter of resignation is just published, addressed by general Washington to the people of the United States of America, and dated 17 September 1796. In that letter is contained the following sentence. The sentiments I am about to deliver, "will be offered to you with the more freedom, as you can only see in them the disinterested warnings of a parting friend, who can possibly have no personal motive to bias his counsel."

To expose the absurdity of this passage, it is not necessary to refine upon the term "personal motive," and to observe that every action of general Washington's life, every peculiarity of his education, every scene in which he was engaged, every sensation he ever experienced, was calculated to produce something more than the possibility of personal motive; since all that, which is peculiar to one man, in contradistinction to his fellow men, is susceptible of being made personal motive.

But, to take the term in its vulgar acceptation, there were certainly very few men in America more liable to personal motive, than general Washington. He had filled, with very little interruption, the first situations in his country for more than twenty years. He takes it for granted indeed that he is exempted from personal motive, because he conceives that his wish to withdraw himself is sincere. But, in the whole period of his public administration, did he adopt no particular plan of politics; and is he absolutely sure that he shall have no personal gratification in seeing his plans perpetuated? Is he absolutely sure that he looks back with no complacence to the period of his public life; and that he is entirely free from the wish, that such principles may be pursued in future, as shall be best calculated to reflect lustre upon his measures? No discerning man can read this letter of resignation, without being struck with the extreme difference between general Washington and a man who should have come to the consideration of the subject *de novo*, or without perceiving how much the writer is fettered in an hundred respects, by the force of inveterate habits.——To return from this example to the subject of the Essay.

Let us for a moment put out of the question the consideration of pleasure and pain, hope and fear, as they are continually operating upon us in the formation of our opinions. Separately from these, there are numerous circumstances, calculated to mislead the most ingenuous mind in its search after truth, and to account for our embracing the shadow of reason, when we imagined ourselves possessed of the substance. One man, according to the habits of his mind, shall regard with satisfaction the slightest and most flimsy arguments, and bestow upon them the name of demonstration. Another man, a mathematician for instance, shall be insensible to the force of those accumulated presumptions, which are all that moral and practical subjects will ever admit. A misfortune, more pitiable than either of these, is when a strict and profound reasoner falls into some unperceived mistake at the commencement, in consequence of which, the further he proceeds in his enquiry, and the more closely he follows his train of deductions, he plunges only the more deeply into error.

SECT. II.

ILLUSTRATIONS.

THE maxims, which the preceding reasonings are calculated to establish, are, that we shall rarely be in the right in allowing ourselves to suspect the sincerity of others in the cause to which they profess adherence; that nothing can be more various than the habits of different minds, or more diversified than their modes of contemplating the same subject; that nothing can be more deceitful than the notion, so general among superficial thinkers, that every cause but their own is destitute of any plausibility of appearance; and that we can never have a just view of the sincerity of men in opinions we deem to be absurd, till we have learned to put ourselves in their place, and to become the temporary advocates of the sentiment we reject.

It may be useful to illustrate these propositions by a specific instance.

The controversy at present most vehemently agitated, is that between new and old systems of political government. The advocates of both parties for the most part see nothing, on the side adverse to their own, but wilful perverseness. They cannot believe that their opponents are sincere and ardent well-wishers to the happiness of mankind. All they discern in one case, is a spirit of monopoly and oppression; and in the other, is a discontented heart, anxious to gratify its cravings by the most rapacious and dishonest means. If each party could be persuaded to see the principle of controversy in the other in a favourable light, and to regard itself and its opponent as contending by different modes for the same object, the common welfare, it would be attended, in this great crisis of the moral world, with the happiest effects.

We will take it for granted for the present that the innovators have the right side of the argument, and will exhibit certain considerations calculated to evince the sincerity and good intention of their adversaries. The instance adduced therefore will be somewhat better adapted for the conviction of the former than the latter.

It may be laid down as an axiom that the enlightened advocate of new systems of government, proceeds upon the establishment or assumption of the progressive nature of man, whether as an individual, or as the member of a society. Let us see how far the principal champions of both hypotheses, are agreed in this doctrine.

The supporters of the systems of government at present in existence, build upon it to a certain extent, as the main pillar of their edifice. They look through the history of man. They view him at first a miserable savage, destitute of all the advantages and refinements of a civilised state, and scarcely in any respect elevated above the brutes. They view him in the progressive stages of intellectual improvement, and dwell with extacy upon the polished manners, the generous sentiments, the scientific comprehensiveness, the lofty flights and divine elevation, which constitute what may at present be denominated the last stage of that progress. They call to mind with horror the fierce and unrelenting passions of savages and barbarians. They see that it has been only by graduated steps that these passions have been controled, in the degree in which they are now controled; and they justly regard personal security as the grand nourisher of leisure, disinterestedness, science and wisdom.

Thus far both parties ought to be considered as

perfectly agreed. The facts, thus asserted by the champion of establishments, are too obvious to be disputed by his opponent; and the progress, which mankind has already made, is one of the most impressive arguments in proof of the progress he seems yet destined to make. It is to be regarded merely as the momentary extravagance of the aristocrat, when he laments the extinction of the age of chivalry; nor is the sally of the democrat entitled to a better name, who, in contemplation of the conceivable improvements of society, passes a general condemnation upon all that it has hitherto effected.

The two parties being thus far agreed, it is at least as much passion and temperature, as sober reason, that leads them wide of each other in what is to follow. The innovator, struck with theoretical beauties which, he trusts, shall hereafter be realised, looks with an eye of elevated indifference and scrutinising severity, upon what mankind have hitherto effected. His opponent, setting out from the same point, the love of intellect and improvement, is impressed with so ardent an admiration of what has been already attained, that no consideration can prevail upon him to commit it to the slightest hazard.

He surely however involves himself in a glaring inconsistency. If all men had been of his temper, the advancement, which he is now contented implicitly to admire, would never have been made. If we praise our ancestors, we should imitate them. Not imitate them by servilely treading in their steps, but by imbibing their spirit. Those of our ancestors who are most highly applauded, were judicious and successful innovators. They realised for mankind what had not previously been attained.

The rational and sober innovator ought to admit, that innovation is a measure attended with peculiar peril, that it should be entered upon with caution, and introduced in portions, small and detached. This is the point, in which the wisest of both parties might learn to agree.

The alarm of the opposite party is by no means unfounded in truth. All men love independence. This is a laudable passion. All men love power. This is a more questionable propensity. From these passions taken together, united with the actual imperfections of the human mind, arises the necessity of political restraint. The precautions that are necessary for the preservation of property, co-operating with the low propensities of selfishness and ignorance, produce a great inequality of possessions; and this inequality is inevitably the source of much heart-burning and animosity.

The evils here alluded to, might perhaps, all of them, have been prevented, if men had been willing to form themselves into small communities, instead of coalescing into great nations*. But if they had always been contented with this, would the arts and improvements of mankind, which easily go on when once originated, have ever been called into existence? There are many things, not absolutely good, which have been good temporarily and under given circumstances. Perhaps luxury, that luxury which is incompatible with a pure and elevated morality, is an instance of this †.

But, granting for a moment that the coalition of mankind into great nations ought never to have taken place, this does not alter the question before us. This coalition actually exists. It constitutes a state exceedingly artificial. It is at war with the strongest propensities of individual man. It therefore requires great caution and extreme vigilance to maintain it. There is probably however not a political theorist in existence, who would say, that it ought to be totally and immediately destroyed. There is not a sober man in the world, with nerves strong enough calmly to face the tremendous issue.

The advocate of establishments says, We have already gained much; the spectacle of human society exhibits much that is admirable; I cannot consent that all this should be put to hazard for

* Political Justice, Book V, Chap. XXII, octavo edition.

† Political Justice, Book VIII, Chap. VII, octavo edition.

the sake of an untried experiment: Let us be aware of our true interest; let us be contented with the things that we have. Surely this man may be eminently both honest and philanthropical.

The rational advocate of new systems of government, would touch actual institutions with a careful hand. He would desire further changes and fresh improvements; but he would consider the task of innovation as an arduous business, nor is there any thing that would excite more the apprehensiveness of his mind, than a precipitate and headlong spirit.

There is nothing perhaps that has contributed more to the introduction and perpetuating of bigotry in the world, than the doctrines of the Christian religion. It caused the spirit of intolerance to strike a deep root; and it has entailed that spirit upon many who have shaken off the directer influence of its tenets. It is the characteristic of this religion, to lay the utmost stress upon faith. Its central doctrine is contained in this short maxim, He that believeth, shall be saved; and he that believeth not, shall be damned *. What it is, the belief of which is saving, the records of our religion have left open to controversy; but the fundamental nature of faith, is one of its most unquestionable lessons. Faith is not only necessary

* Mark, Chap. XVI, ver. 16.

to preserve us from the pains of hell; it is also requisite as a qualification for temporal blessings. When any one applied to Jesus to be cured of any disease, he was first of all questioned respecting the implicitness of his faith; and, in Galilee, and other places, Christ wrought not many miracles, because of their unbelief*. Never were curses poured out in a more copious stream, or with a more ardent and unsparing zeal, than by the meek and holy Jesus upon those who opposed his pretensions †. The short and comprehensive description bestowed upon the refractory to the end of time appears to be this, They have loved darkness, rather than light, because their deeds are evil ‡.

There is a vulgar error closely connected with the subject of this essay, which on account of its extensive influence, deserves to be noticed; I mean the demerit of inconsistency. It is wonderful how great a space this topic occupies in the debates of the English parliament. The greatest luminary of the present house of commons, Mr. Fox, will sometimes occupy one half of a speech upon the

* Matthew, Chap. VIII, ver. 13; Chap. IX, ver. 28, 29; Chap. XIII, ver. 58: Mark, Chap. V. ver. 36; Chap. IX, ver. 23; Chap. XI, ver. 23, 24: John, Chap. XI, ver. 40; Chap. XX, ver. 29.

† Take as an example, Matthew, Chap. XXIII, ver. 33.

‡ John, Chap. III, ver. 19.

most interesting question, with a defence of his own consistency.

It is scarcely necessary to remark, that an argument upon an interesting question, is always much degraded, when it is suffered to involve with it a personal discussion.

Of personal discussions, that of consistency is one of the most frivolous.

Inconsistency is as unfortunate a test of a man's insincerity, as can be imagined.

If by inconsistency we understand some contradiction between one branch of a man's creed and another, this is undoubtedly a defect. It proves that he is imperfect, not that he is dishonest.

But, if by inconsistency we understand, that he does not believe now what he once believed, that his character is changed, and his conduct regulated by different principles, this is scarcely any argument of present defect. Yet this is the sort of inconsistency, the charge of which is most frequently and vehemently repelled.

It is obvious that the man, who, in adjusting accounts with his own mind, is influenced as to the opinions he shall now receive, by the consideration of what it was that he formerly believed, is so far a vitiated character. He ought to be ready to receive the truth, however unlike it may be to his former habits of thinking.

But we are entitled to go further than this, and to affirm that inconsistency, in the sense last explained, is glorious, instead of being shameful. Who is it that is likely, through Shakespear's seven ages of man, to think always alike? The slave of prejudice, or the slave of idleness. The active and independent mind, the genuine lover of and enquirer after truth, will inevitably pass through certain revolutions of opinion.

It may be alleged in behalf of those who are eager in the vindication of the unalterableness of their opinions and principles, that great stress is laid upon this point by the vulgar.

But then, on the other hand, it is to be remarked that, when great and illustrious characters lend their aid to the prejudices of the vulgar, they add much to the vigour of prejudice, and are so far the enemies, not the friends, of the improvement and happiness of mankind.

ESSAY X.

OF POLITENESS.

SECT. I.

BENEFITS OF POLITENESS.

It has been no unfrequent profession among men of a bold temper, and who are smitten with a love for the sublimer virtues, that they are enemies to politeness.

One of the greatest misfortunes incident to morality, as well as to a majority of sciences, flows from the ambiguity of words.

By politeness many persons understand artificial manners, the very purpose of which is to stand between the feelings of the heart and the external behaviour. The word immediately conjures up to their mind a corrupt and vicious mode of society, and they conceive it to mean a set of rules, founded in no just reason, and ostentatiously practised by those who are familiar with them, for no purpose more expressly, than to confound and keep at a distance those who, by the accident of their birth or fortune, are ignorant of them.

In this sense no doubt politeness is worthy of our decisive disapprobation, and in this sense it is to be regretted that there is vastly too much politeness in the world.

Urbanity is a term that has met with a better fortune among our contemporaries, than politeness. Yet, if we have recourse to their etymology, politeness is certainly not less appropriate and laudable. As it descends to us from the Greek, its nature is precisely coincident; as it comes to us through the medium of the Latin word, which signifies to polish, to make smooth, agreeable to the eye, and pleasant to the touch, it is sufficiently adapted to that circumstance in morals which may admit of a substantial vindication.

Morality, or the exercise of beneficence, consists of two principal parts, which may be denominated the greater morality, and the less. Those actions of a man's life, adapted to purposes of beneficence, which are fraught with energy, and cannot be practised but in an exalted temper of mind, belong to the greater morality; such as saving a fellow being from death, raising him from deep distress, conferring on him a memorable advantage, or exerting one's self for the service of multitudes. There are other actions, in which a man may consult the transitory feelings of his neighbours, and to which we can seldom be prompted by a lofty spirit of ambition; actions which the heart can record, but which the tongue is rarely competent to relate. These belong to the lesser morality.

It should seem as if our temper and the permanent character of our minds, should be derived from the greater morality; but that the ordinary and established career of our conduct, should have reference to the less.

No doubt a man of eminent endowments and fortunate situation may do more good by the practice of the greater morality, than he can do mischief by the neglect of the less. But, even in him, the lesser moralities, as they are practised or neglected, will produce important effects. The neglect of them, however illustrious may be the tenour of his life, and however eminent his public services, will reflect a shade of ambiguity upon his character. Thus authors, whose writings have been fraught with the seeds of general happiness, but whose conduct towards their relatives or acquaintance has been attended with any glaring defect, have seldom obtained much credit for purity of principle. With the ordinary rate of mankind it is worse: when they have parted with the lesser moralities, they have nearly parted with every thing.

The great line of distinction between these two branches of morality, is that the less is of incomparably more frequent demand. We may rise up and lie down for weeks and months together, without being once called upon for the practice of any grand and emphatical duty. But it will be strange if a day pass over our heads, without affording scope for the lesser moralities. They furnish therefore the most obvious test as to the habitual temper of our lives.

Another important remark which flows from this consideration, is that the lesser moralities, however minute in their constituent particles, and however they may be passed over by the supercilious as unworthy regard, are of great importance in the estimate of human happiness. It is rarely that the opportunity occurs for a man to confer on me a striking benefit. But, every time that I meet him, he may demonstrate his kindness, his sympathy, and, by attentions almost too minute for calculation, add new vigour to the stream of complacence and philanthropy that circulates in my veins.

Hence it appears that the lesser moralities are of most importance, where politeness is commonly least thought of, in the bosom of family intercourse, and where people have occasion most constantly to associate together. If I see the father of a family perpetually exerting himself for what he deems to be their welfare, if he give the most unequivocal proofs of his attachment, if he cannot hear of any mischance happening to them without agony, at the same time that he is their despot and their terror, bursting out into all the fury of passion, or preserving a sour and painful moroseness that checks all the kindly effusions of their soul, I shall regard this man as an abortion, and I may reasonably doubt whether, by his mode of proceeding, he does not traverse their welfare in more respects than he promotes it.

Rousseau has observed that man is by nature unamiable. There is usually something ambiguous in the use of this term, nature. If he means that man, in the solitary state of existence in which he delights to describe him, and which he represents as the perfection of a human being, has few of the social affections, this cannot be disputed. The savage state, as it exists in some parts of Africa and America, is by no means destitute of affections. There are no where perhaps more affectionate fathers and husbands. They love, as they hate, with uncommon energy and fervour. Their attachment to their guests, their benefactors, and their friends, is ardent and unalterable.

If therefore they appear in any respect unamiable, it is not because they are more selfish, or have fewer affections, than the civilised nations of the world. It is simply because their minds are not subtilised. It is because their intellectual observation has not grown curious and microscopical, and they see things only in masses and in the gross. None more ready than they to perform trying services, to expose themselves to the fury of every element, to suffer all the privations and all the tortures of which our nature is susceptible, for the advantage of those they love. In these cases they can identify themselves with the object of their attachment. But they cannot do so in minuter and more ordinary matters. They have not analysed the elements of the human mind, and scrutinised its history. Gulliver's Houyhnmn is a savage, who cries repeatedly to the unfortunate wanderer to go faster, and never discovers his incapacity or his pain, till it is in the most express manner represented to him. Certain persons calling themselves philanthropists and patriots, are like the savages of which we treat, when they insist almost exclusively upon the greater duties, and represent the petty kindnesses of human life as scarcely worthy the regard of a citizen and a man.

Goldsmith has introduced his Vicar of Wakefield as remarking, that he had ever been a great lover of happy human faces. Such will always be the feeling of him, whose heart is stored with the genuine affections of a man, and in whom cultivation has given incessant activity to philanthropy. How enviable is his state, to whom every door that he frequents,

> Flies wide, and almost leaps from off its hinges,
> To give him entrance;——
> While his approaches make a little holiday,
> And every face is dressed in smiles to meet him! ROWE.

This is one of the great circumstances distinguishing between the civilised and the savage state; the silent communication of the eye, the lively attention that marks every shade of gradation in another's pleasure or pain, the nameless kindnesses that persuade the receiver more forcibly, or, at least, more cordially, of the attachment of the performer, than great services are ever enabled to do.

Again; in civilised society there is a mutual harmony and correspondence between the politeness of the active party, and the state of sensation in the passive. In such persons particularly as have their minds early roused, whether accidentally, or by the judicious proceeding of their institutor, and promise to be, in more than an ordinary degree, useful members of the commonwealth, it is inconceivable how numerous and delicate are their sensations, and how exquisite is their feeling of pleasure or pain. The slightest circumstances, imperceptible to a common eye, and scarcely adverted to by the agent, often produce an indelible impression. There is something exceedingly deceitful in human nature in this respect. A shrinking sensibility will not seldom hide itself under an unaltered exterior. This is frequently illustrated in the education of children. If they are harshly reproved, they disdain perhaps to lament, they are too proud to change a muscle, and we inwardly grieve for their impenetrable hardness, while their soul is secretly torn with conflicting, not seldom with dignified, emotions.

Nor is this sensibility by any means confined to persons of extraordinary talents. The worm that we trample upon, writhes beneath our foot, and is agonised, though in silence. It is a trite observation that one person shall less humble his suitor by a refusal, than another by compliance; so great is the importance that attaches itself to things apparently trivial. That man knows little of human nature, and is either endued with a very small portion of sensibility, or is seldom in the habit of putting himself in the place of another, who is not forward in the practice of minute attentions. When a modest and unassured person enters a room, he is anxious about his gestures, and feels the disposition of every limb and feature as a sort of weight upon his mind. A supercilious look, a dubious smile, an unceremonious accost, from one of the company, pierces him to the soul. On the contrary, at how cheap a rate may he be encouraged and made happy! What kind-hearted man would refuse to procure ease for him at so small an expence?

Perhaps the sort of sensibility here described is to be regarded as a defect. Perhaps, upon a nice adjustment of the value of other men's good opinion on the one hand, and of independence on the other, we shall find that he ought to have been more firm and intrepid. But a judicious moralist will not be abrupt in the suppression of sensibility. The form may be wrong, but the substance ought to remain. In a word, wherever civilisation exists, sensibility will be its attendant; a sensibility, which cannot be satisfied without much kindness, nor without a kindness of that condescending nature, that considers the whole chain of our feelings, and is desirous, out of petty materials, to compose the sum of our happiness.

Politeness is not precisely that scheme and system of behaviour which can only be learned in the fashionable world. There are many things in the system of the fashionable world, that are practised, not to encourage but depress, not to produce happiness but mortification. These, by whatever name they are called, are the reverse of genuine politeness; and are accordingly commonly known by the denomination of rudeness, a word of exactly opposite application. Much true politeness may often be found in a cottage. It cannot however conspicuously exist, but in a mind, itself unembarrassed, and at liberty to attend to the feelings of others; and it is distinguished by an open ingenuousness of countenance, and an easy and flowing manner. It is therefore necessarily graceful. It may undoubtedly best be learned in the society of the unembarrassed, the easy and the graceful. It is most likely to exist among those persons who, delivered from the importunate pressure of the first wants of our nature, have leisure to attend to the delicate and evanescent touches of the soul.

Politeness has been said to be the growth of courts, and a manner frank, abrupt and austere, to be congenial to a republic. If this assertion be true, it is a matter worthy of regret, and it will behove us to put it in the scale as a defect, to be weighed against the advantages that will result from a more equal and independent condition of mankind. It is however probably founded in mistake. It does not seem reasonable to suppose that the abolition of servility should be the diminution of kindness; and it has already been observed that, where the powers of intellect are strenuously cultivated, sensibility will be their attendant. But, in proportion to the acuteness of any man's feelings, will be, in a majority of cases, his attention and deference to the feelings of others.

SECT. II.

RECIPROCAL CLAIMS OF POLITENESS AND SINCERITY.

A REMARK not unfrequently heard from the professed enemies of politeness, is, I dislike such a person; why should I be at any pains to conceal it? Is it not right that the judgment of mankind respecting the character of individuals, should be divulged? I wish to be understood. I feel in myself no vocation to be a hypocrite.

Are the persons who hold this language, wholly unacquainted with the fallibility of human judgment? Be it observed, that they are usually, of all their species, the most capricious, the most hasty in their judgments, and dogmatical in their decisions. Sober and thinking men, are fearful of being misled in a subject so complex and involved as the study of characters; and have no pleasure in delivering their sentiments in this matter, with rapidity of decision, and in a peremptory tone. They are wary and anxious in forming an opinion, and scepticism in enquiry, is eminently calculated to inspire gentleness not imbecility, of delivery and behaviour. Persons who are so ungraciously eager to condemn a character, for the first displeasing appearance, for the merest trifle, for any thing or for nothing, while they pretend to be doing homage at the shrine of sincerity, will generally be found to be merely gratifying their own peevishness and the undue acrimony of their temper.

They do not recollect that the greater part of human virtue consists in self-government, and a resolute counteraction of improper propensities. When I check in myself an unmanly and inordinate lamentation for the loss of a friend, which, being indulged, if I am a man of sensibility, would perhaps destroy me, who is there that will charge me with prevarication in this proceeding? When I refuse to vent the feeling of bodily anguish in piercing cries, as the first impuse would prompt me to do, I am not therefore a hypocrite. In the same manner, if I refuse to treat any person with pointed contempt for every petty dislike, and prefer the keeping my mind always free for the reception of new and opposite evidence, this is no breach of sincerity.

This argument will appear in a still stronger light, if we act upon the great rule of morality, and put ourselves in the place of the individual concerned. On my part, suppose, I am eager to conform to a mistaken law of sincerity, but in reality most probably am chiefly prompted by an unjust and imperious disposition. How is it with my neighbour, whom I am forward to convince of the small degree he occupies in my esteem? He is placed in the most undesirable predicament. He must either defend himself from my assault, by harbouring that unfavourable opinion of me, which easily degenerates into hate; or he must sink, unrelieved, beneath one of the most humiliating and soul-harrowing feelings incident to our nature, that of having brought home, at once to his understanding and his senses, the ill opinion and unfriendly sentiment of a being of his own species. How lightly and thoughtlessly is this desolation frequently inflicted? An offence like this, nothing can aggravate, but the frigid and miserable pretence of the offender, that what he did was the dictate of virtue.

A man conducts himself in a manner I disapprove. I instantly express my contempt towards him, personally, and in the most unqualified terms. —Who made me a judge over him? From what source did I derive my patent of infallibility? He was more concerned in the event, and possibly considered the subject more maturely and patiently than I have considered it. Toleration, and freedom of opinion, are scarcely worth accepting, if, when my neighbour differs from me, I do not indeed burn him, but I take every occasion to insult him. There could be no freedom of opinion, if every one conducted himself thus. Toleration in its full import, requires, not only that there shall be no laws to restrain opinion, but that forbearance and liberality shall be moulded into the manners of the community.

Supposing it certain that the man I censure is a person of depraved character, is this the way to amend him? Is there no conduct that offers itself, but that of punishment? How often does the loud censure, and the "slow-moving finger of scorn *," drive a man to despair, who might have been amended, perhaps rendered the ornament of his species? I ought to reclaim my brother with kindness and love, not to have recourse to measures of insolence and contumely.

This will be still more evident, if we admit the doctrine of a moral necessity, and believe that there is an uniform and constant conjunction between motives and actions. Upon this hypothesis, the man who acts improperly, has a certain train of reasoning on the subject by which his mind is reconciled to the deviation. His understanding is imposed on; there is a cloud of sophistry which

* Shakespear.

rests upon it. How shall this be dispersed? In what manner shall truth be instilled into his mind? Certainly with the dispassionateness of argument, and that conciliation of manners which shall best win on his patience. Who ever thought of enlightening his pupil in the truths of geometry, by transports of rage, or by the cool and biting sarcasms of contempt? If I perceive my neighbour mistaking in some important question, I may pity him: a madman only would be filled with the bitterness of personal resentment.

There is a remark sufficiently memorable which may be deduced from the preceding observations. How far is it compatible with benevolence, that I should speak of a man's character, when he is absent, and present, in the same terms? In answering this question it may be premised that sincerity is a matter of inferior consideration to benevolence. Sincerity is only a means, and is valuable, so far as it answers the purposes of benevolence; benevolence is substantive *.

Perhaps, in the nature of things, there is no contrariety, as to the common intercourses of life, be-

* What is here said of sincerity, is equally true of temperance, activity, perseverance, and every other quality or habit that tends to promote our own happiness, or the happiness of others. They are merely subordinate and ministerial to this great purpose. Sincerity is one of these habits; but, though to benevolence it is only ministerial, it is probably entitled to the very first place among its ministers.

tween the species of sincerity here spoken of, and benevolence. A wise man would speak of the qualities of his neighbour as he found them; "nothing extenuate, nor set down aught in malice *." He would not, even in his neighbour's absence, indulge in sarcastic remarks at his expence; he would not exaggerate his errors; he would not speak of them with anger and invective. On the other hand, his neighbour, if reasonable, would bear to be told of his errors, in plain terms, without softening or circumlocution. So that the language to be used, when I spoke to him if present, or of him if absent, might be reduced to one common standard.

Great inconveniencies arise from the prevailing practice of insincerity in this respect. Its appearances have not failed to be seized by the writers of comedy, as a rich fund of humour; and, with a little exaggeration upon the common modes, nothing can be more irresistibly ludicrous. The variation of tone that a man assumes, when the person of whom he was talking unexpectedly makes his entrance, certainly places the speaker in a pitiful point of view. Yet this insincerity is in a greater or less degree universal; and, if we occasionally meet with a man who, detected in the fact, repeats the same harsh language to the person

* Shakespear.

upon his entrance, it may be doubted whether this proceeding is not rather dictated to him by the sudden irritation of his pride, than by any shade or modification of benevolence.

From hence it has grown into a commonly received rule of civilised life that conversation is not to be repeated, particularly to the persons who may happen to be the subject of it. This rule appears at first sight to be a very strange one. Every man seems to have a just right to know what his neighbours think, or, to use a more appropriate phrase, how they feel, respecting him; and certainly no information can be more interesting. The judgment of his neighbours, is the glass in which he should view himself; by this mirror he should dress his mind, and remove his defects. Not that he should implicitly conform himself to their judgment; but that, by comparing their opinions with each other and with his own, he will best arrive at the truth. Ignorance in this respect corrupts the very vitals of human intercourse. A man frequently does not know what is the opinion entertained of him by his most familiar companion; he is the object of his daily ridicule, and does not suspect it. Yet the knowledge of this opinion is of high importance, both for correction and confidence. Many men go out of the world, profoundly unacquainted with the unanimous sentiment of all their acquaintance respecting them.

The rule however, that conversation is not indiscriminately to be repeated, has something which may be offered in its behalf. If from knowing what all men said of him in his absence, a person could learn what they thought of him, it were much to be wished he should know it, and that man would be a poltroon who would shrink from the having his remarks divulged. But there are so many things said from the mere wantonness of the moment, or from a desire to comply with the tone of the company; so many from the impulse of passion, or the ambition to be brilliant; so many idle exaggerations which the heart, in a moment of sobriety, would disavow; that frequently the person concerned would learn any thing sooner than the opinion entertained of him, and torment himself, as injuries of the deepest dye, with things, injudicious perhaps and censurable, but which were the mere sallies of thoughtless levity.

It has been already seen that, were we in a state of sufficient improvement, the most perfect sincerity in our language respecting the characters of men, would be practicable. It is not at present however to be expected, whether we consider it as it relates to the speaker, or to the person who, in his absence, happens to be the subject of discourse.

It has sometimes been laid down as a rule, that we ought never to speak ill of a person in his absence. But this is ridiculous. Characters, in order to be sufficiently understood, ought pertinaciously to be discussed. There is no duty more clear and unquestionable, than that I ought to endeavour to enlighten my neighbour respecting the character of another, and to guard him against the ill effect of his vices and infirmities. The error therefore does not lie in my speaking ill of a person in his absence.

There is scarcely any speaker so careful of his words, as never to indulge in wanton sallies in descanting on the infirmities of another. There is scarcely any speaker who, in such cases, does not occasionally indulge in invective, and describe the vices of another with that anger and unkindness, which an exalted humanity would teach him to regard as an insult. These sallies and this invective are censurable in whatever way they are considered; but they not seldom change their character and become atrocious, when related to the person who is the subject of them.

Again; as the speaker is frail and imperfect, so also is the person whose errors are the subject of discourse. There are few men at present who can endure to have their errors detailed to them in a plain and unvarnished manner. Yet it is my duty, so far as opportunity serves, to acquaint them with their errors. The medium I shall observe, will be to endeavour by every obvious method to render my tale palatable to them; and particularly to accompany it with proofs of kindness, which probably I little thought of when I spoke of their faults in their absence. Though the subject be the same, my style of treating it will therefore be considerably different.

From these observations it appears that politeness, properly considered, is no enemy to admonition. There is indeed a weak and half-witted humanity, that refuses to incur the possibility of inflicting pain upon its neighbour, where it can be avoided; and would rather allow him to incur the most serious inconvenience, than risk the appearing to his recollection an ungracious monitor. But it is the office of virtue, to view pleasure and pain in a more comprehensive way, and to prefer for another, as for one's self, the less evil to the greater. True politeness is a branch of virtue; and the corner-stone upon which it rests, is, in the minuter and continually recurring incidents of human life, to seek to secure to its neighbour the greatest sum of pleasurable sensation, with the least balance of painful.

Why is admonition so frequently unpalatable? Not so much, as lord Shaftesbury has well observed*, because few people know how to take advice, as because still fewer know how to give it.

* Characteristics, Vol. I, Essay III.

The monitor usually assumes the tone of a master. At this usurpation human independence reasonably spurns. The countenance composed to unusual gravity, and a peculiar solemnity of voice fitted to the occasion, cannot fail to alarm and revolt every man of an ingenuous temper. Why this parade, this triumphal entry as if into a conquered province? Why treat a moral or a practical truth, in a way so different from truths of any other kind? There is a difference of opinion between me and the person whose conduct I apprehend to be imprudent or erroneous. Why not discuss this difference upon equal terms? Why not suppose that I may be ignorant of a part of the question? Why not, as is reasonable, offer what occurs to me, rather as a hint for enquiry, than as a decision emanating from an oracle of truth? Why not trust rather to the reason of the case, than to the arts or the passion with which I may inforce it?

"But I wish to leave a serious impression." Am I so ignorant as to suppose that a large, sober and bland view of the subject, will not produce this effect? Do I imagine that a greater impression ought to be produced, than can thus be produced?

It may further be objected, "I am perfectly sure of the grounds upon which I proceed; why should I be expected to play the hypocrite, and pretend to be uncertain?" To this it can only be answered, It ought not to be expected from you, since you shew yourself thus ignorant of the first principles of morality and reason. The first principle of reason, and that which ought particularly to modify my practical judgments, is, that I should distrust myself and the completeness of my information, both in point of argument and fact.

It is scarcely necessary in this place to enter a caveat against misapprehension, under the form of an eulogium upon the virtue of sincerity. Without habits of entire, unqualified sincerity, the human character can never be raised to its true eminence. It gives what nothing else can so effectually give, an assured, unembarrassed and ingenuous manner. It is the true progenitor of contentment, and of the complacency with which a virtuous man should be able to advert to his modes of proceeding. Insincerity corrupts and empoisons the soul of the actor, and is of pernicious example to every spectator.

Yet sincerity ought not to be practised solely for its own sake. The man who thinks only how to preserve his sincerity, is a glaringly imperfect character. He feels not for the suffering, and sympathises not in the deliverance of others, but is actuated solely by a selfish and cold-hearted pride. He cares not whom he insults, nor whom he injures. There is nothing against which it behoves a well-intentioned man to be more upon his guard, than the mistaking a part for the whole, or the substituting a branch of the tree of beneficence, for the root from which it is derived.

Politeness however, as has abundantly appeared, is, in its genuine sense, seldom or never at variance with sincerity. Sincerity, in its principle, is nearer, and in more direct communication with, the root of virtue, utility, than politeness can ever be. The original purpose of sincerity, without which it is no more than idle rant and mysticism, is to provide for the cardinal interests of a human being, the great stamina of his happiness. The purpose of politeness is of a humbler nature. It follows in the same direction, like a gleaner in a corn-field, and picks up and husbands those smaller and scattered ears of happiness, which the pride of Stoicism, like the pride of wealth, condescended not to observe.

ESSAY XI.

OF LEARNING.

If we examine with a curious and attentive eye those individuals who may be said to have in any degree exerted themselves for the improvement of their intellectual faculties, we shall find ourselves easily able to distinguish those who are usually denominated the self-educated, from every other description of mentally industrious persons.

By the self-educated in this place I would understand not merely those who have not passed through the regular forms of a liberal education; I include, in addition to this, the notion of their not having engaged in any methodical and persevering course of reading, but devoted themselves rather to the labour of investigating their own thoughts, than the thoughts of others.

These persons are well worthy of the intercourse and careful observation of men who are desirous of embracing every means of adding to their own stock of knowledge. There is a striking independence of mind about them. There is a sort of audaciousness of thinking, that has a most happy tendency to counteract that stationariness and sacredness of opinion which are too apt to insinuate themselves among mankind. New thoughts, daring opinions, intrepid enquiries, are thus set afloat, upon which more disciplined minds would perhaps scarcely have ventured. There is frequently a happiness in their reflections, that flashes light and conviction upon us at once.

Yet such persons are often wholly, perhaps always very considerably, deficient in the art of reasoning. There is no sufficient arrangement in their arguments, or lucidness in their order. Often they assign reasons wholly foreign to the question;

often they omit in silence, steps the most material to their demonstration, and which none but the acutest auditor can supply; and this not because they forgot them, but because they never at any time occurred to their minds. They strain words and phrases in so novel a manner as altogether to calumniate their meaning, and their discourse must be translated into the vernacular tongue, before we can fairly make trial of its merits. Their ideas, if I may be allowed the expression, are so Pindarical and unmethodised, that our chief wonder is at the felicity and wisdom which mixes itself among them. They furnish however rather materials of thinking, than proofs of the truth or falshood of any proposition; and if we adopt any of their assertions, we are often obliged to reject their imaginary demonstrations, and invent demonstrations of our own altogether different.

In the mean time this is the favourable side of the picture. Many of the self-educated study themselves into a sort of insanity. They are not only incoherent in their thoughts, and wild in their language: often they adopt opinions the most unequivocally visionary, and talk a language, not merely unintelligible to others, but which is put together in so fantastical and mystical a way, that it is impossible it should be the representative of wisdom in themselves.

There is another feature peculiarly characteristical of the self-educated. Reflecting men of a different description, are frequently sceptical in their opinions. They have so carefully entered into the very souls of the authors they read, and so minutely followed out the whole train of their reasoning, as to enable them to do full justice even to an antagonist's argument. But this to a self-educated man is impossible. He has therefore no doubts. If he is tolerant, it is less in consequence of feeling the weakness of human understanding and the inevitable varieties of human opinion, than through the medium of an abstract speculation, or a generous consciousness, leaning to the side of toleration. It will be strange if, so far as relates to conversation and the ordinary intercourse of human life, he be not frequently betrayed into intolerance. It will be strange, if he do not prove in many instances, impatient of contradiction, and inurbane and ungenerous in his censures of those by whom he is opposed.

It is too common a feature with all disputants, that they think only of their own arguments, and listen, in the strictest sense of the word, only to themselves. It is not their purpose to try whether they may not themselves be convicted of error; they are merely intent upon convincing and changing the mind of the person who differs from them. This, which is too frequent a fault with all men, is peculiarly incident to the self-educated. The generality of men of talent and reflection, were taught first by listening to other men's ideas, and studying other men's writings. The wildness of their nature, and the stubbornness of their minds, have by long practice been broken in to a capacity of candid attention. If I talk to such men, I do not talk in vain. But, if I talk to a self-educated man, it too often happens that I am talking to the air. He has no suspicion that I may possibly be in the right, and therefore no curiosity to know what is capable of being alleged in favour of my opinion. A truly ludicrous spectacle would be to see two such men debating a question, each hearing himself only, and each, however he may cover it with an exterior politeness, deaf to the pretensions of his antagonist.

From this description of a self-educated man it may safely be inferred, that I ought to wish any young person in whose future eminence I interest myself, rather occasionally to associate with individuals of this description, than to be one of their body himself.

It ought however to be remarked that, whatever rank the self-educated man may hold among persons who have exerted themselves for the improvement of their intellectual faculties, he will always, if judicious and able, be regarded by the discerning with peculiar respect, inasmuch as there has been much more of voluntary in his acquisitions, than can well have fallen to the share of those who have enjoyed every advantage of institution and scientifical incitement.

There is a kind of declamation very generally afloat in the world, which, if it could be taken as just and well founded, would prove that the self-educated, instead of labouring under the important disadvantages here enumerated, were the most fortunate of men, and those upon whom the hopes of their species, whether for instruction or delight, should principally be fixed.

How much eloquent invective has been spent in holding up to ridicule the generation of book-worms! We have been told, that a persevering habit of reading, kills the imagination, and narrows the understanding; that it overloads the intellect with the notions of others and hinders its digesting them, and, by a still stronger reason, prevents it from unfolding its native powers; that the man who would be original and impressive, must meditate rather than hear, and walk rather than read. He that devotes himself to a methodical prosecution of his studies, is perhaps allowed some praise for his industry and good intention; but it is at the same time insinuated, that the only result to be expected from such ill-placed industry, is a plentiful harvest of laborious dulness.

It is no wonder that this sort of declamation has been generally popular. It favours one of the most elemental passions of the human mind, our indolence. To acquaint ourselves profoundly with what other men have thought in different ages of the world, is an arduous task; the ascent of the hill of knowledge is steep, and it demands the most unalterable resolution to be able to conquer it. But this declamation presents to us every discouragement, and severs all the nerves of the soul. He that is infected by it, no longer "girds up the loins of his mind *;" but surrenders his days to unenterprising indulgence. Its effect is like that of a certain religious creed, which, disclaiming the connection between motives and action, and between one action and another, instructs its votaries to wait, with pious resignation, for the influx of a supernatural strength which is to supersede the benefit of our vigilance and exertions.

Nothing however can be more ill founded than this imputed hostility between learning and genius. If it were true, it is among savages only that we ought to seek for the genuine expansion of the human mind. They are, of all their kind, the most undebauched by learning, and the least broken in upon by any regular habits of attention. In civilised society, and especially among that class in civilised society who pay any attention to intellectual pursuits, those who have the greatest

* 1 Peter, Chap. I, ver. 13.

antipathy to books, are yet modified in a thousand ways by the actual state of literature. They converse with men who read, though they disdain to read themselves. A sagacious observer might infer beforehand, in its principle outlines, what a self-educated man could do, from a previous knowledge of the degree of improvement existing in the country he inhabited. Man in society is variously influenced by the characters of his fellow men; he is an imitative animal, and, like the camelion, owes the colour he assumes, to the colour of the surrounding objects. But, if men the most austerely and cynically independent in this respect, must be so deeply affected by literature and books at second hand, it were surely better to go at once to the fountain-head, and drink of the spring in all its purity.

The opinion here combated, seems to have originated in the most profound ignorance of the intellectual nature of man. Man taken by himself is nothing. In the first portion of his life, he is more ignorant and worthless than the beasts. For all that he has, he is indebted to collision. His mother and his nurse awaken his mind from its primeval sleep. They imbue it in various respects with subtlety and discrimination. They unfold the understanding, and rouse in turn the whole catalogue of the passions.

The remaining sections of the history of man,

are like the first. He proceeds forward, as he commenced. All his improvements have communication for their source.

Why are men not always savages? Because they build upon one another's structures. Because "one man labours, and other men enter into the fruits of his labour *." It is thus that the species collectively seems formed to advance, and one generation, casualties and extraordinary revolutions being excepted, to improve upon the attainments of another. The self-educated man seems to propose, as far as possible, to divest himself of this fundamental advantage.

If I would do well in any art or science, I should think nothing could be more necessary for me, than carefully to enquire in the first instance what had been done already. I should otherwise most likely only write over again in a worse manner, what had been repeatedly written before I was born. It would be the most atrocious absurdity to affirm, that books may be of use to other men, but not to an author. He of all men wants them most. If on the other hand they be without utility, for what reason is he an author?

The principle of all judgment and taste, is comparison. A man of the soundest texture of mind, would necessarily admire the weakest imitations, if he had seen no better. If I would be a painter,

* John, Chap. IV, ver. 38.

I ought to look, with attentive research, into the works of Angelo, and Titian, and Rubens, and Raffaele. If I would be an historian, I ought to have observed the manner of Herodotus, and Thucydides, and Tacitus, and Livy, or of other eminent historians. If I would be a writer of tragedies, I shall do well to examine the labours of Sophocles, and Shakespear, and Otway, and Racine. These men undoubtedly profited by the success and miscarriages of their predecessors.

The doctrine that first brought this mode of cultivation into disrepute, was that which affirmed genius to be a kind of inspiration, a supererogatory and prodigious gift of heaven, and not produced in the ordinary train of causes and effects. This doctrine is not likely to meet with respectable support in the present age. Natural philosophy has banished prodigies from the material world; and the prodigies of the intellectual world must inevitably follow. It will now probably be admitted that all knowledge makes its approach through the senses, and that, if we find any intellectual faculties peculiarly subtilised and animated, it must have been through the medium of various concurring circumstances, and by the operation of innumerable successive incitements.

The idea, that cultivation and industry are essential to excellence, seems now to be more generally admitted in the art of painting, than in many of the arts of writing. But the same reasons would shew that it was equally true of the one as of the other.

It is extraordinary that any man should have supposed attention hostile to excellence. What a protracted train of unintermitted attention does considerable excellence demand? It is the business of the man who would exhibit it, to produce something new, to state what he has to say in a manner better than it has yet been stated, to hold forth some view of his subject that never yet occurred to any of his predecessors, to deliver what shall arrest the attention of a numerous portion of mankind and fix their attention. Surely this is no sportful task. It is a burthen fit for the shoulders of Atlas.

If I would write a poem, a play, or any other work of fiction, how numerous are the points I have to consider? How judiciously must I select the topic I would treat? How carefully must I reflect upon the

> ————*quid ferre recusent,*
> *Quid valeant humeri**? HOR.

What a comprehensive view must I take of my subject? How accurately ought I to perceive the parts, or branches, as they extend themselves from

* What suits my Genius; what my Strength can bear. FRANCIS.

the trunk, each constituting a well arranged and beautiful whole of itself, yet each depending, for its existence and its form, upon the root by which the entire mass is sustained? From how many sciences ought my illustrations to be drawn? There is scarcely any one branch of knowledge, however apparently remote, from which my work might not be improved, and my ignorance of which will not be apparent to a discerning eye. Lastly, style is a circumstance without which, except in extraordinary cases, no work can expect any permanent success. How carefully ought this to be refined and elaborated? Not so much elaborated by any effort to be exerted at the moment, as by a long train of previous considerations, which have familiarised to the mind beauties the most uncommon and exquisite. What a copious mass of knowledge, previously accumulated, do all these particulars imply?

When we compare the knowledge of any subject to be acquired from books, with that to be acquired from conversation, it is astonishing how unequal they will ordinarily be found. Books undertake to treat of a subject regularly; to unfold it part by part till the whole is surveyed; they are entirely at our devotion, and may be turned backward and forward as we please; it is their express purpose to omit nothing that is essential to a complete delineation. They are written in tranquillity, and in the bosom of meditation: they are revised again and again; their obscurities removed, and their defects supplied. Conversation on the other hand is fortuitous and runs wild; the life's blood of truth is filtrated and diluted, till much of its essence is gone. The intellect that depends upon conversation for nutriment, may be compared to the man who should prefer the precarious existence of a beggar, to the possession of a regular and substantial income.

One of the most prevailing objections to a systematical pursuit of knowledge, is that it imposes upon us a methodical industry, and by consequence counteracts the more unlicensed and dignified sallies of the mind. But the industry which books demand, is of the same species as the industry requisite for the development of our own reflections; the study of other men's writings, is strikingly analogous to the invention and arrangement of our own. A better school cannot be devised for the improvement of individual mind, than for it thus to collate itself with other minds in a state of the highest and most persevering exertion. It is to be feared that, if industry be not early formed, and if that indolence, which in one form or other is always our motive for neglecting books and learning, be uniformly indulged, the mind will never rouse itself to an undaunted subtlety of thought, or acquire the constancy requisite for the invention and execution of any great undertaking.

The reason why reading has fallen into a partial disrepute is, that few men have sufficiently reflected on the true mode of reading. It has been affirmed by astronomers, that the spots discoverable in the disk of the sun, are a species of fuel calculated to supply its continual waste, and that, in due time, they become changed into the substance of the sun itself. Thus in reading: if the systems we read, were always to remain in masses upon the mind, unconcocted and unaltered, undoubtedly in that case they would only deform it. But, if we read in a just spirit, perhaps we cannot read too much: in other words, if we mix our own reflections with what we read; if we dissect the ideas and arguments of our author; if, by having recourse to all subsidiary means, we endeavour to clear the recollection of him in our minds; if we compare part with part, detect his errors, new model his systems, adopt so much of him as is excellent, and explain within ourselves the reason of our disapprobation as to what is otherwise. A judicious reader will have a greater number of ideas that are his own passing through his mind, than of ideas presented to him by his author. He sifts his merits, and bolts his arguments. What he adopts from him, he renders his own, by repassing in his thoughts the notions of which it consists, and the foundation upon which it rests, correcting its mistakes, and supplying its defects. Even the most dogmatical branches of study, grammar and mathematics, supply him with hints, and give a turn to his meditations. Reading and learning, when thus pursued, not only furnish the most valuable knowledge; but afford incitements to the mind of a thousand denominations, and add a miraculous sort of finishing to its workmanship which could have been bestowed by no other means. It furnishes, what is of all things most important, occasions for approbation and disapprobation. It creates a certain manliness of judgment, not indebted for its decisive character to partiality and arrogance, but seeing truth by its own light, even while it never divests itself of the sobriety of scepticism, and accommodated to the office of producing conviction in its intimates and hearers.

To prevent misconstruction it is perhaps necessary to observe, that the tendency of this Essay is to recommend learning. It proceeds upon the supposition that there is a class, and a numerous class of men, by whom severe and profound reading is decried. The term self-educated was defined in the beginning, to mean those who had not engaged in any methodical and persevering course of reading; and elsewhere it was said of them that they held, that the man who would be original and impressive, must meditate rather than hear, and walk rather than read. If there be any singularity in this use of the term, it is hoped at least that the reader will not put a sense upon it in this present instance, which is foreign to the intention of the writer. He is far from thinking all men of learning respectable, and he joins most cordially in the general propensity to withhold from the mere pedant every degree of estimation. The principles intended to be maintained are, that learning is the ally, not the adversary of genius; and that he who reads in a proper spirit, can scarcely read too much.

ESSAY XII.

OF ENGLISH STYLE.

INTRODUCTION.

THE author of this volume does not hesitate to avow that he has in several respects altered his opinion upon the subject of the following Essay, since the first appearance of his book in 1797. And he would be ashamed to continue to contribute in any way to the propagation of what now appears to him to be error.

The object of his Essay was to shew the superiority of the English of the present day over the English of our ancestors. In some respects he still adheres to the same opinion. He believes that on the whole the construction of the language of our best modern writers, the best writers of the age of George the Third, is closer and neater, more free from laxity of structure, and less subject to occasional incongruities, superfluities, unnaturalness and affectation, than that of their predecessors. But neatness, and a sustained equality of march, are not every thing.

Since the publication of this volume the author has been pretty extensively and habitually conversant with the productions of our elder writers. And they have certainly lost nothing with him in a more intimate acquaintance. He admires, and he loves them. They have, many of them, a splendour and an expansive richness of manner, that more than balance the perhaps more laborious exactness of their successors. There is also something in early language, and the new and unhackneyed sense and feeling of words, that is singularly delightful. In Spenser and Shakespear, there is a freshness in all they say, at least in the most admirable parts of their writings, that steals away the soul. It is like flowers, fresh gathered out of the gardens of Paradise. Our words are palled and stale; they have been used too often; we must be content to take up with the leavings of our ancestors. We are born in too late an age, and too chilly a climate. It is as if the happiest genius among the Greeks of the age of the Antonines should have had the presumption to think he could pen an Iliad. And, worst of all, we are born in an age of criticism, where the boldest of us dares not let himself loose to be all that he might have been capable of being. We talk to learned ears, and to persons who from their infancy have been schooled in artificial laws. It would many ways be better, if we addressed hearers and readers of unstudied feelings, and who would confess themselves pleased, without the slavery and the cowardice of enquiring first whether they ought to be pleased.

A part of what I feel on the subject, is aptly expressed in the homely phraseology of Anthony Wood. It is in his article of Chapman, the translator. "Afterwards," says Wood (that is, when he left the university), "he settled in the metropolis, and became much admired by Edmund Spenser, Samuel Daniel, William Shakespear, Christopher Marlow, &c, by all whose writings, as also by those of Sir Philip Sidney, William Warner, and of our author Chapman, the English tongue was exceedingly enriched, and made quite another thing than what it was before."

The purpose of the following pages is rather to

enable the reader to form a comparison, and to determine for himself in what respects the old English writers excelled, and in what respects they fall short of the moderns, than to deliver any thing authoritatively on the subject.

This will best be effected by producing a series of instances.

We will confine ourselves to prose examples. The licence of poetry, and the fetters of versification, have equally in all ages seduced the poets, in some degree to deviate from the received language of the age in which they wrote.

The following specimens were not originally selected with a friendly eye. But they are not on that account in some respects the less qualified to answer the purpose for which they are produced. A selection of Beauties might be calculated to mislead the judgment. The question might then be, not of style, which is the enquiry here intended, but of the genius or profundity of the author. It is by taking the writers in the middle tone of composition, that we can best judge of the successive fluctuations, and improvement or otherwise, of the language in which they wrote.

SECT. I.

AGE OF QUEEN ELIZABETH.

Sir Philip Sidney may be considered in some respects as the earliest of those writers, whom Anthony Wood and others have held up as "exceedingly enriching our language, and making it quite another thing than what it was before;" and his high rank and personal accomplishments have contributed no less than the elegance of his taste and the brilliancy of his imagination, to preserve for him the eminent station he has always held among the fathers of our present English tongue. We will therefore begin with an extract from this writer. Sir Philip Sidney died a young man in the year 1586, and his Arcadia made its first appearance from the press in 1590. The passage here given commences in the second page of that work.

"Alas my *Strephon* (said *Claius*) what needes this skore to recken vp onely our losses? What doubt is there, but that the sight of this place doth call our thoughtes to appeare at the court of affection, held by that racking steward, Remembrance? As well may sheepe forget to feare when they spie woolues, as we can misse such fancies, when we can see any place made happie by her treading. Who can choose that saw her but thinke where she stayed, where she walkt, where she turned, where she spoke? But what is all this? truely no more, but as this place serued vs to thinke of those things, so those serue as places to call to memorie more excellent matters. No, no, let vs thinke with consideration, and consider with acknowledging, and acknowledge with admiration, and admire with loue, and loue with ioy in the midst of all woes: let vs in such sorte thinke, I say, that our poore eyes were so enriched as to behold, and our lowe hearts so exalted as to loue, a maide, who is such, that as the greatest thing the world can shewe, is her beautie, so the least thing that may be praysed in her, is her beautie. Certainely as her eye-lids are more pleasant to behold, than two white kiddes climbing vp a faire tree, and browsing on his tendrest branches, and yet are nothing, compared to the day-shining starres contained in them; and as her breath is more sweete than a gentle South-west wind, which comes creeping ouer flowrie fieldes and shadowed waters in the extreame heate of sommer, and yet is nothing, compared to the hony flowing speach that breath doth carrie: no more all that our eyes can see of her (though when they haue seene her, what else they shall euer see is but drie stubble after clouers grasse) is to be matched with the flocke of vnspeakable vertues laid vp delightfully in that best builded fold."—

"*Claius* was going on with his praises, but *Strephon* bad him stay, and looke: and so they both perceiued a thinge which floated drawing nearer and nearer to the banke; but rather by the fauourable working of the Sea, then by any self industrie. They doubted a while what it should be;

till it was cast vp euen hard before them: at which time they fully saw that it was a man. Whereupon running for pitie sake vnto him, they found his hands (as it should appeare, constanter freinds to his life than his memorie) fast griping vpon the edge of a square small coffer, which lay all vnder his breast: els in him selfe no shew of life, so as the boord seemed to be but a beere to carrie him a land to his Sepulcher. So drew they vp a yong man of so goodly shape, and well pleasing fauour, that one would thinke death had in him a louely countenance; and, that though he were naked, nakednesse was to him an apparell. That sight increased their compassion, and their compassion called vp their care; so that lifting his feete aboue his head, making a great deale of salt water come out of his mouth, they layd him vpon some of their garments, and fell to rub and chafe him, till they brought him to recouer both breath the seruant, and warmth the companion of liuing. At length opening his eyes, he gaue a great groan, (a doleful note but a pleasaunt dittie) for by that they founde not onely life, but strength of life in him."

Hooker was undoubtedly a writer of superior merit. Whoever shall bestow upon him a diligent perusal, will find himself well rewarded by the venerable simplicity of his disposition, the profoundness of his thoughts, and the manliness of his eloquence. The character of his style may be judged of from the following specimens.

Our first extract shall consist of his description of Calvin, in the Preface to his Laws of Ecclesiastical Politie.

"Think not," says the author, addressing himself to the advocates for a further reformation, "that ye read the words of one, who bendeth himself as an adversary against the truth, which ye have already imbraced, but the words of one who desireth even to imbrace together with you the self same truth, if it be the truth; and for that cause, (for no other, God he knoweth) hath undertaken the burthensome labour of this painful kind of conference. For the playner access whereunto, let it be lawful for me to rip up the very bottom how and by whom your discipline was planted, at suchtime as this age we live in began to make first trial thereof.

"A Founder it had, whom, for mine own part, I think incomparably the wisest man that ever the French Church did injoy, since the hour it injoyed him. His bringing up was in the studie of the civil Law. Divine knowledge he gathered not by hearing or reading so much, as by teaching others. For though thousands were debters to him, as touching knowledg in that kind; yet he to none but onely to God, the Author of that most blessed Fountain the book of Life, and of the admirable dexterity of wit, together with the helps of other learning which were his guides: till being occasioned to leave *France*, he fell at the length upon *Geneva*."

We will next refer to a specimen of our author's eloquence, manly indeed, but, as the manner was in the period in which he wrote, somewhat loitering and tedious.

"His [God's] commanding those things to be which are, and to be in such sort as they are, to keep that tenure and course which they do, importeth the establishment of Natures Law. This worlds first Creation, and the preservation since of things created, what is it but onely so far forth a manifestation by execution, what the eternal Law of God is concerning things natural? And as it cometh to pass in a Kingdom rightly ordered, that after a law is once published, it presently takes effect far and wide, all States framing themselves thereunto; even so let us think it fareth in the natural course of the world: Since the time that God did first proclaim the Edicts of his law upon it, Heaven and earth have hearkned unto his voice, and their labour hath been to do his will: *He made a law for the Rain*, He gave his *decree unto the Sea, that the Waters should not pass his commandment.* Now, if nature should intermit her course, and leave altogether, though it were but for a while, the observation of her own Laws; those principal and Mother Elements of the World, whereof all things in this lower world are made, should lose the qualities which now they have; if the frame of that Heavenly Arch erected over our heads should loosen and dissolve it self; if Celestial Spheres should forget their wonted motions, and by irregular volubility turn themselves any way as it might happen; if the Prince of the Lights of Heaven, which now as a Gyant doth run his unwearied course, should, as it were, through a languishing faintness, begin to stand, and to rest himself; if the Moon should wander from her beaten way, the times and seasons of the yeere blende themselves, by disordered and confused mixture, the winds breathe out their last gasp, the clouds yield no rain, the earth be defeated of heavenly influence, the fruits of the earth pine away, as children at the withered breasts of their mother, no longer able to yield them relief; what would become of man himself, whom these things now do all serve? See we not plainly, that obedience of creatures unto the Law of Nature, is the stay of the whole world?" Eccl. Pol., Book I, c. 3. Edit. 1662.

I will add one more extract, recommended to notice by its being quoted by Locke in his Treatise on Government, and seemingly placed as a sort of basis upon which his political system is erected. Locke, Of Government, Book II, Chap. II, §. 5.

"The like natural inducement hath brought men to know, that it is their duty no less to love others then themselves. For seeing those things which are equal, must needs all have one measure: if I cannot but wish to receive all good, even as much at every mans hand, as any man can wish unto his soul, how should I look to have any part of my desire herein satisfied, unless my self be careful to satisfie the like desire, which is undoubtedly in other men, we all being of one and the same nature? To have any thing offered them repugnant to this desire, must needs in all respects grieve them as much as me: So that if I do harm, I must look to suffer; there being no reason that others should shew greater measure of love to me, then they have by me shewed unto them. My desire therefore to be loved of my equals in nature as much as possible may be, imposeth upon me a natural duty of bearing to them-ward fully the like affection." Book I. c. 8.

I proceed now to the mention of Shakespear, a writer whom no ingenuous English reader can recollect without the profoundest esteem and the most unbounded admiration. His gigantic mind enabled him in a great degree to overcome the fetters in which the English language was at that period bound. In him we but rarely trace the languid and tedious formality which often at that time characterised English composition. His soul was too impetuous, and his sympathy with human passions too entire, not to instruct him in the shortest road to the heart.

But Shakespear for the most part is great only, when great passions are to be expressed. His tranquil style is frequently perplexed, pedantical, and greatly disfigured with conceits. Of this we will exhibit some examples. They shall be taken from such of his plays as are supposed to have been written in the reign of James the first.

The following is part of the dialogue between the disguised Duke and Isabella in Measure for Measure, upon occasion of Angelo's atrocious proposition concerning the pardon of her brother.

"*Duk*. The hand that hath made you faire, hath made you good: the goodnesse that is cheape in beauty, makes beauty briefe in goodnesse; but grace being the soule of your complexion, shall keepe the body of it ever faire: the assault that *Angelo* hath made to you, Fortune hath convaid to my understanding; and but that frailty hath examples for his falling, I should wonder at *Angelo*: how will you doe to content this Substitute, and to save your brother?——

"*Isab*. Let me heare you speake farther; I have spirit to doe any thing that appeares not foule in the truth of my spirit.

" *Duk.* Vertue is bold, and goodnesse never fearfull: Have you not heard speake of *Mariana* the sister of *Fredericke* the great Souldier, who miscarried at Sea?

" *Isab.* I have heard of the Lady, and good words went with her name.

" *Duk.* She should this *Angelo* have married: was affianced to her by oath, and the nuptial appointed; between which time of the contract, and limit of the solemnity, her brother *Fredericke* was wrackt at Sea, having in that perished vessell, the dowry of his sister: but marke how heavily this befell to the poore Gentlewoman, there she lost a noble and renouned brother, in his love toward her, ever most kind and naturall: with him the portion and sinew of her fortune, her marriage dowry; with both, her combynate-husband, this well seeming *Angelo.*

" *Isab.* Can this be so? did *Angelo* so leave her?

" *Duk.* Left her in her teares, and dried not one of them with his comfort: swallowed his vowes whole, pretending in her, discoveries of dishonor: in few, bestow'd her on her owne lamentation, which she yet weares for his sake: and he, a marble to her teares, is washed with them, but relents not.——— Goe you to *Angelo*, answer his requiring with a plausible obedience, agree with his demands to the point:——we shall advise this wronged maid to steed up your appointment, goe in your place: if the encounter acknowledge it selfe hereafter, it may compell him to her recompence; and heere, by this is your brother saved, your honor untainted, the poore *Mariana* advantaged, and the corrupt Deputy scaled."

Nothing can be of a style more quaint and uncouth, than the letters that are from time to time introduced in different plays of Shakespear. Take as a specimen the letter of Posthumus to Imogen in the tragedy of Cymbeline.

" Ivstice, and your Fathers wrath (should hee take mee in his Dominion) could not be so cruell to me, as you, (oh the dearest of Creatures) would even renew me with your eyes. Take notice that I am in *Cambria* at *Milford Haven*: what your owne Love, will out of this advise you, follow. So he wishes you all happinesse, that remaines loyall to his Vow, and your encreasing in Love.

" *Leonatus Posthumus.*"

We will only add to these examples, the words in which the Duke communicates to Othello his commission for Cyprus. One would think that no function could require greater simplicity of language.

" The Turke with a most mighty preparation makes for Cyprus: *Othello*, the Fortitude of the place is best knowne to you. And though we have there a Substitute of most allowed sufficiency; yet opinion, a more Soveraigne Mistris of Effects, throwes a more safe voyce on you: you must therefore be content to slubber the glosse of your new Fortunes, with this more stubborne, and boysterous expedition."

We will now proceed to sir Walter Raleigh, a writer more learned than Shakespear, more polished by the varieties of human intercourse, and that with persons of the highest eminence and station, than Hooker.

It is thus that he concludes the Preface of his History of the World.

"J know that as the charitable will iudge charitably: so against those, *qui gloriantur in malitia*, my present aduersity hath disarmed me. J am on the ground already; and therefore haue not farre to fall: and for rising againe, as in the Naturall priuation there is no recession to habit; so it is seldome seene in the priuation politique. I doe therefore for-beare to stile my Readers *Gentle*, *Courteous*, and *Friendly*, thereby to beg their good opinions.—For it is certaine, let vs claw the Reader with neuer so many courteous phrases; yet shall wee euer-more be thought fooles, that write foolishly. For conclusion; all the hope I haue lies in this, That I haue already found more vngentle and vncourteous readers of my Loue towards them, and well-deseruing of them, than euer I shall doe againe. For had it beene otherwise, I should hardly haue had this leisure, to haue made my selfe a foole in print."

From the body of the work we will extract a part of sir Walter's reflections on the deaths of Hannibal and Scipio, in writing which it is evident that his own adversity was strongly present to his mind. Book V, Chap. VI, §. 2.

"Hence it comes, to wit, from the enuie of our equals, and jealousie of our Masters, be they Kings or Commonweales, That there is no Profession more vnprosperous than that of Men of Warre, and great Captaines, being no Kings. For besides the enuie and jealousie of men; the spoyles, rapes, famine, slaughter of the innocent, vastation, and burnings, with a world of miseries layed on the labouring man, are so hatefull to God, as with good reason did *Monluc* the Marshall of *France* confesse, That *were not the mercies of* God *infinite, and without restriction, it were in vaine for those of his profession to hope for any portion of them: seeing the cruelties, by them permitted and commited, were also infinite.* Howsoeuer, this is true, That the victories, which are obtayned by many of the greatest Commanders, are commonly either ascribed to those that serue vnder them, to Fortune, or to the cowardise of the Nation against whom they serue. For the most of others, whose vertues haue raysed them aboue the leuell of their inferiours, and haue surmounted their enuie: yet haue they been rewarded in the end, either with disgrace, banishment, or death. Among the *Romans* we finde many examples hereof, as *Coriolanus*, *M. Liuius*, *L. Æmylius*, and this our *Scipio*, whom we haue lately buried. Among the *Greekes* we reade of not many, that escaped these rewards. Yea, long before these times, it was a Legacie that Dauid bequeathed vnto his victorious Captaine *Joab*. With this fare *Alexander* feasted *Parmenio*, *Philotas*, and others; and prepared it for *Antipater* and *Cassander*. Hereto *Valentinian* the Emperour inuited *Ætius*: who, after many other victories ouerthrew *Attila* of the *Hunnes*, in the greatest battaile, for the well-fighting and resolution of both Armies, that euer was strucken in the world; for there fell of those that fought beside runne-awaies, an hundred and fourescore thousand.—The same vnworthy destinie, or a farre worse, had *Bellisarius*; whose vndertakings and victories were so difficult and glorious, as after-ages suspected them for fabulous. For he had his eyes torne out of his head by *Iustinian*: and he died a blinde begger. *Narses* also, to the great preiudice of *Christian* Religion, was disgraced by *Iustine*. That Rule of *Cato* against *Scipio*, hath been well obserued in euery age since then; to wit, That the Common-weale cannot be accounted free, which standeth in awe of any one man. And hence hath the *Turkes* drawn another Principle, and in deed a *Turkish* one, That euery warlike Prince should rather destroy his greatest men of Warre, than suffer his owne glory to be obscured by them. For this cause did *Baiaret* the second dispatch *Bassa Acomat: Selim* strangle *Bassa Mustapha;* and most of those Princes bring to ruine the most of their *Visiers*. Of the *Spanish* Nation, the great *Gonsaluo*, who draue the *French* out of *Naples:* and *Ferdinando Cortese*, who conquered *Mexico*, were crowned with nettles, not with Lawrell. The Earles of *Egmond* and *Horn*, had no heads left them to weare garlands on. And that the great Captaines of all Nations haue been payd with this copper Coine; there are examples more than too many."

Knolles, author of the General History of the Turks, whose work was published in the year of James's accession to the crown of England, must have a place in our catalogue, in consideration of the encomium pronounced upon him by Dr. Johnson. Johnson, in the hundred and twenty second number of his Rambler, attempts to vindicate the literary honours of his country, as having possessed "historians, whom we may venture to place in comparison with any that the neighbouring nations can produce." For this purpose he mentions Raleigh and Clarendon: and then proceeds as follows:

"But none of our writers can, in my opinion,

justly contest the superiority of *Knolles*, who in his history of the *Turks*, has displayed all the excellencies that narration can admit. His stile, though somewhat obscured by time, and sometimes vitiated by false wit, is pure, nervous, elevated and clear.—There is nothing turgid in his dignity, nor superfluous in his copiousness.—

"Nothing could have sunk this author in obscurity but the remoteness and barbarity of the people whose story he relates. It seldom happens, that all circumstances concur to happiness or fame. The nation, which produced this great historian, has the grief of seeing his genius employed upon a foreign and uninteresting subject; and that writer, who might have secured perpetuity to his name, by a history of his own country, has exposed himself to the danger of oblivion, by recounting enterprises and revolutions, of which none desire to be informed."

The following specimen may not perhaps be found fully to correspond to this lofty eulogium.

"This citie *Mahomet* thought to haue taken vnprouided; and so vpon the suddaine to haue carried it; but was therein much deceiued, finding it strongly fortified and manned both by the Venetians and *Scanderbeg*. Where when he had spent there some time, and to his great losse in vaine attempted the cittie, hee rise vpon the suddaine: and retiring into EPIRVS, came and sat downe againe before CROIA, of purpose by his suddaine comming to haue terrified the citizens: and vainely persuaded, that he had left *Scanderbeg* in DIRRACHIVM, for that in the assailing thereof he had discouered many of *Scanderbeg* his men, and thereby supposed him to haue been there also; the greatest cause why he so suddenly rise and came to CROIA. At his first comming he offered great rewards and large priuiledges vnto the cittizens, if they would forthwith yeeld vp their cittie; otherwise he threatened vnto them all the calamities of warre, vowing neuer to depart thence before he had it; whereunto he receiued no other answere out of the cittie than was sent him by the mouth of the cannon, or brought him by many most braue sallies. *Scanderbeg* in the meane while continually molesting his campe, and euery night falling into one quarter or another thereof." p. 402.

SECT. II.

MILTON AND CLARENDON.

THE age which, next after that of Queen Elizabeth, has obtained the suffrage of the critics, is that of Charles the second. Fanciful observers found a certain resemblance between it and the age of Augustus, the literary glory of which has sometimes been represented as owing to this circumstance, that its wits were bred up in their youth in the lap of republican freedom, and afterwards in their riper age received that polish which is to be derived from the splendour and refinement of a court. Just so, the scene amidst which the wits of king Charles's days passed their boyish years, was that of civil war, of regicide, or of unrestrained republican speculation; which was succeeded by the manners of a gay and licentious court grafting the shoots of French refinement, upon the more vigorous and luxuriant plant of English growth. It is indeed easy to trace in the adventurous sallies of the authors of this period, the remnant and tincture of republican audaciousness.

We will begin with Milton, the oldest of those writers, by whom the reign of Charles the second has been made illustrious. Milton was more than fifty years old at the period of the Restoration, and, though all his larger poetical works were written subsequently to that event, his prose is is almost entirely of an earlier date.

As a specimen of Milton's style, it may be worth while to select that passage from his Reason of Church-Government Urg'd against Prelaty, published more than twenty years before the Paradise Lost, in which he speaks, in little less than a prophetic spirit, of what he purposed to execute, to give substance to his own talent, and for the ornament of his country.

" Although a Poet," says he, " soaring in the

high region of his fancies, with his garland and singing robes about him, might, without apology, speak more of himself than I mean to do; yet for me sitting here below in the cool element of prose, a mortall thing among many readers of no Empyreall conceit, to venture and divulge unusual things of my selfe, I shall petition to the gentler sort, it may not be envy to me. I must say therefore, that after I had from my first yeres, by the ceaselesse diligence and care of my father, whom God recompence, bin exercis'd to the tongues, and some sciences, as my age would suffer, by sundry masters and teachers both at home and at the schools, it was found, that whether ought was impos'd me by them that had the overlooking, or betak'n to of my own choise in English, or other tongue, prosing or versing, but chiefly this latter, the stile by certain vital signes it had, was likely to live. But much latelier in the privat Academies of *Italy* whither I was favour'd to resort, perceiving that some trifles which I had in memory, compos'd at under twenty or thereabout (for the manner is, that every one must give some proof of his wit and reading there) met with acceptance above what was lookt for, and other things which I had shifted in scarsity of books and other conveniences to patch up amongst them, were receiv'd with written Encomiums, which the Italian is not forward to bestow on men of this side the *Alps*, I began thus farre to assent both to them and divers of my friends here at home; and not lesse to an inward prompting which now grew daily upon me, that by labour and intent study, (which I take to be my portion in this life) joyn'd with the strong propensity of nature, I might perhaps leave something so written to aftertimes, as they should not willingly let it die.

"The thing which I had to say, and those intentions which have liv'd within me ever since I could conceiv my self any thing worth to my Countrie, I return to crave excuse that urgent reason hath pluckt from me, by an abortive and foredated discovery. And the accomplishment of them lies not but in a power above mans to promise; but that none hath by more studious ways endeavour'd, and with more unwearied spirit that none shall, that I dare almost averre of my self, as farre as life and free leasure will extend; and that the Land had once infranchis'd her self from this impertinent yoke of prelaty, under whose inquisitorius and tyrannical duncery no free and splendid wit can flourish. Neither do I think it shame to covnant with any knowing reader, that for some few yeers yet I may go on trust with him toward the payment of what I am now indebted, as being a work not to be rays'd from the heat of youth, or the vapours of wine; like that which flows at wast from the pen of some vulgar Amorist, or the trencher fury of a riming parasite; nor to be obtain'd by the invocation of Dame Memory and her Siren daughters, but by devout prayer to that eternall Spirit, who can enrich with all utterance and knowledge, and sends out his Seraphim, with the hallow'd fire of his Altar, to touch and purify the lips of whom he pleases: to this must be added industrious and select reading, steddy observation, insight into all seemly and generous arts and affaires; till which in some measure be compast, at mine own peril and cost I refuse not to sustain this expectation from as many as are not loath to hazard so much credulity upon the best pledges that I can give them. Although it nothing content me to have disclos'd thus much before hand, but that I trust hereby to make it manifest with what small willingnesse I endure to interrupt the pursuit of no less hopes then these, and leave a calme and pleasing solitarynes, fed with cherful and confident thoughts, to imbark in a troubl'd sea of noises and hoars disputes."

The Areopagitica of Milton, or a Speech for the Liberty of Unlicenc'd Printing, notwithstanding the occasional stiffness and perplexity of its style, is one of the most eloquent prose compositions in this or any other language. To give the reader an adequate idea of its beauties, it would be necessary to insert one third of the performance. Let us content ourselves with the following admirable description of the person over whom the licenser will occasionally be called to exercise his jurisdiction.

"If therefore ye be loath to dishearten utterly and discontent, not the mercenary crew of false pretenders to learning, but the free and ingenuous sort of such as evidently were born to study, and love lerning for it self, not for lucre, or any other end, but the service of God and of truth, and perhaps that lasting fame and perpetuity of praise which God and good men have consented shall be the reward of those whose publisht labours advance the good of mankind, then know, that so far to distrust the judgement and the honesty of one who hath but a common repute in learning, and never yet offended, as not to count him fit to print his mind without a tutor and examiner, lest he should drop a scism, or something of corruption, is the greatest displeasure and indignity to a free and knowing spirit that can be put upon him. What advantage is it to be a man over it is to be a boy at school, if we have only scapt the ferular, to come under the fescu of an *Imprimatur?* if serious and elaborat writnings, as if they were no more than the theam of a Grammar lad under his Pedagogue, must not be utter'd without the cursory eyes of a temporizing and extemporizing licencer? He who is not trusted with his own actions, his drift not being known to be evill, and standing to the hazard of law and penalty, has no great argument to think himself reputed in the Commonwealth wherin he was born, for other then a fool or a foreiner. When a man writes to the world, he summons up all his reason and deliberation to assist him; he searches, meditats, is industrious, and likely consults and conferrs with his judicious friends; after all which done he takes himself to be inform'd in what he writes, as well as any that writ before him; if in this the most consummat act of his fidelity and ripenesse, no years, no industry, no former proof of his abilities can bring him to that state of maturity, as not to be still mistrusted and suspected, unless he carry all his considerat diligence, all his midnight watchings, and expence of *Palladian* oyl, to the hasty view of an unleasur'd licencer, perhaps much his younger, perhaps far his inferiour in judgement, perhaps one who never knew the labour of book-writing, and if he be not repulst, or slighted, must appear in Print like a punie with his guardian, and his censors hand on the back of his title to be his bayl and surety, that he is no idiot, or seducer, it cannot but be a dishonour and derogation to the author, to the book, to the priviledge and dignity of Learning."

No author has ever received louder or more frequent applauses than lord Clarendon, author of that most valuable repository of incidents and events, the History of the Rebellion and Civil Wars in England under king Charles the First. He was long held up as the perfect model of an historian. "I have met," says Dr. Felton, in his Dissertation on the Classics, a work formerly of high reputation, "with none that may compare with him in the Weight and Solemnity of his Style, in the Strength and Clearness of Diction, in the Beauty and Majesty of Expression, and that noble Negligence of Phrase, which maketh his Words wait every where upon his Subject, with a Readiness and Propriety, that Art and Study are almost Strangers to."

A short specimen may convince any sober and intelligent reader, that Dr. Felton's eulogium, is considerably exaggerated. Take for example the character he has annexed to the death of lord Strafford.

"Thus Fell the greatest Subject in power, and little inferior to any in Fortune, that was at that time in any of the three Kingdoms; Who could well remember the time, when he led those People, who then pursued him to his Grave. He was a man of great Parts, and extraordinary Endowments of Nature; not unadorn'd with some addition of Art and Learning, though that again was more improved and illustrated by the other; for he had a readiness of Conception, and sharpness of Expression, which made his Learning thought more than in truth it was. His first inclinations and addresses to the Court, were only to establish his Greatness in the Country; where he apprehended some acts of Power from the Lord *Savile*, who had been his Rival always there, and of late had strengthen'd himself by being made a Privy-Counsellor, and Officer at Court: but his first attempts were so prosperous, that he contented not himself with being secure from that Lord's Power in the Country, but rested not, till he had bereav'd his adversary of all power and place in Court; and so sent him down, a most Abject, Disconsolate old man, to his Country, where he was to have the Superintendency over him too, by getting himself at that time made Lord President of the North. These Successes, applied to a nature too Elate and Haughty of it self, and a quicker progress into the greatest Employments and Trust, made him more transported with Disdain of other men, and more Contemning the Forms of business, than haply he would have been, if he had met with some Interruptions in the beginning, and had pass'd in a more leisurely gradation to the Office of a States-man.

" He was, no doubt, of great observation, and a piercing judgment, both in Things and Persons; but his too good skill in Persons, made him judge the worse of Things: for it was his Misfortune, to be in a time wherein very few wise men were equally employ'd with him; and scarce any (but the Lord *Coventry*, whose Trust was more confined) whose Faculties and Abilities were equal to his: So that upon the matter he rely'd wholly upon himself; and discerning many Defects in most men, he too much neglected what they said or did. Of all his Passions, his Pride was most predominant; which a moderate exercise of ill Fortune might have corrected and reform'd; and which was by the hand of Heaven strangely Punish'd, by bringing his Destruction upon him by Two things that he most despised, the People and Sr. *Harry Vane*. In a word, the Epitaph which *Plutarch* records that *Sylla* wrote for himself, may not be unfitly applied to him, "That "no man did ever exceed him, either in doing "good to his Friends, or in doing Mischief to his "Enemies; for his acts of both kinds were most "notorious."

SECT. III.

AGE OF CHARLES THE SECOND.

We now come, strictly speaking, to the age of king Charles the second. Milton and Clarendon, though for their celebrity and merits they could not be omitted, seem rather to belong to an intermediate period.

The style of this period is exceedingly different

from any thing that had gone before. Many of our authors had, during the interregnum, resided on the continent. They studied the French, with the deference that belonged to a class of writers whom they regarded as their masters. It was now first that facility was regarded as the indispensible, and perhaps the first, grace of composition. Their most considerable authors write like men who lived in the world. Their style has much of the charm of what we now regard as polished conversation. Yet, as they caught the exterior and surface of the French character, the consequences were artificial graces, elaborate negligence, feebleness in the choice of words, and inattention in their arrangement. They trusted all to the native powers of invention and taste; and had but a very slight conception that a finished style is only to be obtained by assiduous and unwearied cultivation. Those of our most admired writers in their day who had not lived in France, yet formed themselves in the French school.

The authors most celebrated for the graces of composition in the reign of king Charles the second, were sir William Temple and archbishop Tillotson; nor have any authors in the annals of literature experienced a more copious commendation.

Sir William Temple is undoubtedly an agreeable writer. His thoughts frequently carry the stamp of reflection and good sense, and their impression is by no means counteracted, as we often find it in the preceding periods of our literature, by the alloy of a perplexed or unnatural phraseology.

Take the following passage from his Essay on Popular Discontents as a specimen.

"Princes or States cannot run into every Corner of their Dominions, to look out Persons fit for their Service, or that of the Public: They cannot see far with their own Eyes, nor hear with their own Ears; and must for the most part do both with those of other Men, or else chuse among such smaller Numbers as are most in their way; and these are such, generally, as make their Court, or give their Attendance, in order to advance themselves to Honours, to Fortunes, to Places and Employments; and are usually the least worthy of them, and better Servants to themselves than the Government. The Needy, the Ambitious, the Half-witted, the Proud, the Covetous, are ever restless to get into publick Employments, and many others that are uneasy or ill entertained at home. The Forward, the Busie, the Bold, the Sufficient, pursue their Game with more Passion, Endeavour, Application, and thereby often succeed where better Men would fail. In the Course of my Observation I have found no Talent of so much Advantage among Men, towards their growing great or rich, as a violent and restless Passion and Pursuit for one or t'other: And whoever sets his Heart and his Thoughts wholly upon some one Thing, must have very little Wit, or very little Luck, to fail. Yet all these cover their Ends with most worthy Pretences, and those Noble Sayings, *That Men are not born for themselves, and must sacrifice their Lives for the Publick, as well as their Time and their Health:* And those who think nothing less are so used to say such fine Things, that such who truly believe them are almost ashamed to own it. In the mean time, the Noble, the Wise, the Rich, the Modest, those that are easie in their Conditions or their Minds, those who know most of the World and themselves, are not only careless, but often averse from entering into Publick Charges or Employments, unless upon the Necessities of their Country, Commands of their Prince, or Instances of their Friends. What is to be done in this Case, when such as offer themselves, and pursue, are not worth having, and such as are most worthy, will neither offer, nor perhaps accept?"

Archbishop Tillotson is certainly a writer of some merit. There are few authors who convey more sound sense in more perspicuous expression. It is no mean art of composition, where every sentence comes to us with the force of a proverb, and presents us with "what oft was thought*," but never before set down in so manly a style.

The following passage occurs in Tillotson's Sermon on Sincerity, the last of his clerical compositions.

"Amongst too many other instances of the great corruption and degeneracy of the Age wherein we live, the great and general want of sincerity in Conversation is none of the least. The World is grown so full of Dissimulation and Complement, that Mens words are hardly any signification of their thoughts; and if any Man measure his words by his heart, and speak as he thinks, and do not express more kindness to every man, than men usually have for any man, he can hardly escape the censure of rudeness and want of breeding. The old *English* plainness and sincerity †, that generous integrity of Nature and honesty of Disposition, which always argues true greatness of mind, and is usually accompanied with undaunted courage and resolution, is in a great measure lost amongst us; there hath been a long endeavour to transform us into foreign Manners and Fashions,

* Pope.

† Sincerity is a virtue that can scarcely be too much applauded; but the archbishop was probably mistaken, when he referred us to the old English manners for an example of ingenuous and dignified sincerity.

and to bring us to a servile imitation of none of the best of our Neighbours, in some of the worst of their Qualities. The Dialect of Conversation is now a days so swell'd with Vanity and Complement, and so surfeited (as I may say) of expressions of kindness and respect, that if a man that lived an Age or two ago should return into the World again, he would really want a Dictionary to help him to understand his own Language, and to know the true intrinsick value of the phrase in fassion, and would hardly at first believe at what a low rate the highest strains and expressions of kindness imaginable do commonly pass in current payment; and when he should come to understand it, it would be a great while before he could bring himself, with a good Countenance and a good Conscience to converse with Men upon equal terms and in their own way.

"And in truth it is hard to say whether it should more provoke our contempt or our pity, to hear what solemn expressions of respect and kindness will pass between men, almost upon no occasion; how great honour and esteem they will declare for one whom perhaps they never heard of or saw before, and how entirely they are all on the sudden devoted to his service and interest for no reason; how infinitely and eternally obliged to him for no benefit, and how extremely they will be concerned for him, yea, and afflicted too for no cause. I know it is said in Justification of this hollow kind of Conversation, that there is no harm, no real deceit in Complement, but the matter is well enough, so long as we understand one another, *Et verba valent ut Nummi, Words are like Money,* and when the current value of them is generally understood, no Man is cheated by them. This is something, if such words were any thing; but being brought into the Account, they are mere Cyphers. However it is still a just matter of complaint, that sincerity and plainness are out of fashion, and that our Language is running into a Lye; that Men have almost quite perverted the use of speech, and made words to signify nothing; but the greatest part of the Conversation of Mankind, and of their intercourse with one another, is little else but driving a Trade of Dissimulation; insomuch that it would make a Man heartily sick and weary of the World, to see the little sincerity that is in use, and practice among Men, and tempt him to break out into that Melancholy Complaint and Wish of the Prophet, Jer. 9. *O that I had in the Wilderness a lodging-place, &c.*"

I will add one other passage from the same sermon, which, on account of its striking resemblance, in tediousness and circumlocution, to a passage before quoted from Hooker, may serve as a beacon to shew, how skilful writers are liable to be misled from the path of improvement, by a deferential imitation of their celebrated predecessors.

"Truth and Reality have all the advantages of appearance, and many more. If the shew of any thing be good for any thing, I am sure Sincerity is better; for why does any man dissemble, or seem to be that which he is not, but because he thinks it good to have such a quality as he pretends to? for to counterfeit and dissemble, is to put on the appearance of some real excellency. Now the best way in the world for a Man to seem to be any thing, is really to be what he would seem to be. Besides, that it is many times as troublesome, to make good the pretences of a good quality, as to have it; and if a man have it not, it is ten to one but he is discovered to want it, and then all his pains and labour to seem to have it is lost."

Sprat has been commended by Dr. Johnson, as "an author whose pregnancy of imagination and elegance of language have deservedly set him high in the ranks of literature*."

Our extracts from this author shall be taken from his life of Cowley, as being the most interesting, and not the least finished of his performances.

"Of his [Cowley's] Works that are Publish'd, it is hard to give one general Character, because

* Lives of the Poets.

of the Difference of their Subjects; and the various Form and distant Times of their Writing. Yet this is true of them all, that in all the several Shapes of his Style, there is still very much of the Likeness and Impression of the same Mind; the same unaffected Modesty, and natural Freedom, and easie Vigour, and chearful Passions, and innocent Mirth, which appeared in all his Manners. We have many things that he writ in two very unlike Conditions, in the University and the Court. But in his Poetry, as well as his Life, he mingled with excellent Skill what was good in both States. In his Life he join'd the Innocence and Sincerity of the Scholar, with the Humanity and good Behaviour of the Courtier. In his Poems he united the Solidity and Art of the one, with the Gentility and Gracefulness of the other."

The morality of the following passage is of the noblest kind, but it certainly is not conceived with energy, nor couched in very forcible expressions.

"If any thing ought to have changed his [Cowley's] Temper and Disposition; it was his earnest Affection for Obscurity and Retirement. This, Sir, give me leave to condemn, even to you [Mr. Martin Clifford, to whom the Life of Cowley is addressed], who I know agreed with him in the same Humour. I acknowledge he chose that State of Life, not out of any Poetical Rapture, but upon a steady and sober Experience of Human Things. But, however, I cannot applaud it in him. It is certainly a great Disparagement to Virtue, and Learning itself, that those very Things which only make Men useful in the World, should encline them to leave it. This ought never to be allow'd to Good Men, unless the Bad had the same Moderation, and were willing to follow them into the Wilderness. But if the one shall contend to get out of Employment, while the other strive to get into it, the Affairs of Mankind are like to be in so ill a Posture, that even the good Men themselves will hardly be able to enjoy their very Retreats in Security."

To these extracts, from authors whose attention was particularly devoted to the cultivation of style, led us add a specimen of the manner in which our language was at that time written, from Locke on the Human Understanding. This treatise was published nearly at the period of king William's accession. It has by no means remained without its praise, for the appropriateness and elegance of its composition. Locke was a man of an uncommonly clear and masculine understanding, and greatly superior to many of his most distinguished contemporaries, who, instead of being contented to trace facts and phenomena as he has done, idly bewildered themselves in the invention of fanciful theories. His work forms too memorable an epoch in the annals of literature, not to render it improper that it should be omitted even in this slight essay towards a history of the English language.

It is thus that he expresses himself, in Book I, Chap. I, §. 5.

"Though the *Comprehension* of our Understandings, comes exceeding short of the vast Extent of things; yet we shall have Cause enough to magnify the bountiful Author of our Being, for that Portion and Degree of Knowledge, he has bestowed on us, so far above all the rest of the Inhabitants of this our Mansion. Men have Reason to be well satisfied with what God hath thought fit to give them, since he has given them (as St. *Peter* says,) παντα προς ζωην και ευσεβειαν, Whatsoever is necessary for the Convenience of Life, and Information of Vertue; and has put within the reach of their Discovery the Comfortable Provision for this Life and the Way that leads to a better. How short soever their Knowledge may come of an universal or perfect Comprehension of whatsoever is, it yet secures their great Concernments that they have Light enough to lead them to the Knowledge of their Maker, and the sight of their own Duties. Men may find Matter sufficient to busy their Heads, and employ their Hands with Variety, Delight, and Satisfaction; if they will not boldly quarrel with their own Constitution, and throw away the Blessings their Hands are fill'd with, because they are not big enough to grasp every thing. We shall not have much Reason to complain of the narrowness of our Minds, if we will but employ them about what may be of use to us; for of that they are very capable: And it will be an Unpardonable, as well as Childish Peevishness, if we undervalue the Advantages of our Knowledge, and neglect to improve it to the Ends for which it was given us, because there are some Things that are set out of the reach of it. It will be no Excuse to an Idle and Untoward Servant, who would not attend his Business by Candle-light, to plead that he had not broad Sun-shine. The Candle, that is set up in us, shines bright enough for all our Purposes. The Discoveries we can make with this, ought to satisfy us: And we shall then use our Understandings right, when we entertain all Objects in that Way and Proportion, that they are suited to our Faculties; and upon those Grounds, they are capable of being propos'd to us; and not peremptorily, or intemperately require Demonstration, and demand Certainty, where Probability only is to be had, and which is sufficient to govern all our Concernments. If we will dis-believe every thing, because we cannot certainly know all things; we shall do much-what as wisely as he, who would not use his Legs, but sit still and Perish, because he had no Wings to Fly."

This celebrated author was applied to by the

government of that period, as Milton had been in a similar instance, to write a defence of the principles on which king William was called to the throne. The consequence of this request, was the publication of his Two Treatises of Government, a work highly applauded at that time, and which maintains its reputation, by right of possession probably, to this day.

The first of these Treatises is confined to the refutation of Sir Robert Filmer's Patriarcha. The following passage may serve as a specimen.

" Supposing we should grant, that a Man is *by Nature Governor* of his Children, *Adam* could not hereby *be a Monarch as soon as created*: For this Right of Nature being founded in his being their Father, how *Adam* could have a *Natural Right* to be *Governor* before he was a Father, when by being a Father only he had that *Right*, is, methinks hard to conceive, unless he would have him to be a Father before he was a Father, and to have a Title before he had it.

" To this foreseen Objection, our A. answers very logically, *He was Governor in Habit and not in Act:* A very pretty Way of being a Governor without Government, a Father without Children, and a King without Subjects.—Tho' even this of *Act* and *Habit*, if it signified any thing but our A.'s Skill in Distinctions, be not to his Purpose in this Place. For the Question is not here about

Adam's actual Exercise of Government, but actually having a Title to be Governor: Government, says our A. *was due to* Adam *by the Right of Nature*: What is this Right of Nature? A Right Fathers have over their children by begetting them; *Generatione jus acquiritur parentibus in liberos*, says our A. out of *Grotius*. The Right then follows the Begetting, as arising from it; so that according to this Way of Reasoning or Distinguishing of our A. *Adam*, as soon as he was created, had a Title *only in Habit, and not in Act*, which in plain *English* is, He had actually no Title at all." Book I, Chap. III, §. 18, 19.

SECT. IV.

AGE OF QUEEN ANNE.

We come now to the age of queen Anne. This is the period of English prose, which has generally been attended with the highest and most extensive plaudits. A few scholars indeed have affected to praise the age of queen Elizabeth; but the multitude of readers, for a long time, perhaps to this day, have pitched their tents, and taken up their rest, under the banners of Anne.

Many reasons may be assigned for this. The literary characters of that age were called to fill active situations. Not to mention inferior instances, we may recollect the negotiations of

Prior; the uncommonly important situation Swift held with the Tory administration; and the literary ambition of Bolingbroke, not inferior to the political. The domestic question, which was then secretly at issue, whether the house of Hanover should succeed, or the house of Stuart be restored, animated all hearts, and kept alive all understandings.

To the settlement of the question of the succession, succeeded a national torpor. Literary men were not then aware of the uselessness, not to say incumbrance, of patronage; and patronage could not even in appearance be kept up, under a royal family, by whom our language could neither be spoken nor read. Sir Robert Walpole rendered the case still worse, by the sordidness of his maxims, the phlegmatism of his conduct, and the general propensity he inspired to commerce and gain. The spirit of the nation was sunk; dulness reigned triumphant; and England bid fair to rival, in all that was base and despicable, the republic of Holland.

During this period, the popularity, which the writers under queen Anne had obtained among their contemporaries, had time to sink deep in the hearts of men. Those in whom the love of letters still survived, affirmed, and not without some plausibilities to support them, that the reign of illumination and taste in Great Britain was hastening to a close; and they looked back with affection to Addison, Swift, and their contemporaries, as its last supporters. This appeared to their imagination an Augustan age, about to be succeeded by a long winter of arbitrary sway and intellectual night.

We are able at the present day, when a considerable period of time has elapsed, and these gloomy predictions have by no means been realised, to estimate the merits of these favoured writers with fairness and impartiality.

Let us begin with the writings of Addison. No just observer can recollect the share which belongs to him in the volumes of the Spectator, without feeling that English prose, and the polite literature of his country, are deeply indebted to him. His Papers on Wit, on the Pleasures of the Imagination, on the character of sir Roger de Coverley, and many others, are entitled to no vulgar encomium. Addison was a man of considerable taste, which he has not only demonstrated by the justness and delicacy of the majority of his criticisms, but also by the formation of a style, which is for the most part equally distant from the affectation of a literary fop, and the stiffness of a pedant.

His style is commended by Johnson in the following terms. "[He] sometimes descends too much to the language of conversation; yet if his language had been less idiomatical, it might have lost somewhat of its genuine Anglicism. What he attempted, he performed; he is never feeble, and he did not wish to be energetick; he is never rapid, and he never stagnates. His sentences have neither studied amplitude, nor affected brevity; his periods, though not diligently rounded, are voluble and easy. Whoever wishes to attain an English style, familiar but not coarse, and elegant but not ostentatious, must give his days and nights to the volumes of Addison*."

Nothing can be more glaringly exaggerated than this praise. Addison is a writer eminently enervated; and few authors, distinguished in the *belles lettres*, and of so recent a date, will be found more strikingly loose and unsystematical in their diction.

Let us examine a few passages from writings, of which we are told, that they are "never feeble," and "never stagnate;" that they are "familiar but not coarse, and elegant but not ostentatious."

The following remarks occur in Addison's far-famed and ridiculous commentary upon the ballad of Chevy Chace.

"As *Greece* was a Collection of many Governments, who suffered very much among themselves,

* Lives of the Poets.

and gave the Persian Emperor, who was their common Enemy, many Advantages over them by their mutual Jealousies and Animosities, *Homer*, in order to establish among them an Union, which was so necessary for their Safety, grounds his Poem upon the Discords of the several *Grecian* Princes who were engaged in a Confederacy against an *Asiatick* Prince, and the several Advantages which the Enemy gained by such their Discords. At the Time the Poem we are now treating of was written, the Dissentions of the Barons, who were then so many petty Princes, ran very high, whether they quarrelled among themselves, or with their Neighbours, and produced unspeakable Calamities to the Country: The Poet to deter Men from such unnatural Contentions, describes a bloody Battel and dreadful Scene of Death, occasioned by the mutual Feuds which reigned in the Families of an *English* and *Scotch* Nobleman. That he designed this for the Instruction of his Poem, we may learn from his four last Lines, in which, after the Example of the Modern Tragedians, he draws from it a Precept for the Benefit of his Readers."

The following paragraphs occur in one of the papers, in which the author undertakes to develop the character of sir Roger de Coverley.

"There is one Particular which I have seldom seen but at Sir ROGER's; it is usual in all other

Places, that Servants fly from the Parts of the House through which their Master is passing; on the contrary, here they industriously place themselves in his Way; and it is on both Sides, as it were, understood as a Visit, when the Servants appear without calling."——

"But my good Friend is above these little Instances of Good-will, in bestowing only Trifles on his Servants; a good Servant to him is sure of having it in his Choice very soon of being no Servant at all. As I before observed, he is so good a Husband, and knows so thoroughly that the Skill of the Purse is the Cardinal Virtue of this Life; I say, he knows so well that Frugality is the Support of Generosity, that he can often spare a large Fine when a Tenement falls, and give that Settlement to a good Servant who has a Mind to go into the World, or make a Stranger pay the Fine to that Servant, for his more comfortable Maintenance, if he stays in his Service.

"A Man of Honour and Generosity considers it would be miserable to himself to have no Will but that of another, though it were of the best Person breathing, and for that Reason goes on as fast as he is able to put his Servants into independent Livelihoods. The greatest part of Sir ROGER's Estate is tenanted by Persons who have served himself or his Ancestors. It was to me extreamly pleasant to observe the Visitants from several Parts to welcome his Arrival into the Country, and all the Difference that I could take Notice of between the late Servants who came to see him and those who staid in the Family, was, that these latter were looked upon as finer Gentlemen and better Courtiers."

"One might, on this Occasion, recount the Sense that great Persons in all Ages have had of the Merit of their Dependents, and the heroick Services which men have done their Masters in the Extremity of their Fortunes; and shewn to their undone Patrons, that Fortune was all the Difference between them."——

"I remembred indeed Sir ROGER said there lived a very worthy Gentleman to whom he was highly obliged, without mentioning any thing further."

It were an endless task to hunt this author through all his negligences, uncouthnesses and solecisms. I will only subjoin one further extract, from a paper in which he is recommending, "that the honest Men of all Parties should enter into a Kind of Association for the Defence of one another, and the Confusion of their common Enemies."

The proposed bond of association concludes with the following sentence.

"And we shall upon all Occasions oppose such Persons that upon any Day of the Year shall call Black white, or White black, with the utmost

Peril of our Lives and Fortunes." The author proceeds:

"Were there such a Combination of honest Men, who without any Regard to Places would endeavour to extirpate all such furious Zealots as would sacrifice one half of their Country to the Passion and Interest of the other; as also such infamous Hypocrites, that are for promoting their own Advantage, under Colour of the publick Good; with all the profligate immoral Retainers to each Side, that have nothing to recommend them but an implicit Submission to their Leaders; we should soon see that furious Party-Spirit extinguished, which may in Time expose us to the Derision and Contempt of all the Nations about us."

The meanness of composition in this passage, can only be equalled by the absurdity of its malice, or the impotence of its wit.

We now come to Swift, respecting whom Lowth has authoritatively pronounced, that "he is one of the most correct, and perhaps the best of our prose writers." No author was ever more applauded by his contemporaries: no author ever produced a greater public effect, than he is supposed to have done, by his Conduct of the Allies, and his Drapier's Letters. For his solicitude about accuracy, he deserves to be considered with respect. For the stern and inflexible integrity of his principles, and the profound sagacity of his speculations, he will be honoured by a distant posterity.

We will confine ourselves in our specimens, to his Tale of a Tub and Gulliver's Travels; the two best of his works; the former written with all the rich exuberance of youthful imagination; the latter in his last stage of intellectual cultivation, and, as Milton expresses it, "the most consummat act of his fidelity and ripeness *."

The Tale of a Tub is a work, of perhaps greater felicity of wit, and more ludicrous combinations of ideas, than any other book in the world. It is however, written in so strange a style of "banter," to make use of one of the author's words, or rather in so low and anomalous a slang, which perhaps Swift considered as the necessary concomitant of wit; that it is by no means proper to be cited as an example of just composition. The reader however may not be aware of this; and, to remove the scruples with which he may possibly be impressed, I will adduce a few instances.

"To this System of Religion were tagg'd several subaltern Doctrines, which were entertain'd with great Vogue: as particularly, the Faculties of the Mind were deduced by the Learned among them in this manner:—All which required abundance of *Finesse* and *Delicatesse* to manage with ad-

* See page 357.

vantage, as well as a strict Observance after Times and Fashions." Sect. II.

"A while after there came up *all in Fashion*, a pretty sort of *flame-colour'd Sattin* for Linings." d°.

"To support this Grandeur, which he soon began to consider could not be maintain'd without a better *Fonde* than what he was born to; after much Thought, he cast about at last—." Sect. IV.

"Sometimes he would send them [his bulls] out upon Errands of great importance; where it is wonderful to recount, and perhaps the cautious Reader may think much to believe it, an *Appetitus sensibilis*, deriving itself through the whole Family, from their noble Ancestors, Guardians of the *Golden Fleece*; they continued so extremely fond of *Gold*,——." d°.

"And that which was the good of it, he would —." d°.

The following is a curious example of negligent and disjointed composition.

"But Fashions perpetually altering in that Age, the Scholastick Brother grew weary of searching further Evasions, and solving everlasting Contradictions. Resolv'd therefore at all hazards to comply with the Modes of the World, they concerted Matters together, and agreed unanimously to lock up their Father's Will in a *Strong Box*, brought out of *Greece* or *Italy* (I have forgot which) and trouble themselves no farther to examine it, but only refer to its Authority whenever they thought fit. In consequence whereof, a while after it grew a general Mode to wear an infinite Number of *Points*, most of them *tag'd with Silver*. Upon which the Scholar pronounced *ex Cathedra*, that *Points* were absolutely *Jure Paterno*, as they might very well remember. 'Tis true indeed, the Fashion prescrib'd somewhat more than were directly nam'd in the Will: However that they, as Heirs general of their Father, had power to make and add certain Clauses for publick Emolument, though not deducible *totidem verbis* from the Letter of the Will; or else, *Multa absurda sequerentur*." Sect. II.

Gulliver's Travels is a book in which the author seems to have called up all his vigilance and skill in the article of style: and as the plan of his fiction led to that simplicity in which he delighted, no book can be taken as a fairer specimen of the degree of cultivation at which the English Language had at that time arrived. Swift was perhaps the man of the most powerful mind of the time in which he lived.

The following may serve as a few examples of the loose and incorrect construction with which this performance is written.

"In one of these Cells were several Globes or Balls of a most ponderous Metal, about the bigness of our Heads, and required a strong hand to lift them." Part I, Chap. II.

"When this Inventory was read over to the Emperor, he directed me, although in very gentle Terms, to deliver up the several Particulars. He first called for my Scymiter, which I took out Scabbard and all. d°.

"Even the Emperor, although he stood his ground, could not recover himself in some time." d°.

"His speech was to the following Effect, for I took Notes of it as soon as he left me." Chap. VII.

"These were searched and sought out through the whole Nation, by the Prince and his wisest Counsellors, among such of the Priesthood, as were most deservedly distinguished by the Sanctity of their Lives, and the Depth of their Erudition; who were indeed the Spiritual Fathers of the Clergy and the People." Part II, Chap. VI.

"Upon what I said in relation to our Courts of Justice, his Majesty desired to be satisfied in several Points: And, this I was the better able to do, having been formerly almost ruined by a long Suit in Chancery, which was decreed for me with Costs. He asked, what time was usually spent in determining between Right and Wrong, and what Degree of Expence." d°.

What can be more disjointed and aukward than the construction of the following passage?

"I swore and subscribed to these Articles with Chearfulness and Content, although some of them were not so honourable as I could have wished; which proceeded wholly from the Malice of *Skyresh Bolgolam* the High Admiral: whereupon my Chains were immediately unlocked, and I was at full liberty; the Emperor himself in Person did me the Honor to be by at the whole Ceremony." Part I, Chap. III.

Again: "I told his Majesty that I was come according to my Promise, and with the Licence of the Emperor my Master, to have the Honour of seeing so mighty a Monarch, and to offer him any Service in my power, consistent with my Duty to my own Prince; not mentioning a Word of my Disgrace, because I had hitherto no regular Information of it, and might suppose myself wholly ignorant of any such Design; neither could I reasonably conceive that the Emperor would discover the Secret while I was out of his power: Wherein, however, it soon appeared I was deceived." Chap. VII.

Again: "I walked with Intrepidity five or six times before the very Head of the Cat, and came within half a Yard of her; whereupon she drew her self back, as if she were more afraid of me: I had less Apprehension concerning the Dogs, whereof three or four came into the Room, as it is usual in Farmers Houses; one of which was a

Mastiff equal in bulk to four Elephants, and a Grey-hound somewhat taller than the Mastiff, but not so large." Part II, Chap. I.

Two authors of high eminence and great celebrity, who may be considered as belonging to the age of queen Anne, are Shaftesbury and Bolingbroke. They were both of them men of admirable talents. Shaftesbury devoted himself particularly to the study of the ancients, and proposed in his writings to give a polish and elegance to the English language it had not yet received. His propensities led him to a total seclusion from actual life; and he was unwearied in the labour of turning his periods, and finishing his compositions. Bolingbroke was a man whose very soul was eloquence. The boldness of his genius, and the impetuous torrent of his ideas, seem, when we read, to bear away all opposition before them. Yet, when we are upon the subject of correctness of composition, these authors present us rather with examples to avoid, than examples to imitate. They may serve to illustrate the state of our language, when men, like them, could be so astonishingly erroneous.

Shaftesbury was an author, the whole habits of whose mind appear to have been uncommonly elegant. Yet we trace in him an assemblage the most ill assorted and incongruous. His passion for elegance is immoderate and ungovernable. At one time it leads him to the stiffest and most far-fetched expressions, under the notion of being singularly easy. At another time the same notion induces him to crowd his pages with vulgarisms and buffoonery. It is impossible that so accomplished and original a writer, could have fallen into such egregious errors; if there had at that time been any thing sufficiently stable in our language.

Take the following example from his Soliloquy, or Advice to an Author.

"This was, among the Antients, that celebrated *Delphick* Inscription, RECOGNISE YOURSELF; which was as much as to say, *Divide yourself* or *Be* Two. For if the Division were rightly made, all *within* wou'd of course, they thought, be rightly understood, and prudently manag'd. Such Confidence they had in this Home-*Dialect* of SOLILOQUY. For it was accounted the peculiar of Philosophers and wise Men, to be able *to hold themselves in Talk*. And it was their Boast on this account, 'That they were never less *alone*, than when *by themselves*.' A Knave, they thought, cou'd never be *by himself*. Not that his Conscience was always sure of giving him Disturbance; but he had not, they suppos'd, so much Interest with himself, as to exert this generous Faculty and raise himself *a Companion*; who being fairly admitted into Partnership, wou'd quickly mend his Partner, and set his affairs on a right foot.

"One would think, there was nothing easier for us, than to know our own Minds, and understand what our main *Scope* was; what we plainly drove at, and what we propos'd to ourselves, as our *End*, in every Occurrence of our Lives. But our Thoughts have generally such an obscure implicit Language, that 'tis the hardest thing in the world to make 'em speak out distinctly. For this reason, the right Method is to give 'em Voice and Accent. And this, in our default, is what the *Moralists* or *Philosophers* endeavour to do, to our hand; when, as is usual, they hold us out a kind of *vocal* Looking-Glass, draw Sound out of our Breast, and instruct us to personate ourselves, in the plainest manner." Part I, Sect. II.

This is surely sufficiently quaint and uncouth. What does the reader think of the buffoonery of the following passage?

"We have a notable Instance of this *Freedom* in one of our sacred Authors. As patient as JOB is said to be, it cannot be denied that he makes bold enough with GOD, and takes his Providence roundly to task. His Friends, indeed, plead hard with him, and use all Arguments, right or wrong, to patch up Objections, and set the Affairs of Providence upon an equal Foot." Letter concerning Enthusiasm. Sect. IV.

Again: "There are some, it seems, of our good Brethren, the *French* Protestants, lately come among us, who are mightily taken with this Primitive way. They have set a-foot the Spirit of Martyrdom to a wonder in their own Country; and they long to be trying it here, if we will give 'em leave, and afford 'em the Occasion: that is to say, if we will only do 'em the favour to hang or imprison 'em; if we will only be so obliging as to break their Bones for 'em, after their Country-fashion blow up their Zeal, and stir a-fresh the Coals of Persecution." d°. Sect. III.

The Dedication to sir Robert Walpole, then earl of Orford, prefixed by Bolingbroke to his Remarks on the History of England, has been cited by some persons as the model of the style of the celebrated Junius.

"It is not my design," says he, "to tread the beaten track, and compare you either to FABIUS or CICERO. To insinuate you ever had a type or parallel, is to injure you. No, you are yourself; an original; a nonsuch; nor it is likely posterity should ever produce such another. It is enough for me to give you your own; I aspire to no more; and that I dare not attempt but by figure only."—

"Though I professedly spread the canvas for your portrait, I could not help edging in a slight sketch of my own. I shall not, however, forget that your lordship is to be the principal figure, nor that I ought to be content with an obscure corner in the piece; like your equerry, holding your stirrup, or presenting that head-piece which none but you would presume to put on; or rather as your 'squire, assisting to disarm you; or helping you out of your saddle, &c."

"Whether you are to be cut or drop from the tree, I am afraid to pronounce."

"A tremendous prophecy, my lord, and what you can never be out of the reach of, till you are in your grave."

"The old jingle of *honores mutant mores* you have the glory, my lord, to be an illustrious exception to."

"It is notorious you have now as much to bestow as I expected then."

The conclusion of the following sentence will show that an expression, which has by many been mistaken for a grace of modern rhetoric, can exhibit a title more venerable than they imagined.

"On the stage, indeed, when a master-poet exerts his power over the passions, his victim at the end of the fourth act is frequently made to sing a requiem to his cares and sorrows, as if for ever done away."

These are by no means all the flowers of a similar kind, that might be gathered, out of a Dedication of ten thinly printed pages.

SECT. V.

AGE OF GEORGE THE SECOND.

WE come now to the last period of our investigation; the age of king George the second.

We may select as specimens of this period, Middleton, Sherlock, Fielding and Smollet.

No production of that age has been more extolled as a model of fine writing, than Middleton's Life of Cicero. History had been written among us, before that book made its appearance; but this is the first work in our language that is written in what Englishmen have since been accustomed to regard as the historical style. Middleton is the precursor of the Humes, the Robertsons, and the Gibbons.

But, though this work is to be esteemed upon the whole an able, excellent and elegant production, it is not without considerable defects. Middleton is an eloquent writer, but his verbosity is glaring, and his construction perplexing and tedious. His phraseology is often pedantic, and often unnecessarily loaded with particles. Precision of speech, that conveys its meaning in the most direct and unincumbered manner, is no part of his praise. The vigour of his genius seems to pant and labour under the burthen of his language.

The following passages may serve to illustrate his character.

Speaking of the period, in which it was customary for the young men of Rome to assume the manly gown, the author proceeds: "They were introduced at the same time into *the Forum* or the great square of the City, where the Assemblies of the people were held, and the Magistrates used to harangue to them from *the Rostra*, and where all the public pleadings and judicial proceedings were usually transacted: this therefore was the grand School of business and eloquence; the scene, on which all the affairs of the Empire were determined, and where the foundation of their hopes and fortunes were to be laid: so that they were introduced into it with much solemnity, attended by all the friends and dependents of the family, and after divine rites performed in *the Capitol*, were committed to the special protection of some eminent Senator, distinguished for his eloquence or knowledge of the laws, to be instructed by his advice in the management of civil affairs, and to form themselves by his example for useful members and Magistrates of the Republic." Sect. I.

After enumerating the studies of Cicero, Dr. Middleton concludes: All which accomplishments were but ministerial and subservient to that, on which his hopes and ambition were singly placed, the reputation *of an Orator*." d°.

"This practice [the vote, *ut viderent consules, ne quid respublica detrimenti capiat*], tho' in use from the earliest times, had always been complained of by the Tribuns, as an infringement of the constitution, by giving to the Senate an arbitrary power over the lives of Citizens, which could not legally be taken away without a hearing and judgment of the whole people. But the chief grudge to it was, from its being a perpetual check to the designs of the ambitious and popular, who aspired to any power not allowed by the laws: it was not difficult for them to delude the multitude; but the Senate was not so easily managed, who *by that single vote of committing the Republic to the Consuls*, could frustrate at once all the effects of their popularity, when carried to a point which was dangerous to the State: for since by virtue of it, the *Tribuns* themselves, whose persons were held sacred might be taken off without sentence or trial, when engaged in any traiterous practices, all attempts of that kind must necessarily be hazardous and desperate." Sect. III.

The following is a part of our author's character of Sylla.

"His family was noble and *Patrician*, which yet, through the indolency of his Ancestors, had made no figure in the Republic for many generations, and was almost sunk into obscurity, till he produced it again into light, by aspiring to the honors of the State. He was a lover and patron of polite letters, having been carefully instituted himself in all the learning of *Greece* and *Rome*; but from a peculiar gaiety of temper, and fondness for the company of Mimics and Players, was drawn, when young, into a life of luxury and pleasure; so that when he was sent *Quæstor to* MARIUS *in the Jugurthine war*, MARIUS complained, that in so rough and desperate a service chance had given him *so soft and delicate a Quæstor*." Sect. II.

It must be considered as an argument of the paucity of genius during this period, that we are obliged to have recourse to Sherlock, an author whose character, though unprecedentedly high among his brethren in the church, never rose to the dignity of general fame.

His famous parallel between Christ and Mahomet, which is perhaps the only truly eloquent passage in his works, is indeed happily expressed. He must have been a very cursory observer of style, who does not know, that enthusiasm of sentiment seldom fails to produce a momentary happiness of language. The passage concludes thus:

"When Natural Religion," says the preacher, "has viewed both, ask, Which is the Prophet of God? But her Answer we have already had; when she saw Part of this Scene through the Eyes of the Centurion who attended at the Cross; by him she spoke and said, *Truly this* Man was the Son of God." Vol. I, Discourse IX.

The following passage from the same Discourse, may serve as a specimen of this author's usual manner.

"But here the Question is asked, How shall we distinguish between the Pretences to Revelation, which are so many and various, all of which have an equal Right to be heard, that 'tis endless to look for Religion in such a Croud of Pretenders to it, and difficult to determine the Merit of the several Claims.——

"So that all Religions [in the Heathen World] were esteemed equally good, and the most any Religion pretended to was a local Authority, which reached no farther than the Laws of the Country did: And, unless Men are for giving more to the pretended Heathen Revelations, than ever they claimed for themselves, or was claimed for them by those who introduced them and lived under them, they cannot be brought into this Question, since they have no Relation to us, any more than the many civil Laws and Constitutions of the same Countries had: And Men may as reasonably complain of the great Variety of civil and municipal Laws that distract their Obedience, and then instance in the Laws of the *Medes* and *Persians*, as they now complain of the Variety of Revelations, instancing in such as, if they were true, concern them as little as the Laws of *Persia* do."

Fielding's novel of Tom Jones is certainly one of the most admirable performances in the world. The structure of the story perhaps has never been equalled; nor is there any work that more frequently or more happily excites emotions of the most elevated and delicious generosity.

The style however is glaringly inferior to the constituent parts of the work. It cannot boast of periods elegantly turned or delicately pointed. The book is interspersed with long discourses of religious or moral instruction: but these have no novelty of conception or impressive sagacity of remark, and are little superior to what any reader might hear at the next parish-church. The general turn of the work is intended to be sarcastic and ironical; but the irony is hard, pedantic and unnatural.

The following is part of a sermon, addressed to the supposed mother of the hero, and put by the author into the mouth of his abortive character of Allworthy.

"Love, however barbarously we may corrupt and pervert its meaning, as it is a laudable, is a rational passion, and can never be violent, but when reciprocal; for though the Scripture bids us love our enemies, it means not with that fervent love which we naturally bear towards our friends; much less that we should sacrifice to them our lives, and, what ought to be dearer to us, our innocence.

Now, in what light, but that of an enemy, can a reasonable woman regard the man who solicits her to entail on herself all the misery I have described to you, and who would purchase to himself a short, trivial, contemptible pleasure, so greatly at her expence? For, by the laws of custom, the whole shame, with all its dreadful consequences, falls entirely upon her. Can love, which always seeks the good of its object, attempt to betray a woman into a bargain where she is so greatly to be the loser? If such a corrupter, therefore, should have the impudence to pretend a real affection for her, ought not the woman to regard him, not only as an enemy, but as the worst of all enemies; a false, designing, treacherous, pretended friend, who intends not only to debauch her body, but her understanding at the same time?" Book I, Chap. VII.

Here follow some specimens of the style of irony, or rather buffoonery, in which nearly the whole work is written.

"As this is one of those deep observations which very few readers can be supposed capable of making themselves, I have thought proper to lend them my assistance; but this is a favour rarely to be expected in the course of my work. Indeed I shall seldom or never so indulge them, unless in such instances as this, where nothing but the inspiration with which we writers are gifted, can possibly enable any one to make the discovery." Ch. V.

"The sagacious reader will not from this simile, imagine these poor people had any apprehension of the design with which Mrs. Wilkins was now coming towards them; but as the great beauty of the simile may possibly sleep these hundred years, till some future commentator shall take this work in hand, I think proper to lend the Reader a little assistance in this place." Chap. VI.

Let us add a few passages under the article of style in general. The first is another extract from the sermons of Allworthy.

"But to relieve our brethren only with our superfluities; to be charitable (I must use the word) rather at the expence of our coffers than ourselves; to save several families from misery, rather than hang up an extraordinary picture in our houses, or gratify any other idle, ridiculous vanity; this seems to be only being Christians; nay, indeed, only being human creatures. Nay, I will venture to go farther; it is being in some degree epicures: for what could the greatest epicure wish rather than to eat with many mouths instead of one? which, I think, may be predicated of any one who knows that the bread of many is owing to his own largesses." Book II, Chap. V.

"Allworthy here betook himself to those pleasing slumbers which a heart that hungers after goodness is apt to enjoy when thoroughly satisfied: as these are possibly sweeter than what are occasioned by any other hearty meal, I should take more pains to display them to the reader, if I knew any air to recommend him to for the procuring such an appetite." Book I, Chap. III.

"As to my concern for what is past, I know you will spare my blushes the repetition." Chap. VII.

"The only way, as it appears to me, of solving this difficulty, is by imputing it to that distance which was now grown between the lady and the housekeeper; whether this arose from a jealousy in Mrs. Blifil, that Wilkins shewed too great a respect to the foundling; for while she was endeavouring to ruin the little infant, in order to ingratiate herself with the captain, she was every day commending it more and more before Allworthy, as his fondness for it every day increased. This, notwithstanding all the care she took at other times to express the direct contrary to Mrs. Blifil, perhaps offended that delicate lady, who certainly now hated Mrs. Wilkins; and though she did not, or possibly could not, absolutely remove her from her place, she found, however, the means of making her life very uneasy. This Mrs. Wilkins, at length, so resented, that she very openly shewed all manner of respect and fondness to little Tommy, in opposition to Mrs. Blifil." Book II, Chap. V.

From the examination of Fielding we proceed to that of Smollet.

Smollet has published more volumes, upon more subjects, than perhaps any other author of modern date; and, in all, he has left marks of his genius. He is nevertheless a hasty writer; when he affects us most, we are aware that he might have done more. In all his works of invention, we find the stamp of a powerful mind. In his lightest sketches, there is nothing frivolous, trifling and effeminate. In his most glowing portraits, we acknowledge a mind at ease, rather essaying its powers, than tasking them.

The style of Smollet has never been greatly admired, and it is brought forward here merely to show in what manner men of the greatest eminence in the *belles lettres,* could write forty or fifty years ago.

His most considerable production is Roderick Random. Let the reader take as a specimen of his style, the story of Mrs. Sagely, in the beginning of the second volume, as related by herself.

"It is of little consequence to tell the names of my parents, who are dead many years ago; let it suffice to assure you, they were wealthy, and had no other child than me, so that I was looked upon as heiress to a considerable estate, and tiezed with addresses on that account. Among the number of my admirers, there was a young gentleman of no fortune, whose sole dependence was on his promotion in the army, in which at that time he bore a lieutenant's commission.—I conceived an affection for this amiable officer, which in a short time increased to a violent passion, and, without entering into minute circumstances, married him privately.—We had not enjoyed one another long, in stolen interviews, when he was ordered with his regiment to Flanders; but before he set out, it was agreed between us, that he should declare our marriage to my father by letter, and implore his pardon for the step we had taken without his approbation.—This was done while I was abroad visiting; and just as I was about to return home, I received a letter from my father, importing, that since I had acted so undutifully and meanly, as to marry a beggar, without his privity or consent, to the disgrace of his family, as well as the disappointment of his hopes, he renounced me to the miserable fate I had entailed upon myself, and charged me never to set foot within his doors again.—This rigid sentence was confirmed by my mother, who, in a postscript, gave me to understand that her sentiments were exactly conformable to those of my father, and that I might save myself the trouble of making any applications, for her resolutions were unalterable.—Thunder-struck with my evil fortune,

I called a coach, and drove to my husband's lodgings, where I found him waiting the event of his letter."——

It is unnecessary to transcribe the remainder of the passage. Suffice it to say that it is in vain that, in any part of it, we should search for the scholar, the man of education, or the man of taste. The composer of fictitious writings indeed, sometimes lowers his style to suit the meanness or absurdity of his personages. But this ought never to be done, except where it is attended with comic effect. It is the office of the poet and the novelist to adorn the style of their characters, and to give to real life the most impressive form. We do not suppose the real Hamlet always to have spoken with that felicity or that energy of diction, which Shakespear has bestowed on him. Mrs. Sagely's narrative might have been written with simplicity; but it should have been written with elegance. On the contrary we find little in it above the style of a servant-maid over her winter fire.

Respect for the great name of Smollet, will not suffer me to pass over in silence his History of England, the most important of his compilations. It is not to the purpose of the present enquiry to observe that the general concoction of the work, reminds us rather of the promptings of the bookseller, than of the talents of its author. It is not however to be wondered at, that the style of a work, thus crudely composed, should not be such as to put contemporary authors to the blush.

In the volume in which the war of 1739 is narrated, Smollet talks of the "inequality of the match" between Sir Robert Walpole's pamphleteers, and their antagonists; and adds, that "he resolved to seize the first opportunity to choak those canals through which the torrent of censure had flowed upon his character." He says that, to avoid a rupture with Spain, the minister "endeavoured to obtain some sort of satisfaction by dint of memorials and negociations." Walpole, he observes, objected to certain resolutions proposed by the opposition, that "they would cramp the ministers in their endeavours to compromise these differences." He describes the earl of Ilay, as "staunch to the minister, and invariably true to his own interest." Having brought the pretender in his narrative as far as Fort William, he tells us that he "forthwith marched to Perth." In undertaking to account for the miscarriage of the invader, he has the following remark: "He was at the same time regaled with the promise of powerful succours from France, though the ministry of that kingdom were never hearty in his cause: nevertheless they foresaw, that his appearance in England would embarrass the government, and make a considerable diversion in their favour." Upon the war of 1739 he observes generally: "England, from being the umpire, was now become a party in all continental quarrels; and instead of trimming the balance of Europe, lavished away her blood and treasure, in supporting the interest and allies of a puny electorate in the North of Germany."

SECT. VI.

CONCLUSION.

THE whole of the preceding extracts is drawn, as much as possible, from the earliest editions of the respective works: since various circumstances of orthography, capitals, and other minute articles, properly enter into the history of the language, and serve to render the portrait here attempted to be delineated more entire and complete.

It was proposed to draw our specimens from the authors in each successive period who have been most highly and publicly commended. There are other writers who have obtained the suffrage of individuals of great authority and taste, and who may in some respects be superior to the authors here used. But these will probably be allowed by the impartial enquirer, to afford a sufficient basis upon which to rest our inference.

It was remarked in the beginning of the present Essay, that on the whole the construction of the language of our best modern writers, the best writers of the age of George the Third, is closer and neater, more free from laxity of structure, and less subject to occasional incongruities, superfluities, unnaturalness and affectation, than that of their predecessors.

So far is well. But neatness, and a sustained equality of march, are not every thing.

We shall particularly fall into absurdity, and be the enemies of our own improvement, if because we surpass our predecessors in one thing, we neglect and despise them. Infinite instruction is to be derived from their assiduous perusal.

We observed in a former Essay *, that it was perhaps impossible to understand one language, unless we were acquainted with more than one: but that the man who is competent to, and exercised in the comparison of languages, has attained to his proper elevation: language is not his master, but he is the master of language: things hold their just order in his mind, ideas first, and then words: words therefore are used by him as the means of communicating or giving permanence to his sentiments; and the whole magazine of his native tongue is subjected at his feet.

This observation applies with perhaps still greater force to the study of our own language, as it has been written by authors in successive ages.

* Part I, Essay VI.

It is by this sort of comparison of century with century, that we become acquainted with the genius and treasures of our native tongue, and learn the different changes and revolutions that have attended it. It is like the study of the character of an eminent man. If we only see him on high days and collar days, we shall know but little about him. We must observe him in his retirement, in his family, in his familiarities, in his relaxations, in his sports, if we would thoroughly understand him, or (to pursue the parallel in which we are engaged) if we would know all the uses that may be made of him.

It is necessary that he who would write well the English of the present day, should study our elder authors, for this reason also. There are great treasures in our native tongue, of which he will remain in complete ignorance, who is acquainted only with the writings of his contemporaries.

Ut silvæ foliis pronos mutantur in annos;
Prima cadunt—
Multa renascentur quæ jam cecidere.

We should read the authors of a forgotten age, that we may revive combinations and beauties that never ought to have perished. We may gain raciness and strength from, it may be, their rude strength; we may give muscle and force and variety, to what might otherwise run the risk of becoming too tame or too monotous; we may learn from them copiousness and an occasional exuberance of expression; and we may infuse a freshness and living spirit into what might otherwise withar and fade.

There is no art, the subject of human diligence and industry, more subtle and difficult of acquisition, than that of writing an excellent style. Two things are especially necessary, a flowing eloquence of language, and an exquisite propriety of diction.

It almost impossible that we should write a good style in a language to which we are not natives. To write a good style requires so much minute observation, and is a quality produced by so vast a multitude of slight and evanescent impressions, that it cannot be expected to fall to the lot of a foreigner.

Before we can be masters of this qualification, we must have an accurate notion of the meaning of words, the delicate shades of meaning by which they are diversified, and the various ideas and associations they are calculated to excite: and we must have an extensive acquaintance with their history. Our words must in general be considered as having been expressions of the perceptions of our external senses, before they were expressions of abstraction; and it is incumbent upon us, as much as possible, to bear in our minds the pictures to which they were originally annexed, that we may judge how far they are decorous in themselves, or congruous with each other. We must not suffer them merely to ring upon our ears, and then be repeated by us like children, without any direct investigation of their force. Nay, after we have become acquainted with this, we have still much to learn. Many words and phrases, neutral or even elegant in themselves, have been debased by an application to trivial or ignoble objects. On this account, a phrase will sometimes impress a foreigner with dignified sensations, which to a native shall appear altogether ludicrous and contemptible. In this respect we are very imperfect judges of the writings of the ancients, as we have scarcely any acquaintance with their familiar conversation.

When our choice of words is determined, we have next to combine our words into phrases, and our phrases into periods. Here the idiom of the language in which we write must be accurately understood, and for the most part rigidly adhered to. It is probably of little consequence whether the idiom of the English language, for instance, be Gallic or Teutonic, whether it come from the East or the West. But it must have an idiom; it must be, to a considerable degree, uniform and consentaneous to itself. Those Gallic modes of speaking, which have been introduced by our best writers, ought not probably to be rejected, merely because they are Gallic. Even new and unauthorrised forms of expression may be introduced into a living language, provided it be done sparingly, provided they be decisively beautiful or expressive, and provided they do not so depart from the genius of the language into which they are introduced, as to stand out from the substance with which they are meant to coalesce. Let us dare to enrich the language in which we write, by design; but let us not debauch it by inadvertence.

He that would write a good style must have a clear understanding and a comprehensive mind. He must have that ductility of thought that shall enable him to put himself in the place of his reader, and not suffer him to take it for granted, because he understands himself, that every one who comes to him for information will understand him. He must view his phrases on all sides, and be aware of all the senses of which they are susceptible. He must so choose his words, and so limit his expressions, as to produce an unallayed perspicuity. There is no fault in writing so great as ambiguity and obscurity.

He must have an ear for the harmony of language. This has been found by experience to be by no means the same thing as a musical ear. The most exquisite musician may want it; and he that has no delight in concords of inarticulate sound, may possess it in a sovereign degree. When he has formed to himself this species of taste, he must employ the sort of music it recommends, with a frugal hand. He must not pall his readers with a satiety of sweetness. What is most necessary, is that he should avoid the too frequent recurrence of what is broken, abrupt and discordant. The true music of a good style, is rather a philosophically just arrangement of ideas, than a laborious cultivation of the arts of sound.

Lastly, he must have a decisive and ardent thirst after simplicity. This is the first of all beauties. This is the basis and ground-work of every beauty. Even in the most ornamented composition, in the "torrent, tempest and whirlwind" of eloquence, there must be "begotten a temperance, that may give it smoothness*." He that is not penetrated with a love of simplicity, may write sounding bombast or gaudy nothings; but can never be truly either pathetic or sublime.

A good style is essential to our obtaining from others a just consideration of our thoughts. There can be nothing eminently winning and insinuating without it. He that writes a bad style, erects a barrier between himself and his reader, and does not allow his reflections and notions to obtain a fair hearing. A man of taste will often be found, either wholly unable to proceed in reading a work thus disgraced, or proceeding with disgust, and performing his journey through it as a wearisome

* Shakespear.